THE GOSPEL ACCORDING TO

The New York Times

Gift from Publishers to JNT 26-10-00

THE GOSPEL ACCORDING TO

The New York Times

.. No. 51,279   WEDNESDAY   ON

How the world's most powerful news organization shapes your mind and values

WILLIAM PROCTOR

BROADMAN
&HOLMAN
PUBLISHERS

Nashville, Tennessee

© 2000
by Inkslingers, Inc.
All rights reserved
Printed in the United States of America

0–8054–2347–8

Published by Broadman & Holman Publishers, Nashville, Tennessee

Dewey Decimal Classification: 071
Subject Heading: JOURNALISM

Library of Congress Cataloging-in-Publication Data

Proctor, William.
    The gospel according to the New York times : how the world's most power-
ful news organization shapes your mind and values / William Proctor.
    p.cm.
ISBN 0–8054–2347–8 (pb)
1. New York times. I. Title.

PN4899.N42 N377 2000
071'.471—dc21
                                                              00–030392

1 2 3 4 5   04 03 02 01 00

DEDICATION

To news addicts everywhere—
especially those who have been hoodwinked into believing
that there is any such thing as objectivity in journalism.

CONTENTS

PART IV: RESPONDING TO THE NEW FUNDAMENTALISM

PREFACE

This book has been in the works for almost three decades, beginning with my first intensive exposure to the *New York Times* as a New York City reporter in the early 1970s.

During that period, as legal correspondent and head of the Manhattan Criminal Courts Bureau for the New York *Daily News*, I gained great respect for the intelligence and reporting skills of the reporters at the "other paper across town." Since that experience, however, it has become increasingly apparent to me that the *Times* is pursuing a highly potent, largely clandestine, and unnoticed strategy to promote a particular worldview—not only in editorials, op-ed columns, or other opinion pieces, but also in news stories. In many instances, news stories, pictures, reviews, op-ed pieces, and editorials actually seem orchestrated to promote deeply held values that are an integral part of the *Times'* corporate culture.

To explore this possibility further, I embarked during 1995 on more focused research into possible techniques that might lie behind the *Times'* news coverage. This book represents the culmination of my investigation. In brief, my methodology can be divided into four categories:

- Analysis of significantly played news stories, editorials, op-ed columns, reviews, and other articles in the *Times* from the summer of 1995 through the summer of 1999.

- Comparison of the *Times'* coverage of news events during this four-year period with the coverage of the same events by other publications and news outlets, including the *Wall Street Journal*, the *Palm Beach Post*, leading medical and legal journals, and selected TV and radio news reports.
- An examination of references to the *Times* and reprints of *Times* articles in other news media outlets.
- Exploration of links between current and former *Times'* employees and outside organizations, institutions and movements that support or promote the *Times'* viewpoints.

Although most of the names mentioned in this book—such as those of *Times* columnists and reporters—are the actual names of the individuals, a few names and identifications have been changed to protect privacy and confidentiality. In most cases, I have signaled changes in names or identifying characteristics by putting the first use of the person's name in quotations. For a further explanation of my research techniques and a summary of some of the findings, please see the Appendix.

Finally, a question that will arise at the outset in the minds of many readers is the extent to which my own biases and beliefs may have shaped my critique of the worldview and comprehensive belief system that emerges from the pages of the *Times*. This is a fair question, and I shall gladly address it in some detail after the publication of the book by anyone who chooses to ask. However, since the main issue at hand is what the *Times* believes, not what I believe, I have chosen to keep most of my personal views to myself.

Still, I will say this much: Readers shouldn't assume that I necessarily oppose a particular *Times'* "doctrine" just because I identify it as part of the paper's "gospel." In fact, in researching and writing this book, I have been surprised at the number of times I have found myself actually agreeing, at least in part, with the paper's belief system.

In any event, my purpose has not been to promote my own convictions, but instead, to cast further light on the beliefs and veiled proselytizing techniques of the world's most powerful news institution. It is absolutely essential that everyone who is exposed to the mass news media understand the enormous influence of the *Times*, which is widely recognized as the primary agenda-setter for other national news organizations. Only with knowledge such as this can the average reader hope to filter news reports with truly critical eyes and ears and be in a position to make independent judgments, not only about pressing issues of the day, but also about his or her most important personal beliefs.

William Proctor
Vero Beach, Florida

ACKNOWLEDGMENTS

In reflecting on those who have influenced my thinking on the issues related to this book, I realized that I am indebted to far too many reporters, editors, and others in the news business to even attempt to provide a list of names. Instead, I have elected to express a general recognition of those who introduced me years ago to the field of big-city journalism at the New York *Daily News*.

When I first entered the newsroom in Manhattan, I was a trained lawyer and fresh out of service as a defense counsel and military judge in the Marine Corps' Judge Advocate General division. But my heart was in writing, so I naturally gravitated toward a line of work in which I could spend all my time doing what I loved best.

During the years I spent at the *News*, I learned firsthand the basic rules of good journalism, and I have my more experienced colleagues on the paper to thank for that. Also, my former colleagues and competitors at the *New York Times*, the *New York Post*, *Newsday*, and the Associated Press instilled in me insights and principles of newsgathering that have influenced my research and writing profoundly in subsequent years and have helped immeasurably in the preparation of this book.

My Broadman & Holman editor, Len Goss, has provided much-needed editorial guidance, and John Landers has applied his usual superb skills in ushering the book to final publication. Also, I'm grateful to my publisher, Ken Stephens, and to Bucky

Rosenbaum, for their belief in this book and their ongoing support of my writing efforts.

I want to make it absolutely clear that the observations and conclusions in these pages are entirely my own. The help I've received from others in no way implies that they are responsible for the admittedly rather controversial contents that follow.

William Proctor

PART I

THE RISE OF A NEW FUNDAMENTALISM

CHAPTER 1

THE NEW AMERICAN FAITH

Personal beliefs and moral standards are in turmoil—and have been for several decades. Yet two basic questions persist:

- First, why is this decline in our values and behavior taking place?
- Second, what, if anything, can we do to reverse the downward trend—and protect our families and children from moral and spiritual danger?

Often, what was viewed as a bedrock personal virtue or social standard only a few years ago is now seen as an optional lifestyle choice. What was once definitely wrong may now be accepted as quite all right—so long as you feel comfortable and nobody gets hurt.

It's easy to become so immersed in the fashions and enthusiasms of the present that we forget the possibility that there may have been good reasons for the principles and convictions of the past. It's also easy to forget the warning of a certain prophet: "Woe to those who call evil good, and good evil."

Yet if the average American in 1960 could have peered into the future and seen the philosophical and spiritual earthquakes that would transform the cultural landscape of the United States by the year 2000, the likely response would have been shock and consternation.

To understand what some of these changes are—and how dramatically they have affected certain individuals—consider how several actual men and women have been transformed by what might best be described as a series of profound cultural conversions. (Names and identifying characteristics have been changed to protect privacy and confidentiality.)

THE ROMANTIC CONVERSION

"Jennifer" was reared in a conservative religious family, where premarital or extramarital sex were explicitly forbidden. Her mother frequently warned her of the dangers of disease, unwanted pregnancy, and abusive men.

But when Jennifer struck out on her own to pursue her career in a large Midwestern city, she quickly found that these restrictive sexual views put her in a very small minority among her peers. In fact, she couldn't seem to find anyone who followed the traditional morality of her parents. Also, everything she read or saw on TV or in the movies suggested that the healthy norm for a single person was sexual activity, not abstinence.

So Jennifer decided to begin an affair with a man she was seeing at work. As it happened, he was still married, though separated from his wife. Her paramour did finally get divorced, and Jennifer expected that their relationship would eventually blossom into marriage. But after a period of six years of cohabitation, her companion left her for another woman, whom he married within a few months.

Jennifer was devastated and began to question whether the moral course she had chosen for her relationships was wise. But she eventually entered into another cohabitation arrangement with a second man.

Today, she would still like to get married and start a family. But if this current relationship doesn't work out—and problems are already emerging—she is contemplating taking what she calls "the Jodie Foster route" of having a child as a single parent.

THE SEXUAL ORIENTATION CONVERSION

"Paul" experienced homosexual urges from a young age, though he found he was also drawn sexually to some women. During his teenage years, he spent some time mulling over what seemed "normal" lifestyles led by gay men who were described in various mainstream newspapers and magazines he read. He was also impressed by similar depictions in a number of movies and television shows.

Still unsure about his sexuality, Paul found his small town to be too confining and traditional to allow him an opportunity to "discover who I really am." So he decided in the early 1990s to move to a large metropolitan area, which he knew had a large, openly gay community.

Almost immediately after his arrival, Paul cast aside any heterosexual feelings he harbored and entered into a series of gay liaisons until he finally settled down with one male companion for a period of a couple of years. Unfortunately, by then he learned that he was HIV positive. He died of AIDS in the mid-1990s.

THE REPRODUCTIVE CONVERSION

"Pamela" had grown up believing that abortion was wrong, but she wasn't quite sure why. She just accepted that standard because her church and family said it was right.

Then, when Pamela launched her career, she moved in with her boyfriend. On occasion, they had unprotected sex.

When Pamela discovered she had become pregnant, she went into a panic: "I can't afford to have a child! What about my career? Besides, my boyfriend doesn't want to get married and start a family."

The idea of getting an abortion began to seem quite reasonable to her. For one thing, she knew other young women who had undergone procedures to terminate their pregnancies. None of her friends opposed the idea.

Also, everything she read made it clear that abortion was a perfectly acceptable option. In fact, it was usually presented as a reasonable back-up method of birth control. Among the arguments that were most compelling to her were that any woman should have the right to control her future, and any pregnant woman should have the final say over her own body.

Finally, after she entered the second trimester of her pregnancy, Pamela decided to have an abortion.

THE GREEN CONVERSION

"Sophie," who was in her mid-forties, never thought much about the environment until she read a powerful book arguing against the dangers of global warming. After this experience, she found herself reading closely every article on corporate abuses of the environment in the newspaper and listening closely to any television reference to the subject.

Finally, Sophie joined several activist groups and began attending pro-environmental demonstrations. Her "faith" began to extend well beyond simple protection of the woods, air, and seashore. She actually began to affirm an eclectic form of animism and Native American spirituality, sensing that there were multiple "spirits" in the rocks, trees, and sky.

Sophie's growing commitment to animism and radical environmentalism filled a void in her life brought on by an inner crisis of meaning. An attempt on her own, without the help of trained clergy, to recapture her traditional childhood religious training hadn't quite satisfied her, and she found herself wondering more and more about the purpose of her existence.

In a further attempt to find some answers, Sophie embraced a branch of Hinduism, which emphasized the powers of meditation.

Her new spiritual interests caused her to become a vegetarian and work for a radical animal rights group and to continue pursuing the more general environmentalist philosophy she had been developing.

Sophie felt she had found something to live and work for—something bigger than herself that seemed to have the potential to change the world for the better.

THE INTERNATIONAL CONVERSION

"Will" grew up with strong patriotic feelings about the United States and actually wanted to enlist in the Marine Corps at one point.

"A strong America means a safer world," he often said.

Furthermore, he was quite suspicious of putting too much faith in the United Nations or American alliances with foreign governments because he felt these arrangements could work against the United States.

But as he grew older, Will regularly listened to a contrary international viewpoint on public television and public radio. Those media influences, plus regular articles and editorials in his newspaper, confirmed his increasing conviction that the United States needed to de-emphasize American power abroad and rely instead on multinational military forces, which could intervene to prevent human rights violations in foreign nations.

Over a period of a few years, Will found himself becoming less concerned if American troops were placed under foreign commanders, or if the United Nations was given added powers. In fact, in the next election, he voted for candidates who advocated reduced American power abroad and put heavy faith in trusting the goodwill of other nations and the power of international cooperation.

THE CREATION CONVERSION

"Mark" was a regular churchgoer who had always believed in his church's interpretation of the biblical six-day creation, though he wasn't too clear about details. For example, he didn't know how the dinosaurs fit into the picture or how the ancient dates most scientists assigned to the appearance of different species fit in with the biblical chronology.

But Mark was an intelligent guy and very concerned about having a well educated image among his professional peers as well-educated. The more he read and heard about evolution, radiocarbon dating, and the like, the more convinced he became that he couldn't take the biblical account at face value. Besides, he noted that the secular media, which he respected highly, consistently referred to any attempt to take the Bible seriously or to reconcile biblical and scientific arguments as "fundamentalism," "unscientific," or "antiintellectual."

Eventually, Mark became too embarrassed about his church's position to continue attending services. Currently, he has few connections to established religion.

A CULTURAL REVOLUTION?

During the past few decades, American beliefs and practices have shifted on so many issues that some observers are now convinced that we have undergone a genuine cultural revolution.

Reflect for a moment on your own attitudes and those of family members or friends. Do you see major mutations in personal, social, or political beliefs that remind you of the experiences of some of the individuals described above?

Most people I know can point to many such "cultural conversions." And many fear that at least some of these changes may portend an ominous future for our society as a whole.

In other words, certain changes—such as those that contribute to the breakdown of the traditional family and marriage—may reflect a wide-ranging deterioration in morality and ethics. A sampling of prevailing American beliefs, taken from recent studies and surveys on trends in the last half of the twentieth century, tends to support the conclusion that we may have something to worry about.

For example, many Americans now believe that:

- *Having children outside of marriage is socially acceptable.*

Since the late 1960s, many celebrities, including film and rock stars, have shown no compunction about having children out of wedlock. This attitude has surfaced in gossip columns, in television "newsmagazines," and among the general public in regular news stories—and is supported by studies that have compared current and past behavior patterns.

In 1960, for instance, barely 5 percent of all births in the United States occurred outside of marriage. By 1980 that figure had risen to nearly 20 percent, and by 1992, nearly one-third of all babies were born out of wedlock (National Center for Health Statistics; *NYT,* 5/30/95, p. A5; *Miami Herald*, 6/7/95, p. 1A; Bennett, p. 46).

- *The "traditional" concept that the ideal family consists of a husband, wife, and children living under the same roof is now outdated.*

The percentage of American households consisting of married couples with children has declined sharply. According to U.S. Census Bureau data, married couples with children comprised only 25 percent of all American households in 1997, a precipitous drop from 40 percent of all households in 1970.

- *Divorce is not only an acceptable alternative to a difficult or challenging marriage, but often, the best solution.*

The divorce rate in the United States more than doubled between 1960 and the mid-1990s. Half of all marriages now end in divorce, and more than half of these divorces involve families with children.

Furthermore, an estimated 15 percent of all children in divorced families will experience the remarriage of a parent and then a second divorce before they turn eighteen years of age (*NYT*, 3/19/95, p. 1; 5/30/95, p. A5; Bennett, pp. 58–59).

• *Abortion is acceptable as a last-ditch method of birth control.*

Abortions have soared since 1972, a date that is just prior to the 1973 U.S. Supreme Court decision of *Roe v. Wade*, which established a constitutional right to abortion.

The number of abortions stood at about 600,000 in 1972, but after *Roe v. Wade*, quickly moved up to 1.2 million in 1976, 1.6 million in 1980, and a plateau of about 1.7 million in the early 1990s (Alan Guttmacher Institute; Bennett, pp. 68–69).

Those who worry about such changes in our personal convictions, standards, and behavior patterns frequently ask what, if anything, can be done to turn the moral tide in America. In particular, they wonder what they can do on a personal level to protect their families and children from the negative influences that are constantly threatening the traditional home and spiritual values.

As we'll see in the following pages, there are powerful steps that individuals and groups can take to counteract the decline in our society and to protect their loved ones. But first, before we can act intelligently and effectively, we must ask and answer an essential preliminary question:

• *Why have these and other dramatic cultural shifts been occurring during the past few decades?*

Obviously, a number of factors are involved, including presidential policies, new legislation, and landmark court decisions. But few of the political or governmental steps could have made headway without public support. In other words, a significant transformation in public morality and values has been necessary.

So we are left with an even more fundamental question:

• *What has caused public attitudes to change in such a short period of time?*

The responsibility must in large part be laid squarely at the feet of the mass media, which have burgeoned beyond every expectation in the past three to four decades. National news organizations and the immense entertainment industry regularly expose the average man, woman, and child to a steady barrage of new moral and social standards. Even more important, these media outlets consistently report or display many of the earth-shaking changes in morality and values in such a way that they appear natural and normal.

So the non-traditional new values are presented as an inevitable part of "progress," or the "maturing" of a civilized society. The impression is that intelligent, sophisticated people will always accept these tremendous changes as fair and beneficial; the uneducated and religiously closed segments of the population will not.

Finally, we come to the most basic question of all:

- *Is there a single, guiding hand behind the media blitz that is changing our lives?*

A considerable body of evidence, described in some detail in the following pages, suggests strongly that there is indeed a single journalistic hand that sets the public agenda for all others—and that is the self-proclaimed "newspaper of record," the *New York Times.*

CHAPTER 2

THUS SAITH THE TIMES . . .

You may envy New York City. You may mock it. You may even hate it. But you ignore it at your peril, for the bible of contemporary American culture—the holy scripture that canonizes the values and beliefs that control much of your life—is published there. And its name is the *New York Times*.

As this story of the *Times'* influence unfolds, you will encounter a comprehensive worldview that may seem familiar—and rightly so. Most likely, you are exposed to the *Times'* values-laden messages every single day in the news reports that reach you through your own newspaper, local television, radio outlets, and the Internet.

If you take time to analyze those messages, you will soon surmise that you are dealing with a well-designed belief system, which touches every aspect of life. In effect, you are being exposed to a *gospel*, but one that is a far cry from the traditional good news of Matthew, Mark, Luke, and John. Rather, this gospel is rooted in a kind of secular theology that purports to convey infallible social, moral, and political truth—a truth that the paper fervently promotes with all the zeal of the fieriest proselytizer.

Although the gospel according to the *New York Times* encompasses many specific beliefs and doctrines—which we'll discuss in some detail in the ensuing pages—all point to a basic and *absolute* tenet, which can be summed up in this statement of faith:

> To be a good person and a productive member of society—and to attain maximum self-realization—I must believe in the values, rights, and standards of behavior established by the *Times*.

> Conversely, the more I deviate from the *Times'* worldview, the greater the danger that I'll become a bad person and a drag on society—and never realize my full potential as a human being.

Another way of phrasing this statement of faith might go like this: The highest aspiration anyone can harbor in life is to be conformed to the image of the *Times*.

Now, if you happen to live outside Manhattan, all this may sound like irrelevant drivel or New York poppycock. But in fact, no matter who you are or where you live, you are touched by the *Times* in more ways than you may realize.

ARE YOU TOUCHED BY THE TIMES?

Those who live and work outside the city usually have little idea of the far-reaching power that the *Times* wields over their cultural, political, and personal values. The influence impacts the average non-New Yorker—who may never have bought or read a copy of the *Times*—through a complex of media tentacles that originate in the paper's editorial and business offices on West 43rd Street, just off Times Square in Manhattan.

Well-orchestrated news, editorial, and op-ed pieces from the *Times* slither out to other media organizations, including the major broadcast stations and networks. No responsible news anchor, editor, or producer can allow a day to go by without a substantial dose of the *Times*.

Every politician, scholar, or other opinion leader who operates on the national or international stage—from U.S. presidents . . . to cabinet members . . . to senators . . . to corporate CEOs . . . to university professors—must know what is in the *Times*. Furthermore, if they are called to account by the paper for their behavior, they must be prepared to respond to pertinent findings or charges, or suffer the consequences.

What are the implications for *you* when one news media behemoth becomes the virtually infallible cultural bible for movers and shakers on the national and international scene?

Here's one way of understanding your personal challenge. If you analyze the *Times'* coverage of particular political or social issues—including relevant editorials, strategically placed and written news stories, op-ed pieces, and pictures—you may find, as I have, that certain of your personal beliefs conform rather closely to the messages conveyed by the newspaper. But on other issues, you may discover that you part company radically with the *Times*.

Unfortunately, most of us don't always read analytically—and that's where our problems begin. You may be in such a hurry in the morning that you feel you have time only to skim headlines, editorials, the "leads" of a few major stories, and some prominent pictures. Or if you typically settle down with the paper in the evening, you probably just want to relax and enjoy yourself. You don't feel like thinking too deeply after a hard day at work.

In other words, day after day, year after year, you move passively through news reports, for the most part accepting the words and concepts on each page at face value. In effect, you become an uncritical literalist as you absorb the information, opinions, *and underlying belief system* that emerge on the newsprint before you.

So what's the problem with this seemingly innocuous practice of enjoying the paper every day?

The danger is that the *Times*, perhaps more than any other media leader, has developed extremely potent and effective mechanisms to stamp its views and basic assumptions about life on our minds. Even more ominous is the evidence that this subtle process of proselytizing is changing our basic attitudes and beliefs, and most of us don't ever know it.

More specifically, what enables the *Times* to shape American social, political, and cultural values? The beginning of an answer lies at the very source of the paper's power—the *Times*' premier position in the world of journalism.

WORDS FROM ON HIGH

Leading journalism scholars and other news organs and institutions consistently place the *Times* at the top in any newspaper ranking. Columbia University's Melvin Mencher, author of the classic textbook, *News Reporting and Writing*, which has been used in many college and university journalism courses, sums up the feeling this way:

> "Some newspapers regularly figure in lists of the country's best newspapers. At the head of the list, invariably, is the *New York Times*, the nation's newspaper of record" (p. xviii).

Mencher's sentiments about the superior status of the *Times* are echoed in the results of a 1995 study on newspapers from The Freedom Forum Media Studies Center: "the *New York Times* has long been considered America's paper of record."

Interestingly, the Freedom Forum is a foundation established by one of the *Times*' arch-competitors, Allen H. Neuharth, former chief executive officer of Gannett Company, the news media conglomerate. Neuharth also founded *USA Today*, the national newspaper that vies directly with the *Times* for circulation supremacy in the United States.

History speaks

Certainly, solid achievements support the *Times*' top billing among its peers and competitors. These are apparent after even a cursory look at the historic record.

The *Times* has been publishing definitive, award-winning, policy-shaping national and international stories under the ownership of the Ochs-Sulzberger family for more than 100 years.

Actually, the paper's immediate ancestor, the *New-York Daily Times*, published its first issue on September 17, 1851, but the modern-day powerhouse didn't emerge until nearly fifty years later.

The newspaper was effectively bankrupt when Adolph S. Ochs bought it in 1896. He immediately placed the soon-to-be-legendary implied promise on the editorial page: "All the News That's Fit to Print." Then, in February 1897, apparently thoroughly taken with the slogan, he moved it to a box on the front page—called in newspaper parlance, the "ear"—where it remains to this day. With that gesture, one of the most remarkable turnarounds in news media history began (see Davis, pp. 172–198; Berger, p. 2).

Today—after decades of strong family leadership culminating with that of the present chairman and publisher, Arthur Ochs Sulzberger Jr., Adolph Och's great grandson—the paper has become financially healthy and profitable and has ascended to the very zenith of American journalism. By 1999, the *Times'* stories and reporters had accumulated seventy-nine of the coveted Pulitzer prizes, a number that far exceeded that of any other newspaper.

In 1998, when the *Times* reached seventy-seven Pulitzers, *Editor & Publisher*, the main organ of the newspaper industry, trumpeted the achievement this way:

> "Casting its shadow over journalism the way a swaggering Babe Ruth used to dominate baseball, the *New York Times* has won three 1998 Pulitzer Prizes, raising its record to 77, more than double the awards of any other newspaper" (April 18, 1998, *www.mediainfo.com*, p. l).

Newsweek magazine has gone as far as any competitor in singing the praises and acknowledging the quasi-religious status of the *Times*. A September 15, 1997, article begins with the observation that the *Times* "is printed on sacred parchment paper" (p. 76).

Later in the article, the writer becomes more specific in his reverence—as he recognizes the power of the *Times* not only over competitive newspapers, but also over network TV news organizations:

"The *Times* is special, not so much for the paper itself as for its effect on everybody else. Preeminent among a tiny handful of papers including the *Wall Street Journal* and the *Washington Post* (*Newsweek*'s sister publication), the *Times* sets the agenda for what the network-news divisions and a host of other news outlets do" (p. 76).

In this same vein, Joseph C. Goulden, in his otherwise critical *Fit to Print: A. M. Rosenthal and His Times*, states that, like good students, the other media outlets follow the lead of the *Times*. Furthermore, he says, the nation's leaders and scholars regard the paper as so influential that for them, a *Times* report is the same as "certifiable historical fact" (Goulden, p. 16).

To symbolize the spiritual ascendancy of the *Times* in our culture, Ellis Cose gives the third part of his book, *The Press*, a telling title: "The Cathedral: The New York Times." Having thus identified the true temple of news worship, he goes on to pay proper homage:

> "*The New York Times* ranks as the preeminent newspaper in the United States. It is not the oldest paper in the nation, or in New York, but it has the strongest sense of history and tradition. And—as is the nature of preeminent institutions—it is shrouded by the densest cloud of mystery; a change in its masthead is scrutinized by journalists in a manner usually reserved for leadership change at the Kremlin" (Cose, p. 187).

The *Times*' own staff has also been known to view the paper with near-religious fervor. Former reporter John Corry captured the in-house veneration this way: "The *Times* was the *Times*, as much myth as institution, and if you worked there, it was home, church, and family" (Corry, pp. 26–27).

When seemingly responsible people begin to refer to a secular communications company as a "cathedral" and a "church," which is "shrouded by mystery" and published on "sacred parchment paper," the boundaries of mere newsgathering have been crossed.

But don't assume that such reverential views are limited to some remote Manhattan elite, or for that matter, that the main outreach of the *Times* is restricted to New York City. Far from it!

Instead, you can be certain that this preeminent paper is perched in some fashion on your very doorstep—or in your TV or computer—whether you live in California, Florida, Tennessee, Louisiana, or North Carolina.

WHY YOU CAN'T ESCAPE THE TIMES

There are several important reasons why you can't escape the *New York Times*, and the first is the paper's vast circulation. The *Times* is in an extremely strong position to exploit its reputation as the most influential news institution in the United States—if not on the entire earth—because by some measures it is the most widely read newspaper in this country.

According to statistics released by the newspaper industry's Audit Bureau of Circulations (A.B.C.) in May of 1999, *USA Today* had the highest daily circulation in the United States with more than 1.8 million average weekday sales, and the financially oriented *Wall Street Journal* came in second. The *New York Times* placed third in weekday sales, with more than 1.1 million.

But even more impressive, the average circulation of the influential Sunday edition of the *Times* was almost 1.7 million according to the A.B.C. calculations. The combined weekday and Sunday total enable the *Times* to proclaim on its Web page that it is the "largest seven-day newspaper in the country."

The paper is also easily accessible through ordinary paper routes: the company advertises home delivery in 181 American cities and 43 states. In view of such outreach, don't be surprised if somebody in your office or on your block subscribes. Many others you know probably pick up the paper at their local 7-Eleven or newsstand.

Furthermore, contrary to the general decline in newspaper circulation across America, readership of both the daily and Sunday editions of the *Times* is still on the increase according to the 1999 A.B.C. report.

But wide circulation, steady growth, and an unrivaled top reputation in the journalistic community are only some of the reasons for the *Times'* influence. The pervasive power of the paper becomes even more evident when we consider how the *Times* permeates our entire culture, including the editorial content of other media both in the United States and abroad.

THE TENTACLES OF THE TIMES

As we have already seen, the "cathedral" of American journalism is centered in Manhattan at the headquarters of the flagship newspaper on West 43rd Street. What many don't realize, however, is that the *Times* also owns the *Boston Globe*, which is widely recognized as the leading newspaper in New England, with fifteen Pulitzer Prizes to its credit.

Furthermore, in July 1999, the *Times* strengthened its grip on New England by replacing the *Globe's* publisher—who was a member of the family that had run the Boston paper for 126 years—with the *Times'* own senior vice president from New York.

A Boston radio commentator who had written both for the *Times* and the *Globe* seemed less than happy about the change when he observed, "All the commercial media in Boston are owned or controlled by distant emperors" (*NYT,* 7/13/99, 1999, p. C8).

But New England occupies only one corner of the *Times'* communications empire. The company also owns twenty-one regional newspapers, which can be found in such far-flung locations as Sarasota, Florida; Wilmington, North Carolina; Santa Barbara, California; Tuscaloosa, Alabama; and Thibodaux, Louisiana. Add to these the Times Broadcast Group, with CBS, NBC, and ABC television affiliates in Virginia, Tennessee, Alabama, Oklahoma, and Illinois.

Radio stations, magazines, and an extensive syndicate and news service also contribute to the *Times'* outreach from coast to coast. The *New York Times* Syndicate, which disseminates the paper's news stories and opinion pieces, has more than two thousand clients on five continents. The *New York Times* News Service boasts six hundred fifty clients in more than fifty countries.

In fact, through reprinted articles in papers that subscribe to the Syndicate and News Service, the Manhattan "bible" has probably become part of your own daily diet of news. To evaluate the extent to which you may have fallen under the spell of the "distant emperors" in New York City, check the small print under some of the articles you read today for some reference to the *New York Times* as the news source. Most likely, you'll find you're reading the "newspaper of record" more often than you think.

In researching this book, one of the papers I read regularly for a couple of years was the *Palm Beach Post*, a Cox Newspaper publication with wide readership in east central Florida. Though owned by an entirely different company—which also publishes the *Atlanta Journal-Constitution*—the *Post* sometimes ran so many reprints from the *Times* that on occasion I felt I was rereading the *Times* itself.

For example, during the first two weeks in early November 1996—a crucial news period that included the Clinton-Dole presidential election—multiple *Times* articles were reprinted in the *Post*. Many, sometimes more than one at a time, appeared on the front page of the Palm Beach paper. Furthermore, not only did the *Post* give prominent play to many *Times* stories, but also, like the *Times*, it endorsed Bill Clinton for president.

The Internet is becoming another important medium through which the *Times* conveys its message. The organization's growing array of Internet offerings at its Web site, *www.nytimes.com*, includes the *New York Times on the Web*, which provides the current day's major stories without charge. Other Internet efforts by the *Times*—including a joint venture with the bookseller barnesandnoble.com and with TheStreet.com, an on-line financial news service—are multiplying at disconcerting speed. So, it's reasonable to assume that the paper will be at the forefront of future technological media breakthroughs and that its influence will increase, even as the scope of the Internet increases.

The company even owns a half interest, with the *Washington Post*, in the *International Herald Tribune*, the English-language newspaper with circulation of more than two hundred thousand that is read by opinion leaders throughout the world.

To top off its sprawling influence, the *Times* company has developed an educational arm to pull in students ranging in age from middle school through college. The *New York Times Learning Network* provides quizzes and other activities based on the paper's daily content, and the *New York Times College Program* promotes the publication as a learning resource in colleges and universities. In other words, the next generation is already fast becoming a captive audience of the paper.

Of course, this description of the wide-ranging corporate power of the *Times* could easily describe many other major international companies. But when that company is a communications organization with the power to shape the opinions and beliefs of millions, special scrutiny seems to be in order.

REFLECTIONS ON THE TIMES FROM ANOTHER MANHATTAN NEWSROOM

I first became aware of the far-reaching power of the *Times* when I ran the Manhattan Criminal Courts Bureau and served as legal correspondent for the New York *Daily News*. Of course, the *News*, the *New York Post*, and *Newsday* all exerted considerable clout on the New York scene. Still, there was a subtle assumption and occasionally even a sense of deference that the *Times* was indeed what it claimed to be: the "newspaper of record."

An article in other papers might bestow fleeting fame or notoriety and could certainly go a long way toward promoting a local or statewide political campaign, or furthering a regional cause or issue. But coverage by the *Times* could project a story onto the national or international stage and might even make it a part of history.

The impact of the *Times* on television reporters was evident to me from the moment I started covering court cases for the *News*. I still recall television reporters crowding into the Manhattan Criminal Courts newsroom during major trials, which showcased such nationally renowned defense lawyers as F. Lee Bailey and the late William Kunstler. More often than not, the first step these TV journalists took to prepare for the interviews they had planned was to pore over the previous day's report in the *Times*.

More recently, I tried for a few weeks to keep track of the number of times that Ted Koppel of ABC's *Nightline*, Charlie Rose of PBS, Brian Williams of NBC, and other television and radio commentators mentioned a *Times* story. Some would even interview a *Times* reporter as *the* authority for the topic they were discussing. But the cases quickly became so numerous that I soon abandoned the exercise.

I've also witnessed in a close and personal way the impact that the *Times* can have on its readers when a product or service receives a favorable mention in the paper. A number of years ago, a specialized national newsletter I cofounded and edited was given a favorable review in a *Times* article. My partner and I enjoyed an immediate quadrupling of our subscriptions around the country.

Such a result wouldn't surprise the opinion leaders, upscale New Yorkers, and others who revere the words of the *Times*. During the twenty-plus years I lived in Manhattan—as well as in the subsequent years that I have operated outside the city—I have frequently heard friends or business associates offer one of these clinchers as definitive proof to end an argument:

"The *Times* says . . ." or
"The *Times* supports . . ." or
"The *Times* disagrees . . ."

With such a citation of authority, the discussion is usually closed.

THE POWER OF THE SELF-SERVING STATEMENT

The *Times* doesn't hesitate to sound its own horn—just in case someone has missed the point. In a guest column called "Writers on Writing," the writer Henry Bech began with this verbal obeisance: "One . . . of the spiritual burdens of being a New Yorker is an undue reverence for the *New York Times* . . ." (3/1/99, p. B1).

In a similar vein, the novelist and journalist Ward Just, writing in the *Times Book Review*, referred to the publication as "the nation's most important newspaper" (3/7/99, p. 7).

Perhaps the most blatant adulation came in the *Times'* review of the book, *The Trust: The Private and Powerful Family Behind The New York Times*, written by Susan E. Tifft and Alex S. Jones, a former press reporter for the *Times*. The guest reviewer, Christopher Ogden, wrote, "Presidents, nations, corporations, causes and citizens have all wanted something—ideally approval or at least recognition—from the world's most influential newspaper." Furthermore, "The authority of The Times remains unequalled today" (9/22/99, p. B8).

Even the paper's interns can't escape the implied imperative to kowtow at key moments. Writing a blurb on Monica Lewinsky in a *Week in Review* story, an unnamed editorial assistant began, "I have just completed my first week of work at the *New York Times*, the newspaper of record...." (2/7/99, p. 7).

It would be easy to dismiss such statements as mere self-serving twaddle by a publication obsessed with its own self-importance or by writers who want to ensure a regular flow of assignments from the temple on Times Square. But the philosophical authority of the *Times* can and does have immediate, practical impact—such as by swaying readers' ballot decisions through strong editorial endorsements.

Nearly every time I encounter a voting line in Manhattan, I see many people perusing and underlining the *Times* recommendations for different offices. They are clearly ready to accept, without question, the paper's guidance in casting their ballots. (Typically, candidates anointed with the *Times* imprimatur are liberal Democrats.)

I must confess that I am not immune to the seductive pull of the "gray lady," as the paper has been nicknamed—not only for its traditionally somber black-and-white look and layout (though touches of color have been added), but also in honor of its serious reputation. Even today, operating from my editorial headquarters in Florida, I find that no morning is complete without my "*Times* fix." I have a deeply ingrained need to get the latest word on health and fitness from Jane Brody, science from John Noble Wilford, and medicine from Lawrence K. Altman. The "Beliefs" section, produced by religion writers Peter Steinfels and Gustav Niebuhr, usually fascinates me. Finally, I can't put the paper down without checking the page-one treatment of the current national or international crisis.

But over the years I have discovered a darker side to the all-encompassing influence of the *Times*. Any institution that wields such vast power over individual minds and attitudes, and by inference over cultural movements and political decisions, must be monitored closely. And if necessary, such an institution must also be called to account—or even exposed—when its influence over personal beliefs and values becomes excessive or inappropriate.

EXPLORING THE DARK SIDE OF THE GRAY LADY

As part of the research for the various articles and nearly eighty books I have written, I have closely followed the *Times'* coverage of current events for almost three decades—through daily reading, studying, and filing of *Times* articles.

In preparing for this book, I've devoted more than four years to special analysis of thousands of *Times* news stories, editorials, op-ed pieces, columns, and reviews. As part of the study, I've also evaluated a significant number of references to the *Times* in other publications. The materials that form the main basis for this current inquiry were published mostly from the summer of 1995 through the summer of 1999. (For a more detailed explanation of my methodology, see the Preface and the Appendix.)

As a result of this investigation, I have moved inexorably to the conclusion that the *Times* is engaged in the ongoing promotion of its own well-defined, comprehensive "gospel." In other words, the Manhattan conglomerate—especially at the highest administrative levels—is not a bastion of unbiased, objective news coverage. Instead, all evidence points toward an organization that sees itself as the primary guardian of a great worldview and what the paper regards as a virtually infallible set of guiding truths that demand to be disseminated widely and promoted ardently.

The main vehicle through which the *Times* spreads its gospel involves a subtle but highly potent process of journalistic proselytizing that I call "Culture Creep." When accepted uncritically by those exposed to the *Times'* influence, Culture Creep has the potential to shape individual minds, alter personal beliefs, and produce broad-based social and political changes.

HOW THE TIMES SHAPES MINDS AND MOVEMENTS THROUGH CULTURE CREEP

In a nutshell, Culture Creep works this way:

The process begins with the people who set editorial policy at the top of the *Times'* hierarchy. An in-depth examination of the paper's editorial choices over a four-year period suggests strongly that those in charge affirm a set of clear-cut beliefs, or doctrinal points about what is important and worthy of veneration in life and what is not. Specifically, the *Times'* doctrines include deep convictions about such matters as foreign relations, human rights, genocide, welfare, capital punishment, censorship, gun control, cosmology, human nature, political conservatism and liberalism, sexuality, education, abortion, and religion.

To be sure, over the years the *Times'* publisher, executive editor, and other executives have been known to disagree with one another about story assignments and editorial positions. But when all is said and done—and the paper finally hits the streets and the Web site each day—a remarkable consensus has emerged about basic values and beliefs. The *Times'* consistency in affirming a comprehensive and distinctive worldview is reminiscent of the unwavering allegiance to a common creed, or a specific statement of faith that one might expect in a fundamentalist religious body.

Also, much like an evangelical religious body, the *Times* has developed highly effective techniques for "spreading the gospel." The basic way the paper proselytizes is through headlines and pictures that implant a particular message in the reader's mind; the strategic selection of facts that support a particular viewpoint; subtly slanted writing; and placement (or "play") of mind-shaping stories in prominent spots throughout the paper.

A story that the *Times* considers particularly important will usually be put on the front page or assigned to some other eye-catching position. The article will typically be introduced with a headline that leans toward the desired belief. A complementary "lead" (the first few sentences of the story) may be given a subtle slant or spin, which reinforces the headline. A "kicker"—or dramatic concluding statement or quote for a story—establishes the final impression with a memorable thought or viewpoint that the editor and writer want to fix in the reader's mind.

But words are only part of the story. An accompanying picture may promote the desired message even more powerfully than any text. In addition, a story containing a message that the paper wants to push will often be coordinated with editorials and op-ed pieces that reflect the *Times'* overriding viewpoint.

Finally, important stories and opinion pieces are disseminated through the Times Syndicate, the Times News Service, and other media outlets under the paper's control. At the same time, unrelated newspapers, talk shows, and television and radio networks will inevitably pick up on the story.

Nor is that the end of it. When the *Times* considers an issue or position to be particularly significant, it employs the Culture Creep technique in one form or another again and again, over a period of weeks, months, and even years. As the paper hammers away at favored issues, some opinion leaders may gradually begin to change and even experience full-blown "conversions" to the *Times'* positions. In addition, those university scholars, media moguls, and government leaders who already hold the "correct" views may be inclined to intensify their advocacy of *Times*-approved doctrines.

Finally, as the word spreads far and wide, the general public gets on board. Given enough time, a dominant media organization, operating through the irresistible force of Culture Creep, can shape a society—and actually re-create the people in that society in the organization's own image.

How does this mechanism of Culture Creep work in practice on the *Times?* Consider the play given during a one-month period in 1998 to the explosive and divisive issue of homosexual rights.

A CASE STUDY IN CULTURE CREEP

The attitude of the American people toward homosexuality has changed dramatically since the gay rights movement gained steam in the 1970s—and the *New York Times* has taken the lead in pushing for the shift in mainstream attitudes.

A 1998 study by the pro-gay rights advocacy group, the National Gay and Lesbian Task Force, revealed that in 1987, 75 percent of the American people disapproved of same-sex relationships. But by 1996, that disapproval rating had dropped by nearly 20 percentage points to 56 percent *(www.ngltf.org/Press/execorder.html*; also see *NYT*, 3/31/98, p. 15).

Of course, it's not possible to establish an ironclad cause-and-effect relationship between what the *Times* has written and promoted and a change in public attitudes toward a particular issue. But given what we know about the tremendous power that the *Times* wields over national media and opinion leaders, a highly suggestive case can be made for a link between the ongoing *Times'* news coverage and editorial statements, and the public's changing beliefs on this important issue.

Some activists have criticized the *Times* for being slow to respond to gay rights issues, but in fact, the paper took relatively early positions that were sympathetic to the concerns of homosexuals. For example, on August 8, 1982, the *Times* led the way in referring to "acquired immune deficiency syndrome" and "A.I.D.S." (later shortened to "AIDS") to describe the devastating, lethal epidemic that was spreading among homosexual men. The *Washington Post* became the second major national newspaper to begin regular coverage of AIDS ("Covering . . . ," *Columbia*

Journalism Review, p. 1).

During the early 1980s, the *Times* began listing the living members in same-sex relationships as "companions" in its obituaries. A few years later, in the late 1980s, the paper started to employ the term "gay" as a synonym for homosexual (Tifft, pp. 616, 687; Goulden, pp. 405–406). Also, with the advent of the 1990s, the paper's obituary pages became more heavily loaded with deaths of young homosexuals who had died from AIDS.

As the 1990s unfolded, the *Times* ran many news stories that assumed as fact that homosexuals deserved a special civil and human rights status—one designed to place them at least on the same legal plane as minorities, women, or those persecuted abroad because of their ethnic status (see "TWO STEPS FORWARD FOR HOMOSEXUALS," 11/16/95, p. A12).

A Spring Campaign

To illustrate more precisely how the *Times* employs its peculiar brand of Manhattan mind control, consider this sequence of articles promoting gay marriage during a period of several weeks in 1998:

- *April 17, 1998: A front-page story describes how clergy are increasingly performing gay "marriages."*

On the jump page inside the paper, the story continued below a dramatic and sympathetic headline that spanned all six columns of the page:

LAWS ASIDE, SOME MEMBERS OF CLERGY ARE QUIETLY
BLESSING GAY 'MARRIAGE'

Perhaps most striking of all, the inside page was dominated by a two-column picture showing two lesbians kissing in front of a Unitarian Universalist church. The caption for the picture included this editorialized line, which suggested, almost subliminally, the trend that the *Times* expected the reader to accept as a given for the future: "Same sex religious unions like theirs are becoming more common."

- *April 18, 1998: religion writer Peter Steinfels features quotes from a book author who places same-sex relationships on the same plane as regular marriage.*

Steinfels chose the following pro-gay-marriage statements from the author, a heterosexual mother who had written a book on sexual fidelity: "Homosexuality can be moral or immoral in exactly the same ways and for exactly the same reasons as heterosexuality."

Steinfels then went on to quote her as saying that sexual orientation shouldn't "exclude anyone from matrimony in the sacramental sense" (p. B6).

- *May 3, 1998: A major, sympathetic feature on actress Anne Heche and her lesbian love affair with TV comedian Ellen DeGeneres appears in the Sunday "Summer Movies" section (p. SM2).*
- *May 6, 1998: a news story entitled "REFORM RABBIS TO AVOID VOTE ON ALLOWING SAME-SEX UNIONS," keeps the issue of gay marriage at the forefront of public consciousness (p. A16).*

Then, the *Times'* spring campaign reached a climax with the overt promotion of a practical measure designed to enhance the legal status and rights of gay couples:

- *May 13, 1998: a prominent news story heralds a bill proposed by Mayor Rudolph Giuliani to give "domestic partners," including gay couples, the same rights and benefits as spouses in city contracts, housing, and death benefits (p. A28).*

The story was introduced by a four-column headline, "GAY GROUPS REJOICE IN MAYOR'S MOVE AS CRITICS DEPLORE IT," and a laudatory subhead, "A milestone for the birthplace of the gay rights movement." But a close reading of the article, which was heavily weighted toward the gay position, revealed an almost total absence of the "deploring" that was promised in the headline. Specifically, less that 20 percent of the more than 18 column inches allotted to the story included any negative elements at all—and most of those that did focused on problems the mayor's actions might create for his national political ambitions. In fact, the reporter devoted barely five lines, or less than 3 percent of the entire story, to addressing specific moral, familial, or social arguments against or questions about Giulani's proposal!

Now remember, we're talking here about what purports to be a news story. Yet by no stretch of journalistic standards could such a skewed selection of facts in such a controversial and important story be considered evenhanded or fair. Even more important, a failure by the "newspaper of record" to provide an in-depth discussion of the arguments of all sides in stories involving such a major shift in social policy seems to border on irresponsibility. Regardless of the beliefs of the publisher, editors, or reporters, the public deserves a less biased presentation of the facts in a supposedly straight news account. To serve the public properly, stories that blend fact and opinion or editorial bias in this way should be signaled clearly as "opinion," or at least as "news analysis." In this reporting the "newspaper of record" fell far short.

But in offering this critique, I don't want to be misunderstood. I'm not suggesting that we should expect reporters and editors to operate atop some unachievable pedestal of objectivity. In fact, as I've said, I don't believe complete objectivity in a news story is possible. Nor do I believe that the time-honored principle of balance in news writing and reporting necessarily requires that exactly 50 percent of an article—even on a highly explosive topic—should be allotted respectively to the pros and cons of an issue. But when practically no space is accorded to an opposing viewpoint in what purports to be a regular news account, questions about bias automatically arise.

The Editorial Coup de Grace

Finally, the *Times* capped this particular campaign to promote gay relationships with a strong editorial, which also appeared on 5/13/98 (p. A26).

Entitled "EQUALITY FOR DOMESTIC PARTNERS," the editorial took an official position that strongly favored the mayor's "enlightened legislation." Giuliani "should be applauded" for "following in an honorable tradition of tolerance and equality that even conservative audiences should understand," the *Times'* editorial page declared.

What was the final result of this *Times'* effort on behalf of the gay rights agenda?

On June 24, 1998, the New York City Council passed the measure extending the rights of "domestic partners" overwhelmingly by a vote of 39 to 7. Among other things, the bill gave "domestic partners" much the same status as married spouses, including visitation rights in city hospitals and jails, certain property rights, allowance for bereavement leave, and child care for city employees (New York City Council Newswire, p. 1).

The Council noted that by the end of April 1998 approximately eighty-seven hundred couples had registered as domestic partners in New York City under provisions in previous mayoral executive orders. Of those, about 45 percent were registered as "same-sex couples," and 55 percent were registered as unmarried heterosexual couples (Local Law, p. 1).

Mayor Giuliani signed the bill into law on July 7, 1998.

Of course, this one-month campaign represents only one battle in an ongoing war the *Times* has waged in favor of the gay rights program. The full operation of the mechanism of Culture Creep is far too complex and comprehensive to explain in this short introduction. As we'll see in later chapters, the *Times* continuously utilizes numerous variations on these techniques, often spanning periods of a year or more, to fix particular beliefs in the public consciousness. The example cited above is just a taste of how news stories are placed and slanted to move the public to take actions that may profoundly change cultural assumptions and even the basic fabric of our society.

Now here is a preview of what is to come in the following pages of this book, beginning with a brief introduction to "Manhattan Fundamentalism," which is the focus of chapters 3–5.

AN INTRODUCTION TO MANHATTAN FUNDAMENTALISM

The "Manhattan Fundamentalism" promoted by the *Times* is a well-defined but also rather rigid package of viewpoints which the paper disseminates widely to influence political, social, and personal beliefs and behaviors.

An overriding assumption in the paper is that if you disagree with the *Times'* position on an important doctrine, you're probably not well informed. Or you're not well educated; or you're unsophisticated; or you're close minded. Worst of all, you may be labeled "intolerant."

As the *Times* uses this last term, any person or group that disagrees with a *Times'* belief—especially as to religious faith, social policy, or moral behavior—is in danger of committing the mortal sin of "intolerance." Yet as we'll see, the titans of the *Times'* have stumbled into a paradox here: the paper itself often expresses virulent intolerance toward those who dare to diverge from certain of its stated doctrines. In short, nonconformity often isn't tolerated in the news sanctuary on West 43rd Street.

Chapter 3 will unmask in more detail the clandestine operation of Culture Creep, as the *Times* practices its distinctive method of converting unbelievers to Manhattan Fundamentalism. Then in chapter 4, we'll discuss the most basic tenets of Manhattan Fundamentalism—a term, by the way, that is *not* an oxymoron, first impressions notwithstanding.

Chapter 5 will explore the *Times'* "plan of salvation," both for America and for the broader international community. In that section, you'll get a close look at the *Times'* utopian hopes for the future—and how the paper plans to move American society, and eventually the rest of the world, in its own preordained direction.

THE DEADLY SINS AND RULING SPIRITS OF THE TIMES

Because the *Times'* editorials and even a significant number of news stories are often communicated with a quasi-religious fervor, it seems appropriate to use spiritual terminology to describe many of the efforts of its writers and editors. So chapters 6–12 will scrutinize the "seven deadly sins," or major behaviors and beliefs that the *Times* loves to hate and attack.

These include:

- The sin of religious certainty—especially evangelical Christian and Roman Catholic certainty
- The sin of conservatism—especially "right-wing" Republican politics
- The sin of capital punishment
- The sin of broken public trust—including ethical violations in business, government, and the non-profit sector
- The sin of the Second Amendment—or virtually any form of private gun possession
- The sin of censorship—or placing any restrictions on freedoms of the press, speech, or expression
- The sin of limiting in any significant way a woman's right to abortion

Then in chapters 13–16, we'll investigate the "cultural spirits" the *Times* has enshrined at its cultural cathedral just off Times Square. These represent hallowed preconceptions, movements, social policies, and isms that may be worshiped as ultimate truth. Separate discussions focus on the spirits of multiculturalism, globalism, sexual freedom, environmentalism, entitlements and welfarism, scientism, and naturalistic humanism.

The final chapters of the book will provide some thoughts and suggestions about how individual readers—as well as groups and organizations that question the *Times'* worldview—can launch a counterattack against the encroachment of media-driven values.

Now, let's move on to a more detailed examination of exactly how the *New York Times* may be playing with *your* mind and *your* belief system through the process of Culture Creep.

CHAPTER 3

WELCOME TO THE WORLD OF CULTURE CREEP

T he most powerful news organization on earth, the *New York Times*, employs a highly versatile array of journalistic devices to mold the American mind and draw the lightly committed and unwary into the paper's web of beliefs and values.

Some readers, after considering the exact nature of the *Times'* "doctrines," may decide that the *Times'* positions are consistent with their own beliefs. For these readers, there's no reason for concern.

But the majority of readers will probably determine that at least one and often many of the *Times'* beliefs vary significantly from their own. In that case, there is reason for concern—because of the powerful and effective techniques of persuasion that this unique paper has developed over the past century for exercising influence over public opinion.

The low-profile and often overlooked mechanisms through which the *Times* operates will be referred to throughout this book as Culture Creep, a concept you have already been introduced to in the previous chapter. It's so easy to be intellectually blindsided by this subtle process that even the most independent thinkers may be unaware of how their opinions and beliefs are gradually being nudged in new directions.

What are the specific characteristics of Culture Creep? To what extent is this process jeopardizing your freedom to think freely or influencing your personal belief system? To answer these questions, it's necessary first to dispose of an important negative issue—what Culture Creep is *not*.

WHAT CULTURE CREEP IS NOT

In most cases, the following three categories of news coverage should not be confused with Culture Creep.

Category One: Straight Facts on Current Events

Culture Creep may not be a factor in the reporting of straight facts about certain current events—such as natural disasters, wars, the outcome of diplomatic negotiations, or corporate or governmental decisions.

A front-page, four-column lead story in the August 18, 1999, paper was headed, "THOUSANDS KILLED AS BIG QUAKE HITS CITIES IN WESTERN TURKEY—AN ANXIOUS SEARCH—MANY PINNED IN RUBBLE—GOVERNMENT SEEKS AID IN EXCAVATING." The *Times* is at its best when communicating the facts about a big breaking international story such as this one.

Similarly, a front-page headline in the August 5, 1999, paper read, "DOW CHEMICAL SAYS IT PLANS TO BUY UNION CARBIDE." For the most part, this story also represented a straight report about an important event in the business world and didn't involve any obvious attempt to change beliefs or opinions. The information was presented in such a way that it could be useful to investors or others having some dealings with these companies—but with a minimum of editorializing.

Category Two: Warnings about the General Welfare

Secondly, Culture Creep is often not a factor when the paper is issuing warnings to the public about possible dangers to the general welfare—such as the threat of terrorism or arms proliferation.

A front-page story on January 22, 1999—headlined, "CLINTON DESCRIBES TERRORISM THREAT FOR 21ST CENTURY"—illustrates this point. In that story, the *Times* provided a straightforward account from the president about the danger that terrorists may try to conduct chemical or germ warfare on American soil in the next few years. A useful sidebar article that contained excerpts from an interview with the president on this subject was also included (pp. A1, A9).

Category Three: Health and Quality of Life News

Culture Creep does not usually sneak into reports about medical breakthroughs, scientific findings, or other news that may affect our health or quality of life.

For example, one "Science Times" and "Health & Fitness" section in the paper (8/3/99) was filled with helpful stories for parents. One article revealed that contrary to previous reports, the practice of playing Mozart and other classical music for babies and toddlers may not help youngsters' brain development (p. D1). In another report, personal health expert Jane E. Brody provided parents with information and tips on ways to keep toilet training from becoming a power struggle (p. D7). Finally, the paper ran a feature on the new Spark fitness program which health experts have designed to put kids into better shape (p. D8).

Such useful, balanced, and well-reported articles keep me buying the paper every day. But you'll notice that in each of these categories, I've included a qualifier, such as "usually" or "often." The reason is that editorializing and journalistic proselytizing can sometimes enter into even these traditionally "straight" areas of news coverage.

For example, a report about a new cholesterol-lowering drug may contain unadorned facts that are useful to anyone with a lipid-related cardiovascular problem. But it's reasonable to assume that a decidedly slanted or partisan report about a new pill that induces abortions, coupled with pro-abortion editorials and op-ed columns, represents a journalistic package designed to nudge the reader into changing social policy positions and personal beliefs.

The Decline of "Straight News" Coverage

To get a broader picture of how the *Times* covers different stories—and which types of coverage may be most subject to Culture Creep—let's take a look at a 1997 study from the Committee of Concerned Journalists. This group, sponsored by the Project for Excellence in Journalism and the Medill News Service Washington Bureau, examined 6,020 stories in sixteen news outlets over a twenty-year period. The data compiled on the *New York Times* revealed that the publication of "straight news" on the *Times'* front page declined from 49.8 percent in 1977 to 16.2 percent in 1997!

In a 1995 study by the Freedom Forum Media Studies Center, news coverage in the following papers was analyzed from January 3 to 27, 1995: the *Times*, the *Atlanta Journal-Constitution*, and the *Des Moines Register*. In descending order, the top ten stories (in number of words) covered by the *Times* were:

1. 104th Congress convenes, 44,988 words
2. Russian-Chechen separatist fighting, 29,809 words
3. Earthquake in Kobe, Japan, 29,386 words
4. O. J. Simpson's double murder trial, 22,778 words
5. President Clinton's State of the Union speech, 16,017 words
6. Mexico's devaluation of peso against dollar, 14,608 words
7. Wars in Yugoslavia, 12,469 words

8. Federal budget deficit, plans to balance budget, 11,469 words
9. Israeli-Palestinian conflict, 11,324 words
10. Abortion clinic protest violence, 8,243 words

The other two papers contained a roughly similar mix of stories in their top ten. But because of the huge size of the *Times'* "news hole"—the space reserved in the paper for editorial matter as opposed to advertising—the *Times'* reporting of these stories was, in fact, quite different from the other two papers. The researchers estimated that the total size of the national-international news hole in the *Times* during the period studied was 493,059 words—as compared with only 152,908 words in the *Atlanta Journal-Constitution* and 142,043 words in the *Des Moines Register*.

From such analyses, we can make several interesting observations:

Many of the top stories highlighted by the *Times* certainly do involve straight news coverage. These involve such issues as the earthquake in Kobe, the wars in the Balkans, and even the sensational O. J. Simpson murder trial. To its credit, the *Times* has usually tended to play it straight on these types of stories.

But other topics—such as the political coverage and abortion violence—are ready-made for editorializing. And as we'll see, the *Times* often takes full advantage of this fact to promote its views through Culture Creep.

Over the past couple of decades, the *Times* has allotted increasing amounts of news space to stories that can be manipulated to promote the paper's belief system.

This situation has arisen, in part, because the *Times* devotes much less space to "straight news" than it did two decades ago—a drop of almost 70 percent according to the Concerned Journalists' study.

Also, because the *Times* has much more total space in its news hole than other papers, the company has more "running room" to promote its views.

For example, the Freedom Forum Media Studies Center study showed that abortion coverage ranked tenth in the *Times* and the *Des Moines Register* and ninth in the *Atlanta Journal-Constitution*.

But the group indicated that the larger amount of space available to the *Times* presents a dramatically different picture of the coverage of abortion. In fact, with its vastly larger news hole, the *Times* devoted three times as much ink to abortion as the Atlanta paper, 2.8 times as much as the Iowa paper, and almost five times as much as ABC network newscasts that were studied.

A Mixed Picture

The *Times* thus presents us with a mixed picture. It is undeniably a paper that continues to be a daily repository of useful information. Also, the paper still possesses some of its long-standing, built-in drive to engage in old-fashioned "crusading journalism," which thrives on exposing crimes and nefarious plots against the public interest. For example, a team of *Times* reporters won the 1998 Pulitzer Prize for international reporting as a result of a series of reports that unveiled political corruption among high Mexican officials in the war against drugs in Mexico.

More recently, the *Times* ran a lead story on the front page reporting charges that Bosnian leaders had stolen up to $1 billion in relief aid (8/17,99, p. A1). ABC's *Evening News* picked up on the story that night and explicitly acknowledged the *Times'* role in breaking the story.

Unfortunately, the pursuit of these important journalistic functions, as well as the *Times'* basic credibility, may now be in jeopardy, as editors and reporters increasingly blur the lines between opinion and straight news coverage. What the paper often presents as an ordinary news account is actually a tract in disguise—an editorialized Trojan horse that slips into the reader's psyche and surreptitiously begins to shape social, political, and even spiritual beliefs.

How can you, the reader, recognize and protect yourself from this mind-molding process?

The first step is to understand some specific danger signals that may emerge in news coverage—"red flags" that indicate the *Times* may have moved from fact to propaganda, and is most likely engaging in some form of Culture Creep.

There are at least six "red flags" that can signal the presence of Culture Creep:

1. Corporate conflicts of interest
2. Personal biases of reporters or editors
3. Skewed story selection
4. Slanted story presentation
5. Strategic omission of facts or of the "other side of the story"
6. Reliance on a like-minded pool of experts—who have apparently been chosen because their views reinforce those of the paper

In the remainder of this chapter, we'll explore the first three of these red flags. These signal background conflicts and biases that may determine which stories or viewpoints are selected to run in each issue.

Then in the following chapter, we'll deal with the other three red flags—which focus on how a desire to spread a certain cultural philosophy can influence the nuts and bolts of actually putting a particular story together.

BACKGROUND CONFLICTS AND BIASES: THE FIRST THREE RED FLAGS OF CULTURE CREEP

A decision to engage in propaganda—or the spreading of specially selected facts, ideas, and charges to promote a particular cause or worldview—usually arises from a strong set of basic beliefs or vested interests. Because so many people these days have shallow or non-existent personal philosophies, a true believer with a well-thought-out set of convictions and a gift of persuasion can often convince non-believers rather easily.

But if you understand the propagandist's philosophical assumptions and preconceptions—and also can identify and understand links to other organizations and philosophies—you'll be in a better position to evaluate the arguments you hear and read.

The first three red flags of Culture Creep concern some of the most important background conflicts, biases, and assumptions that drive the corporate moguls, editors, and reporters at the *Times*.

RED FLAG #1: CORPORATE CONFLICTS OF INTEREST

An entire volume could be written exploring the connections of the *New York Times* with other organizations and corporations—and how this cobweb of contacts has enhanced the prodigious power, and also compromised the ingrity, of the publication. But even the few illustrations I've included here should provide a reasonably good sense of how potential conflicts of interest may affect news coverage.

First, let's dispose of the question of hypocrisy. In this regard, it's important to recognize that the *Times* gives lip service to avoiding conflicts of interest. In fact, in a lead editorial on July 14, 1998, (p. A18) entitled "DON'T CALL IT JOURNALISM," the rulers of the paper huffed and puffed with more than a touch of self-righteousness about how various media giants were departing from the purest principles of journalism.

Painting with a condescending, holier-than-thou brush, they warned such media giants as Disney, CBS News, Time Warner, and CNN that their souls would be in mortal danger if they continued to commit the unpardonable journalistic sin of conflict of interest. Specifically, the *Times* decried the tendency of these organizations to mix entertainment and slanted news presentations with "journalism's high purpose," which is to channel unadulterated information to the public. "A news consumer deserves to know about conflicts of interest," the paper solemnly cautioned its lesser comrades.

But could it be that that the hands that produce the *Times* are themselves not entirely clean and free of conflicts of interest?

The beginnings of an answer to this question may be found in the paper's treatment of *Corpus Christi*, a 1998 play by Terrence McNally, which many conservative church people found to be highly offensive because of such touches as the depiction of Jesus as a homosexual (5/28/98, pp. A28, B1, B10).

Although the Manhattan Theatre Club had scheduled the play for production, the Club cancelled it because of the intensity of protests from the Christian community—and especially from the Catholic League for Religious and Civil Rights. A threat of violence was also reported against the theater and the playwright.

On May 28, 1998, the *Times* weighed in with a scathing editorial, taking the Catholic League to task for its protests and also criticizing the Manhattan Theatre Club for caving in to the pressure.

The final result was that the club rescheduled the play, and it opened in the fall of 1998. But the *Times* didn't tell the whole story. To set the stage, remember the paper's chief pronouncements against conflicts of interest that plague other media organizations:

"A news consumer deserves to know about conflicts of interest" (my emphasis).

What the *Times* didn't tell its readers in that May 28, 1998, *Corpus Christi* editorial—or in a feature story published the same day—was that the *New York Times* Company was one of the Manhattan Theatre Club's "top corporate donors," according to Playbill, the program distributed to all theatergoers (*WSJ*, 10/16/98, p. W13).

Furthermore, the *Times* has made a great deal of space available to the Manhattan Theatre Club for public relations purposes. A one-year search of the paper's archives, ending in August 1999, turned up four hundred articles mentioning the Club and its productions, or more than one per day! Such publicity is money in the bank for any cultural institution in New York City, both for ticket sales and donations. So any suggestion that the club might lose its major news outlet would be enough to strike fear into the heart of even the most intrepid fund raiser.

These connections raise all sorts of interesting questions.

First of all, did the *Times'* "news consumers"—the readers and the thousands of media outlets that carry its reports around the world—deserve to know that the paper had a direct financial connection with the very organization that was at the center of the paper's reporting and editorializing?

Ethics 101 should tell us that viewpoints and actions will be influenced by financial involvement. At a minimum, full disclosure seems the only ethical way for a reputable newspaper to handle such a conflict of interest, yet the *Times* chose to violate this principle of journalism—a principle that it had previously reprimanded other media organizations for transgressing.

Second, an outside observer might question whether the *Times* should have applied pressure on the Manhattan Theatre Club to reschedule the play—when the Club relied for its very existence on major donors such as the *Times*, not to mention the paper's unmatched publicity machine.

Third, this *Corpus Christi* affair is only one instance of the *Times'* reporting on an issue in which it was enmeshed in a conflict of interest. It's reasonable to wonder on how many other occasions the *Times* has pronounced judgment on a topic in which it had some hidden vested interest.

It would be hard enough for a completely independent Manhattan cultural institution to withstand the impact of a *Times* editorial commanding it to resurrect a cancelled play. But suppose an implied financial threat is added to the mix—such as a loss of donations in this current era of governmental cutbacks for arts projects, and a squeeze on the publicity that helps produce donations. In such a situation, the temptation could become overwhelming for a theater to bend to the will of a powerful newspaper-contributor. (We'll go into this *Corpus Christi* affair in more detail in chapter 5.)

The topic of conflicts of interest involving the *Times* might indeed be fodder for a very long book. For example, one might explore the ties of the *Times* with the Pulitzer Prize organization—

which awards the top prizes for journalism. If a paper, reporting team, or individual journalist wins a Pulitzer, that's regarded in the newsgathering field as incontrovertible evidence of having risen to the top of the field. And as mentioned in the first chapter, by 1999 the *Times* had won seventy-nine Pulitzers, or about double the number of any other paper.

What should be made of the fact that *Times'* employees or former employees are typically represented disproportionately on the Pulitzer Prize Board? At least three of the current twenty board members—including Seymour Topping, the administrator of the prizes—have had some significant *Times* connection.

Topping was a *Times* foreign correspondent, foreign editor, managing editor, or editorial director of the company's regional newspapers for thirty-four years. William Safire is a longtime op-ed columnist for the paper, and Tom Goldstein, now the dean of the Columbia Graduate School of Journalism, was a *Times* legal and business reporter.

The previous year's chairperson of the board was Geneva Overholser, an alumna of the *Times'* editorial board. Furthermore, numerous *Times'* staffers have served or currently serve as the jurors who actually vote on the awards.

To be sure, the *Times'* Pulitzer winners usually seem worthy enough. But are they *more* worthy that the many fine, hard-working reporters from other news organizations whose papers don't have so many intimate connections with the awarding process?

Even more important, do the links of the *Times* to the Pulitzer's decision-making process amount to a self-perpetuation of the *Times'* reputation as the nation's greatest news organization?

Suppose for a moment that an egalitarian movement took hold among journalists across America—with the *Times* being accorded the same clout and influence on the Pulitzer Board and Pulitzer administrative operations and juries as, say, the Vero Beach, Florida, *Press Journal*.

It's just possible that such an equitable revamping of the Pulitzer organization might result in many fewer Pulitzers to the

Times and many more to deserving lower-profile news organizations. With a long-term drought of Pulitzers—which are often cited as signs of the *Times'* superiority—some might even begin to question if perhaps another institution should be anointed with the title "newspaper of record."

So corporate conflicts of interest—or just circumstances that give the appearance of unclean hands—are indeed an important red flag that may signal media bias and Culture Creep. But tainted organizational connections don't exist only at the corporate level. Writers and editors may also become mired in social movements or interest groups, which can give rise to questions about the fairness of their reporting.

RED FLAG #2: PERSONAL CONNECTIONS OF REPORTERS OR EDITORS

Those who report, write, and edit at the *New York Times* don't operate in a journalistic ivory tower. They are real flesh-and-blood people like you and me who have prejudices, political opinions, spiritual beliefs, and pet causes. Furthermore—regardless of what some news pundits or journalism professors may say to the contrary—these reporters and editors can't possibly keep their biases completely out of their reporting. Complete objectivity is simply not a possibility.

So if a reporter or editor has voted for a certain political party or feels strongly about certain political issues, his news reports on related topics are likely to reflect his personal views in some way.

A poll conducted by the Freedom Forum and the Roper Center on voting patterns in the Washington press corps, including reporters at the *New York Times*, revealed that 89 percent of the city's journalists and 60 percent of the editors had voted for Bill Clinton for president in 1992. Furthermore, 61 percent of the journalists regarded themselves as "liberal" or "liberal to moderate," and only 9 percent said they were "moderate to conservative" or "conservative." The other 30 percent saw themselves as straight "moderate" (*lib.ucon.edu*, p. 2).

This profile of Washington journalists suggests that, at the very least, we should examine their dispatches closely for bias. The need for such scrutiny intensifies when the paper with the most influential Washington Bureau, the *Times*, consistently gives editorial endorsements to Democratic candidates at all levels of government.

The Freedom Forum-Roper findings dovetail nicely with results of another study done in 1980 by S. Robert Lichter of George Washington University and Stanley Rothman of Smith College (9/8/93, p. B12; Freedom Forum, *www.fac.org*, pp. 1ff).

These two researchers interviewed 240 journalists from leading media outlets in New York and Washington. The organizations included: the *New York Times*; *Washington Post*; *Wall Street Journal*; *Time*; *Newsweek*; *U.S. News & World Report*; and the news departments at CBS, NBC, ABC, and PBS. A follow-up study covering 196999–1998 by S. Robert Lichter, Linda S. Lichter, and Daniel R. Amundson was released in April 200 by the Center for Media and Public Affairs *(www.cmpa.com)*. Organizations analyzed were the same, except that PBS and the *Wall Street Journal* were excluded. Among other things, these studies revealed these characteristics of the reporters (1980 figures are listed first):

- 86 percent of the New York-Washington journalists seldom or never attended religious services. (That number had dropped to 70 percent in 1995.)
- Half had no religious affiliation at all (22 percent in 1995).

By contrast, only 42 percent of all Americans have consistently said they seldom or never attended church or synagogue (Jan. 7–10, 2000, CNN/USA Today/Gallup Poll).

Other findings also raised questions about potential biases:

- 90 percent of the journalists were pro-choice on abortion (97 percent in 1990s). Yet only 48 percent of the general public considered themselves "pro-choice" in Gallup polls conducted in early 2000.
- 75 percent of the elite journalists disagreed with a statement saying that homosexuality was wrong (73 percent in

1990s). Yet only 34 percent of Americans in 1982 and 50 percent in 1999 said that they thought homosexuality was an "acceptable lifestyle," according to Gallup.

- 54 percent of the elite journalists didn't regard adultery as wrong. Yet 90 percent of men and 94 percent of women in the U.S. in the 1990s believed that extramarital sex was "always wrong" or "almost always wrong," according to a *Times* report (7/4/98, p. A13).

- A mere 15 percent of the elite media "strongly agreed" that abortion, homosexuality, and adultery were immoral.

Furthermore, according to the 2000 report, only 7 percent of the religion news reports by these organizations dealt with theological or spiritual beliefs. The emphasis was on non-spiritual issues, such as politics.

As might be expected, those who want to uphold the illusion of unbiased reporting and objectivity in newsgathering have attacked the Lichter-Rothman investigation on numerous fronts. The Freedom Forum, the foundation established by Allen H. Neuharth of Gannett News Media, cited a host of critics, including the *Columbia Journalism Review* and a team of prestigious Indiana University journalism professors. A major argument emerging from these critics was that the study wasn't representative—that the researchers focused on the elite northeastern media outlets, and as a result, their basic approach and methodology skewed their results.

But of course, that's just the point. The greatest influence on all news media in the United States and abroad emanates from the Northeast. Consequently, the beliefs of journalists linked to the New York-Washington, D.C., axis are the main ones the average news consumer should be concerned about.

In this regard, consider the *pontifex maximus* of *CBS Evening News*, the retired and revered network anchor, Walter Cronkite. I became a trusting fan back in the mid-1960s while I was attending Harvard Law School. As a member of an eating club, the Lincoln's Inn Society, I enjoyed withdrawing to a lounge upstairs after the evening meal and settling down in front of a television set with a full cup of coffee and a chocolate chip cookie.

In that setting, the avuncular "Walter," as we called him affectionately, would present the news and pontificate as we sipped and munched. I had every reason to assume at the time that he was delivering his news "straight," with no slant toward one side or the other. It wasn't until much later that I learned Cronkite had a rather biting and aggressive set of political and religious views.

In particular, the former anchor-icon received extensive press coverage in 1997 for his no-holds-barred attack on conservative Christian political activists in a fund-raising letter he did for a group called the "Interfaith Alliance." According to one report, the organization had been formed to counter "religious political extremists."

In his polemic, Cronkite launched a broad attack on conservative Christian activists, including the popular political consultant Ralph Reed. I was somewhat puzzled by Cronkite's choice of Reed, who had always seemed to me the epitome of the rational man—even when I disagreed on particular positions he espoused. But Cronkite was apparently in a mood to take no prisoners, as he railed against the evangelical activists for "wrapping their harsh right-wing views in the banner of religious faith."

Reading between the lines, I surmised that Cronkite had been stewing over this issue for some time. He had reportedly taken political and religious sides when he met the relatively liberal Alliance representatives during the filming of a documentary he was doing on the religious right in 1994 (*Palm Beach Post*, AP, p. 2A).

Understandably, after reading about Cronkite's attack on the conservative Christian political activists, I began to wonder just how fair-minded he had really been as I had watched him years ago when I was a naïve law student, drinking in his pronouncements on politics along with my coffee. I soon discovered that Cronkite's hostility was only the tip of an anti-conservative-Christian iceberg that was floating just beneath the surface among the northeastern news media.

Guilt by Very Close Association?

To understand how these prevalent anti-Christian attitudes may play out in practice, let's turn to a common mechanism that may signal strong bias on the part of reporters and columnists—a dynamic that might best be called "guilt-by-very-close-association."

Suppose, for instance, that a staff writer has been associated with a particular belief, organization or group that promotes a certain social policy—or is consistently recognized for furthering the mission of an advocacy group. In such a case, the group's viewpoint is likely to be reflected in some way in the articles the journalist writes.

Two cases in point have been prominent *Times'* op-ed columnists—Frank Rich, who still writes for the *Times* as this book goes to press, and Anna Quindlen, who in 1994 left the paper.

- First, Frank Rich—one of the most virulent opponents of Christian conservatives and one of the nation's most outspoken and radical supporters of abortion and gay rights—has made no secret of his biases in his columns and has received due recognition for his advocacy.

In 1997, for instance, Rich received the "Outstanding Newspaper Journalism" award from the Gay & Lesbian Alliance Against Defamation (GLAAD) for his supportive coverage of homosexual issues. In addition, he receives regular recognition and accolades from this group and other gay organizations, such as Gay and Lesbian News page and Gay Place News on the Internet *(www.ReligiousTolerance.org,* p. 2; www.GLAADAlert, p. 1; *www.gayplace.com,* p. 3).

Rich, it should be noted, is the same man who has written such intemperate tirades as "GODZILLA OF THE RIGHT," a May 20, 1998, op-ed assault on James Dobson, the Christian psychologist and author, and founder of Focus on the Family (p. A23). Apparently, Dobson's main offense was disagreeing with Rich on such issues as school prayer, partial-birth abortion, and gay rights. (The *Times'* regular op-ed columnists write their own headlines, by the way. So Rich must be given full credit for the unusual dose of venom delivered by his article [*Booknotes*, p. 15].)

Among other things, Rich compared Dobson to David Duke, the former Ku Klux Klanner, and accused the mild-mannered family relations expert of "blackmail" of Congress, saying he "looks like a guy who would smack you down if you gave him any lip."

The *Times* editorial page, though somewhat less crazed in its rhetoric, takes basically the same position as Rich on key social policy issues such as abortion and homosexual rights—as later chapters will demonstrate. Furthermore, both Rich and his editorial overseers make liberal use of such inflammatory terms as "religious right" and "bigot" to refer to Christian conservatives.

For example, a search of the *Times*' on-line archives for a full year (July 1998 through July 1999) turned up 936 articles using the term "religious right"—or an average of almost three articles per day! Furthermore, it would take an extraordinary team of investigators to turn up any positive references to those unfortunate enough to be linked to this epithet.

- Anna Quindlen, who won the Pulitzer Prize for commentary in 1992 as a *Times* columnist, has gained a wide reputation as a strong abortion rights supporter.

This reputation stemmed largely from articles she wrote for the paper up to the time she left in 1994. A best-selling collection of her columns, reprinted in *Thinking Out Loud*, which was published in 1993 while she was still on staff at the *Times*, featured many pro-abortion pieces.

She led off the abortion section of the book by protesting, rather disingenuously, that she was "deeply ambivalent about abortion" (Quindlen, p. 215). But then a couple of pages later, she became more straightforward about her beliefs—which, incidentally, are also reflected regularly on the *Times*' editorial page:

"The profile of most feminists on the issue [abortion]— and I am feminist, have been nearly all my sentient life—is that we believe flatly that women cannot be free unless they can control when they will carry a pregnancy to term" (pp. 217–218).

The columns she chose for her book, which were written from about 1990–92, reveal that she favors no restrictions on abortion, such as waiting periods or parental consent laws (p. 247). She also came out swinging against the presidential candidacy of George Bush, who affirmed an anti-abortion position: "Surely Republican women must consider how they will explain to their daughters their reelection of a man who will attempt to rescind the basic human right of bodily integrity [i.e, the right to an abortion]" (p. 248).

Is there anything unseemly in Quindlen's efforts to foist her pro-abortion views on the public? Of course not. An op-ed columnist is, by definition, supposed to have strong opinions and express them on paper.

But one might also reasonably ask, Would the *Times* have picked her for this role if she had been an equally outspoken pro-life advocate?

Again, the answer is, of course not. After all, a pro-life writer in Quindlen's position would seriously dilute the impact of the paper's promotion of its radical pro-abortion agenda, which appears frequently in the editorials on the opposite page.

Both before and after she left the *Times*, Quindlen reinforced her advocacy of abortion and other liberal issues by taking advantage of public forums well beyond the op-ed pages of the paper. In an interview by C-Span *Booknotes* interviewer Brian Lamb on May 16, 1993, which was conducted while she still worked for the *Times*, she identified herself as more liberal than President Bill Clinton. She also described the "liberal position on abortion"— which she acknowledged was the topic of many of her columns— as "a matter of individual choice and personal liberty" (p. 10).

Her own "individual choice" approach to abortion seems relatively traditional. She wrote on one occasion that she would not consider having amniocentesis when pregnant because she would have the child regardless of any findings about genetic defects (*Col. J. Rev.*, p. 2). But her views on "personal liberty" for those who do want to terminate a pregnancy are definitely at the extreme end of the pro-abortion spectrum.

Quindlen's public reputation as an abortion advocate had become so well-established by the spring of 1999 that she had to withdraw as commencement speaker at Villanova University after some of the pro-life students, alumni, professors, and activist groups protested her scheduled appearance (*Washington Times*, p.1).

In addition, her formal affiliations as an abortion promoter include service on the boards of the Planned Parenthood Federation of America and the National Abortion and Reproductive Rights Action League (NARRAL) Foundation ("Commencement," *Mt. Holyoke Alum. Quar.*, p. 16). Among other things, she has written the preface to *Choices: Women Speak Out About Abortion*. This volume was released by the NARRAL Foundation to commemorate the twenty-fifth anniversary of *Roe v. Wade*, the U.S. Supreme Court decision that established a national right to abortion *(www.feminist.com*, p. 1). In addition, Quindlen moderated a major discussion on *Roe v. Wade* featuring pro-abortion luminaries on a national teleconference sponsored by Stanford Law School *(Roe v. Wade*, Stanford, p. 1).

What is the significance of Quindlen's extensive abortion advocacy both before and after her tenure on the *Times?*

First of all, one must ask a basic question. Has a person with such deep ties to one side of an issue—whether a regular reporter or a columnist—abandoned any claim to credibility as a disinterested journalist who is ready to explore all viewpoints in the search for truth?

It goes without saying, of course, that Quindlen can't possibly make any claim to objectivity or balance in her reporting on this issue. To her credit, she admits in *Thinking Out Loud* that objectivity was "suspect" in her news stories and "preposterous" in her opinion pieces (Quindlen, p. xxv).

Second, as we'll see, one of the *Times'* basic beliefs is that a woman should have a virtually unlimited right to an abortion. The paper has promoted this position for years, not only in news stories and editorials, but also overwhelmingly through op-ed page writers such as Quindlen.

Quindlen is particularly effective because she is such a good essayist. In contrast to a polemicist like Frank Rich, who often bludgeons the reader from the first paragraph with vitriolic, sneering accusations against his opponents, Quindlen employs guile. She teases the reader, sometimes by withholding her conclusions until the last paragraph or sentence. Or she may punctuate her arguments with strategic concessions to the opposing side, or accounts of the personal breast-beating that she has inflicted on herself before reaching her inevitable, left-wing conclusions.

Yet even as Quindlen agonizes publicly, she is constantly, albeit quietly, building her case against traditional values. Her expert writing—along with her strong extracurricular advocacy, both now and before she left the paper—have established her as a formidable opponent of those who affirm more conservative moral beliefs and as an important cog in the *Times'* ongoing proselytizing program.

But the paper doesn't rely only on its hired guns. Even high U.S. officials may be anointed to carry the torch of the true faith, so long as their beliefs pass muster with those of the dozen or so gurus who divine what is to go on the editorial page. As an illustration, consider how the *Times* used former President Gerald R. Ford to push another of the paper's pet issues—affirmative action.

For a Democratic paper like the *Times*, finding a leading Republican politician who is ready to spread the paper's beliefs must have seemed a dream come true. The newspaper didn't waste a moment taking full advantage of President Ford's willingness to lend his name to an op-ed piece endorsing affirmative action under the rather alarmist headline, "INCLUSIVE AMERICA, UNDER ATTACK" (8/8/99, p. 15).

In this Sunday column, Ford reminisced about the prejudice he had observed against blacks in games played in the South when he was a football player at the University of Michigan. Then, employing one of its classic one-two punches, the *Times* followed up the next day with a lead editorial, "THE NEW AFFIRMATIVE ACTION FIGHT" (Aug 9, 1999, p. A18). In that piece, the paper excoriated what it called the "anti-affirmative action camp in California" for its "pernicious attack" on special efforts to recruit minorities and women for jobs and college slots.

The key factor here is not whether you or any newspaper reader rejects or supports affirmative action in one form or another. These days, most people want minorities to get a fair break, both economically and educationally—despite the considerable difference of opinion about how to achieve these ends.

Rather, the lesson to be learned from this incident is the way that the *Times* subtly promotes its own viewpoint—in this case a comprehensive form of government-imposed affirmative action. Readers on consecutive days found themselves subjected to hard intellectual pummeling, first from the op-ed page and then from the editorial side. The ripple effect in such a situation can be enormous, as other newspapers and television stations around the country pick up the story, and the momentum accelerates because a former U.S. president has been pulled on board the *Times'* bandwagon.

The expression of such strong social and political beliefs by prominent or influential columnists, as well as by nationally revered guest columnists who toe the *Times'* line, help create a powerful, monolithic corporate voice for influencing the general public. But stacking the op-ed page represents only one step up the slope of slanted coverage at the paper. In addition to the proselytizing whipsaw created by one-note, complementary editorials and op-ed pieces, the paper employs Culture Creep to ensure the promotion of its gospel through careful story selection.

RED FLAG #3: SKEWED STORY SELECTION

There may be eight million stories in the big city, but only a relative handful are chosen to run in the *Times*—and many of those serve to spread the paper's social and political gospel.

To understand how the story selection process works and how editorial interest in a concept, person, or viewpoint can skew that process, take three names that have dominated history: "Jesus Christ," "Buddha," and "Hitler." Which of these do you think would interest the *Times* most, and which would get the most space?

A simple way to get a reading is to go to the archives search page on the paper's Web site and do a search of the past year. When I conducted such a search covering July 9, 1998 through July 9, 1999, I ended up with these results:

- Jesus Christ—205 articles, or fewer than one per day.
- Buddha—109 articles, or half as many as Jesus received.
- Hitler—540 articles, or about one-and-a-half per day.

Now, I wouldn't want to infer too much from this finding. But the comparison does show how a seemingly innocent decision to focus on one person or topic can easily outweigh the coverage of other topics. Moreover, the sheer weight of coverage in the paper is one way to impress on the reader's mind what is important and what is not.

The Weight-of-Coverage Dynamic

To illustrate how weighting the coverage given to a particular issue can further the process of Culture Creep, let's continue with the above example of the three dominant historical figures, Jesus, Buddha, and Hitler.

If you read about Hitler more than twice as often as you read about Jesus Christ, then you may subconsciously begin to assume that Hitler is at least as worthy of your attention, if not more worthy. It's not that Hitler becomes *better* than Jesus in your mind, or that the *Times* is trying to implant that belief. Rather, the weight of the coverage suggests simply that it may be more important to understand the demonic dictator than any spiritual figure, including Jesus.

After all, these top editors and writers, whom you trust implicitly, have devoted many more (more than 70 percent more) stories to the Nazi ruler than they have to Jesus and Buddha combined!

A Snapshot of the Times' Story Selection

The simple one-year search procedure described above revealed the following profile of the *Times'* level of interest in certain issues. The figures represent the number of articles published on the indicated topic during the 365-day period from July 9, 1998, through July 9, 1999.

- "Abortion"—980 articles.
- "Welfare"—1,522 articles.
  ✚Related topic: "Entitlement"—115 articles.
- "Gay"—1,481 articles.
  ✚Related topic: "Lesbian"—351 articles.
  ✚Related topic: "Homosexual"—346 articles.
- "Women's rights"—372 articles.
  ✚Related topic: "Sexual harassment"—508 articles.
  ✚Related topic: "Feminist"—423 articles.
- "Ethical"—673 articles.
- "Education"—6,317 articles.
- "First Amendment"—647 articles.
  ✚Related topic: "Press freedom"—488 articles.
  ✚Related topic: "Censorship"—231 articles.
- "Globalization"—173 articles.
  ✚Related topic: "Refugee"—638 articles.
  ✚Related topic: "Genocide"—376 articles.
  ✚Related topic: "Holocaust"—963 articles.
- "Multicultural"—233 articles.
  ✚Related topic: "Racial"—1,617 articles.
  ✚Related topic: "Immigrant"—1,148 articles.
  ✚Related topic: "Minorities"—1,132 articles.
  ✚Related topic: "Ethnic diversity"—148 articles.
- "Gun control"—696 articles.
- "Death penalty"—640 articles.

✠Related topic: "Capital punishment"—358 articles.

As you reflect on these results, remember that the weight of coverage—that is, the frequency with which a paper discusses a topic—can be a fairly accurate barometer of the corporate belief system. Furthermore, the more you are exposed to those beliefs, the more likely it is that *your own beliefs* may be affected through the subtle process of Culture Creep.

Sometimes you may be quite comfortable dwelling on things in the paper that reinforce or deepen beliefs you have arrived at independently. For example, regardless of your personal political or spiritual orientation, if you sort through some of the issues surveyed above, you will most likely find that you are generally in agreement with a number of the *Times'* positions. Along with the paper, you will probably affirm conduct that is "ethical"; you will condemn the factors that led to the "Holocaust"; and you will sympathize with calls to relieve the plight of "refugees."

On the other hand, your personal convictions may not coincide with those of the *Times* on other subjects, such as "abortion," "gun control," or "capital punishment." In such a case, you have several choices:

Option #1: You become angry or frustrated, and decide to avoid completely the news reports or organizations you dislike. Instead—if you read or listen to the news at all—you immerse yourself exclusively in those publications, writers, or commentators you agree with.

Option #2: You continue to read and listen *uncritically* to excessive numbers of stories that conflict with your beliefs—and later discover that your own belief system has changed.

You may find that ten years ago you didn't believe in abortion in any form. But today, you think it's acceptable, so long as the procedure occurs during the first trimester of pregnancy. In fact, if your beliefs on this subject were relatively weak or unformed to begin with—and you tend to accept everything you read at face value—you might find that you've moved even further, to condoning "partial-birth abortion" right up to the moments just before a full-term birth.

Or ten years ago you may have been convinced that a Divine Hand was directly involved every step of way the as animals and humans appeared on earth. But today you take the position that God was involved only at the beginning, but then he took his hand off the process and evolution took over completely.

In effect, you've become a Deist—though to your credit, you still haven't quite moved to the totally naturalistic and atheistic position implied in the *Times'* reports. Typically in those stories, no room is made for God at all, even as the First Cause.

If you happen to be a regular, generally uncritical devotee of the *Times*—or of one of the countless newspapers and radio and TV outlets that the paper influences—you may well find that your beliefs on certain issues have shifted radically over the years. Yet most likely, you won't even be aware that a change has occurred until you compare your beliefs today with those you held a few years ago.

Option #3: You continue to read and listen to skewed news coverage—but through the experience and skills you have developed in dealing with Culture Creep, you are able to evaluate the reports *critically* and use them to your best advantage.

When you encounter a new idea or argument that you feel can be incorporated into your personal belief system—without unacceptable compromise of your deepest convictions—then you make appropriate adjustments. Even when such changes aren't possible, you can still learn to sift through and interpret the slanted information.

Such an effort is absolutely essential to put you in a good position to respond persuasively to those who hold beliefs contrary to yours. Every good lawyer or debater knows that to present his own case well, he must also devote at least as much time to studying the other side's facts and arguments. Only by knowing your

opponent thoroughly can you anticipate his objections and for-
mulate the most powerful responses.

The first of these three options characterizes the religious separatist. He chooses to leave the world entirely rather than expose
himself to news reports or opinion pieces that may seem unset-
tling or too difficult to answer.

The second option describes the person with a relatively shallow or rudimentary worldview. If you don't have firm beliefs, then
you'll tend to be tossed about by every cultural wind, which blows
in a new belief, theory, or pattern of facts.

Those in this second category are most susceptible to the
impact of Culture Creep and will quickly become true believers in
the gospel propagated by the *Times*. The media giant is simply too
powerful—and its writers and reporters too intelligent, confident,
and skilled at their craft—for any regular reader without a firm set
of personal convictions to withstand the power of their arguments
and intellect.

The third option represents the ideal of what might be called
the "reader-scholar." This individual has developed a firm philosophy of life—probably founded on a traditional religious faith.
Because of her personal spiritual commitment, she will often find
her beliefs at odds with certain reports she reads in the *Times* or
hears on network news programs. (As we have already seen, many
of these reports are deeply influenced by the social and political
agenda of the *Times* and its staff.)

At the same time, the person pursuing the third option wants
to increase her knowledge of the world around her and perhaps
employ that knowledge to expand and enhance her own worldview. She may even be motivated to join with like-minded
thinkers to seek ways to turn the tables on the *Times* and its followers and take some steps to help others reverse the process of
Culture Creep.

To this end—after she learns in detail how the paper is shaping
minds and beliefs—she may endeavor to unmask these strategies
in conversations with those whose beliefs may not be as well

formed as hers. An underlying assumption that drives such a person is the conviction that her worldview is better for individuals and society at large than the philosophy being propounded in the *Times*.

That's not arrogance. Rather, it's an attitude that reflects personal conviction and self-confidence. In effect, as sages have taught in another culture and era, the reader-scholar demonstrates that she is *in* the world of the *New York Times* but not *of* that world.

But choosing a story is only the first step in the editorial process of Culture Creep. Once an editor or publisher has selected the topic for a particular day's paper, the story must be written—and here is where the serious work of propaganda begins.

_____ CHAPTER 4

ALL THE BIAS THAT'S FIT TO PRINT

Up to this point, we have explored certain background factors that may set the stage for bias—including the *Times*' corporate conflicts, the tendency of writers to become advocates, and the skewed process of story selection. But three more red flags still remain—warning signs of Culture Creep that involve the all-important hands-on process of actually turning out stories, columns, and editorials for the paper.

Red Flag #4: Slanted Story Presentation

In most cases, the *Times* orchestrates its coverage by employing a layered approach to advocacy. The four key layers that reporters and editors use in serial fashion to mold and shape your mind include:

- The not-the-news news story—also known as the opinion piece in disguise
- The editorial blast
- The op-ed "hit"
- The bombardment

In a typical daily edition of the *Times*, you find yourself confronted not just with one article that supports a particular viewpoint, but with an entire series of slanted news presentations that push an entire secular theology. The result is an editorial package that moves the *Times* closer and closer to journalism as opinion, and further and further from the classic journalistic ideals of objectivity, balance, and fairness.

The First Layer of Advocacy: the Not-the-News News Story

The first layer of the *Times'* advocacy consists of news stories that are really opinion pieces in disguise. They often introduce the paper's preferred point of view with a number of clandestine tactics that may escape notice unless the reader is watching for them. These include:

- Editorializing, or inserting personal beliefs into news accounts
- Specially crafted leads (the first few sentences or paragraphs)
- "Kickers" (endings), which highlight a "send-off" thought
- Headlines-with-a-message
- Strategic selection of facts and quotations
- Pictures that really *are* worth one thousand words

A quick lesson in how to editorialize. The first of the above news story tactics represents a journalistic line in the sand that has been crossed increasingly during the last few decades—to the decided detriment of reliable reporting.

At one time, most good reporters swore allegiance to the sacred dictum that news reporters should avoid editorializing—or the insertion of opinion into their newswriting. In the relatively recent past, most traditional, reputable newspapers rode close herd on the practice of editorializing because they were convinced that tainting a regular news report with such subjectivism would open the door to blatant bias on the news pages. Opinion was to be reserved for the editorial page. The news reporter was expected to keep his personal views to himself, and as far as possible, to relate the facts and the facts alone.

Of course, many reporters—especially those on the more sensationalistic publications—didn't follow this rule. Some of the most colorful and interesting newswriting, going all the way back to the founding of the Republic, involved reporters and editors who had axes to grind. And they didn't hesitate to push their points of view in news stories as well as on the editorial page.

But the *New York Times* was always regarded as different. As I've already suggested, the paper earned its reputation as the somber "gray lady," not just because of its staid physical appearance, but also because its reporters and editors refused to succumb to the temptation of becoming so colorful that they crossed the line into opinion and propaganda.

That standard might have seemed stodgy to the flashy tabloid reporters who were provoking controversy after controversy. But the *Times* was committed to writing serious news, which treated issues and people fairly and with balance.

The *Times* today follows a different philosophy. The line between news and opinion has all but disappeared. Consider a few pertinent illustrations.

A front-page story published in August 1999 described how Rwandan Hutu guerrillas were creating major problems for the government of Congo (8/4/99, pp. A1, A4). But the story could as easily have been an editorial. The headline and subhead on the jump page made it clear where the *Times* stood on the issue: "BRUTAL RWANDANS IMPERIL CONGO PEACE—THE GUERRILLAS ARE AMONG THE WORLD'S MOST VIOLENT. WHO WILL DISARM THEM?"

Few would argue with the outrage expressed through these headlines—but that's not the point. When a news organization begins to express such strong opinions and actually issues a call to arms in its news stories, and not just on its editorial or op-ed page, the floodgates are open for abuses.

Let's move to the realm of politics for a moment. Everyone knows the *Times* is a strong supporter of the Democratic Party and usually endorses Democrats over Republicans or Independents in most elections.

But surely a few non-Democrats read the paper in search of balanced, fair news accounts, and millions of others are influenced directly or indirectly by the *Times* through other news outlets. So it doesn't seem too extreme to expect the paper to draw some reasonably clear line between news and opinion on political issues.

Once again, the *Times* falls short.

For example, a close reading of the *Times*' coverage of the Clinton-Lewinsky scandal and the subsequent impeachment reveals news stories that support in one way or another the *Times*' editorial position. In brief, the paper proclaimed in many different ways that the president should *not* resign, should *not* be impeached by the House (predictable views for a Democratic paper about a Democratic president), and should certainly *not* be kicked out of office in a Senate trial. But the *Times* did strongly disapprove of Clinton's antics in the Oval Office and opined that a congressional censure would be in order.

A front-page story published on September 30, 1998, was slanted so as to make a strong pitch against impeachment. Again, the headline says plenty: "IN A TYPICAL COMMUNITY, TYPICAL FOLKS BACK CLINTON" (pp. A1, A11). In other words, if you are a normal, clear-thinking American, you'll support the president, not his opponents.

In this story, a local newspaper in Canton, Ohio, had called for Clinton's resignation after Monica Lewinsky's infamous stained dress had come to light. But the local paper discovered it was out of step with local public opinion. The quotes and interviews in the story were weighted heavily in favor of the Democratic and *Times*' viewpoint, which staunchly opposed both resignation and impeachment.

The most prominent pictures were captioned with this concluding quote: "This isn't impeachable." And the story ended with a classic kicker, a quote from a steelworker who declared: "I'm just voting straight Democrat."

The message in this "news" story was clear and consistent with the *Times'* editorial stance—no resignation and no impeachment. But the presentation was sufficiently subtle that the typical reader would have to study the article to identify the subliminal message that was being conveyed.

On other topics, such as traditional Christianity, subtlety may be shoved out the West 43rd Street window. In a Lincoln Center review of a gospel performer—which admittedly must contain opinion, but certainly *shouldn't* contain bigoted remarks against a particular religious faith—Neil Strauss delivered this rather awkward taunt:

> ". . . because religion, especially Christianity, tends to proselytize, in life and in music, it is like a root that tries to wrap itself around the tree that grows out of it (or any other tree in the area for that matter) and pull it back into the ground" (7/9/99, p. B5).

Because this intended gibe isn't phrased too clearly, you may have to read the remark more than once to get the meaning. But the writer's point seems to be that because Christianity condones evangelism (the *Times* doesn't?), one cannot expect anything that arises from that faith—even gospel music—to have any chance to blossom or grow to its full potential.

If this is indeed what Strauss meant, he may have provided us with an accurate summary, albeit rather convoluted, not only of his own position, but the position of his paper as well. The overwhelming weight of the evidence in the pages of the *Times*—which by all indications has designs on becoming the American cultural bible for the twenty-first century—points to an utter disdain for the teachings and the Bible of traditional Christianity.

Consider, for instance, what message you would most likely take away from this headline if you just glanced at it: "TEACHING VALUES WITHOUT TAKING A PAGE FROM THE BIBLE" (6/1/99, p. A15).

This headline suggests strongly that in the serious world of public education, the Bible is passé. In the body of the story, the writer furthered this assumption by emphasizing U.S. Supreme

Court decisions that prohibit sectarian prayer in public schools and highlighting cultural movements that promoted non-religious "character" and "interactive skills" education. In fact, the story emphasized that at one California school, the words "virtues" and "values" were rejected as "too shaded by religion."

Editorializing through loaded language. Another way of identifying editorializing in a news story is to look for "loaded language."

I've already mentioned how the *Times* uses terms like "religious right" to dismiss anyone with a Christian faith who happens to be slightly to the right of political center. Other propagandistic weapon-words favored by the paper include "literal" or "literalist" for those who follow a classic, traditional approach to scriptural interpretation. (For example, for Christians that includes those who believe in such accounts as the bodily resurrection of Christ and miraculous healings. For Orthodox Jews, that would mean accepting as a miracle the parting of the Red Sea.)

The paper often uses the term *fundamentalist* to pigeonhole traditionalists of many faiths—including Islam, Judaism, and Christianity—as anti-intellectual, anti-social, bigoted, mean-spirited, or even violent.

To understand how loaded language works, let's examine the terms used to describe those who support or oppose abortion. Remember: the *Times* favors strongly the unlimited right of a woman to have an abortion. If, in fact, the paper's reporters or editors are guilty of editorializing in their news stories, we would expect them to use biased language to further this particular viewpoint.

Common sympathetic terms used to describe those who oppose abortion or support it are, respectively, "pro-life" and "pro-choice." Activists on both sides of the issue prefer these labels because they avoid the unappetizing "A-word." Common *un*sympathetic terms are "anti-abortion" and "pro-abortion" for precisely the same reason—they employ the dreaded word.

A 365-day search of articles on the *Times'* Web site, from July 9, 1998, through July 9, 1999, revealed that the frequency of use of the sympathetic words was practically the same:

- "Pro-life," 67 articles
- "Pro-choice," 61 articles

This finding would suggest a lack of bias in coverage. But a radically different picture emerged when we compared the frequency of use of the two negative terms:

- "Anti-abortion"—169 articles
- "Pro-abortion"—14 articles

As you can see, articles using the loaded, negative term "pro-abortion" are virtually non-existent. But "anti-abortion" appeared an average of almost every other day during that one-year period in 1998–99.

In other words, the *Times* relied on the well-worn tactic of attaching a negative term to its enemies, but avoided using the comparable negative term when referring to its allies. Obviously, the paper had the option to characterize the pro-life movement activists more positively—such as by calling them "defenders of rights of the unborn" or even "rights of the fetus." But instead, the *Times'* writers chose to identify the abortion opponents negatively, or primarily in terms of what they were *against*.

This loaded-language tactic is consistent with the overall tone and fact selection in the *Times'* news stories, editorials, and columns on abortion over the years. Consistently, the paper has stressed not only that the pro-life activists are opposed to abortion but has also pictured them as being against other potentially worthy principles—such as a "woman's right to control her own body" and women's rights in general.

But there is much more to news media Culture Creep than using editorialized language in a news story. To get a broader picture of how slanted stories are assembled, let's take a look at a quick snapshot of news coverage of one aspect of the 1999 Littleton, Colorado, school shootings.

Two ways to cover Columbine. Two completely different messages can be conveyed by different organizations covering the same event. Consider, for instance, how the *Times* and the Associated Press handled two days of coverage of the return of students to Columbine High School in Littleton, Colorado, at the end of the summer of 1999.

By the time school opened on Monday, August 16, much had already been written about the trauma experienced by the students, who had lost many friends during the shooting rampage by two classmates on April 20. Yet references in various papers and national news programs suggested that many people around the country continued to wonder how the survivors would cope and if there were any sources of hope and optimism they could rely on when they returned to classes for the new school year.

The *Times* and the Associated Press provided dramatically different answers to these concerns. First of all, a relatively long Sunday story in the *Times* was headlined rather blandly, "A FRESH COAT OF PAINT AND A NEW START: COLUMBINE STUDENTS, WARY YET EAGER, PREPARE FOR NEW SCHOOL YEAR" (8/16/99, p. A16).

The headline conveyed the weary message that this was a story in need of an update. But the paper seemed also to be implying, "Don't expect the victims of the disaster to have found any real meaning or answers in the tragedy!"

In fact, no one—reporter or editors—appeared to be particularly interested in going beneath the surface to explore emotional or spiritual responses or insights that the intervening months might have produced.

The lead, sprawling over three long paragraphs, dwelt on the already exhaustively covered blood, mayhem, and bullet-riddled walls of the library, which local officials had closed off from view. The reporter ended the lead with the depressing observation that the school "faces the rather daunting challenge of seeking normalcy in a place that could never be the same after what happened there" (p. A21).

The body of the story referred to concerns about the need for stricter gun control, the psychological scars suffered by the students, and the prognosis by a child psychologist that the recovery process would be slow and painful.

In the kicker, or final paragraph, a teacher from the school was quoted as saying, "there will be some tears" and sad memories. He concluded on a note of very guarded optimism: ". . . kids are geared up to do what they need to do to have a real school again" (p. 21).

The pictures accompanying the article reinforced the negative mood of the story itself. One depicted a young couple embracing and mourning at the Littleton cemetery near the graves of the victims.

The second picture bordered on the macabre. A school architect was shown gesturing in front of lockers that were being used to seal off the school library from view. In the caption, the editors made sure everyone got the point, as they reminded readers that the library was "the site of most of the killings during the massacre on April 20."

As true as much of this information may have been, it was old news and did nothing to apprise the reader about any breakthroughs in the recovery process.

The next day, Monday, August 16, the *Times* apparently became so depressed by its own uninspired reporting that it gave up on this phase of the story. In the national edition, the editors did not even run an article—only a picture of a Littleton minister, Rick Barger, talking to small children (no high school students!) about returning to school. The caption was headlined, again in rather flat fashion, "PREPARING FOR SCHOOL IN LITTLETON."

Now contrast this doleful, hopeless scenario presented by the *Times* with the story that Richard N. Ostling did for the Associated Press. His report, which focused on how religious faith was helping students overcome the horrors of the school shooting, was headlined in the America Online version, "CHRISTIANS HELP COLUMBINE STUDENTS" (*AOL News*, 8/16/99, p. 1). Another headline for this AP story, plastered on the front page across six full columns of a Florida newspaper, read, "Spirit-filled Columbine Students Head to Class" (*VBPJ*, p. 1).

The dramatic difference in the respective treatments of the stories emerged first of all in the headlines. The *Times*' headlines and subheads kept the report downbeat to the point of being depressing. No hope was promised, and the story provided none.

The headlines for the AP story, on the other hand, made it clear that the reporter had uncovered spiritual resources in the community in the form of the Christian faith. There is no mention of this emotional and moral support system in the *Times*' back-to-school coverage.

Following the hopeful tone set in the AP headlines, Ostling's uplifting lead was short and to the point. His first sentence read this way: "The weekend before the reopening of Columbine High School, area Christians tapped spiritual resources to help teenagers and the community lift lingering clouds of grief and fear."

A major part of his article focused on an evangelistic rally for three thousand teenagers and also a series of back-to-school Sunday services held by nineteen Catholic and Protestant churches in the area. Ironically, the idea for the Sunday services originated with the very same Lutheran minister—Rick Barger—who was pictured rather nondescriptly in the *Times*' Monday paper. But the *Times* said nothing about his efforts in helping the community move toward spiritual recovery.

Ostling also quoted local church members as saying, "Littleton has become a symbol both of inexplicable evil and of restoration."

In the words of a Lutheran pastor who had assumed leadership of the recovery, "God has done awesome work in this community. These last few months, I feel, have been one of the biggest Spirit-filled movements of the 20th century. God has invaded a country to bring us from darkness into light."

Perhaps most significant of all, Ostling set the story in historical context by observing that the "Littleton carnage produced Evangelical Protestants' most important martyr in decades,

Cassie Bernall, who experienced a dramatic conversion two years ago. She reportedly told a gunman 'yes, I believe in God' and was immediately shot dead."

The Associated Press writer closed his article by reporting on how Littleton teens had spread out on Sunday to speak and sing at twenty religious events across Colorado and in other states.

Finally, in the Florida paper mentioned above, the photograph accompanying the AP story stood in stark contrast to the one chosen by the *Times*. Teenagers were pictured with hands raised, singing "their praise to God" during an inspirational rally.

In evaluating the use of pictures with a story, it's important to remember that editors in accounts like the Littleton shooting often have many options about which pictures to run. Their final choices frequently say something about their view of the events covered—and about the value system they are projecting to their readers.

An Anti-supernatural Bias? Why was there such a decided difference between these two sets of reports?

There are several possible reasons. For one thing, the *Times*, as an institution, has a strong bias against what has been called "intrinsic religion," or inner spiritual experience that can deeply influence one's life. Those with this bias could be expected to minimize or eliminate any suggestion that personal spiritual bonds, or exposure to a moving church or worship service, might help people cope with a disaster such as Littleton. In this regard, remember the Lichter study cited on p. 48: only 7 percent of religion news reports by the elite New York and Washington news organizations deal with spirituality.

This limited view of religion and of the power of personal spiritual experience apparently starts at the top on the paper. A review of the book, *The Trust*, in the *New York Times Book Review* on September 26, 1999 (p. 9), highlighted this comment by publisher Arthur Ochs Sulzberger Jr.:

> "I have the *Times*, that's my religion, that's what I believe in."

The authors of *The Trust* went even further in their text, saying ironically that "those who worked for the Sulzbergers worshiped in the same pew as the family," and that the publisher was "voicing a sentiment shared by many at the paper" (p. 591). Also, the *Times* clearly rejects any possibility that events can be explained in supernatural terms. Those who control the paper make the assumption that it's futile for them or their readers to attempt to understand events in terms other than what can be grasped by the five senses, or explained by psychologists and other therapists. Because such natural and psychological explanations fell short in the Littleton situation, the mood projected by the *Times'* accounts was downcast and pessimistic—and ultimately reflected inadequate reporting and editing.

To sum up, the *Times* missed the real follow-up story on the Columbine High School incident because the paper, as a corporate entity, wears spiritual blinders. Referring to a transcendent dimension to explain or understand human events isn't possible because, according to the *Times'* worldview, God doesn't exist. Or if he is out there somewhere, he remains at the very periphery of human affairs—perhaps existing only as the deistic initiator of the universe, or else as an extremely distant and impersonal divine presence who finds the details of our existence rather irrelevant.

Columbine and the Token Article Strategy. Although the *Times* missed the real story on the return of the Columbine students to school in 1999, it's important—and instructive—to recognize that the paper did devote space a few months earlier to an excellent, if token, article on the spiritual dimensions of the tragedy.

One *Times* reporter, Sara Rimer, caught a vision of the spiritual dimensions of the aftermath of the shooting in a story published on June 6, 1999, under the headline, "COLUMBINE STUDENTS SEEK ANSWERS IN THEIR FAITH" (p. 22). She went into some detail describing how Christian students found assurance and solace in their belief that they and their slain friends were in God's hands. She wrote:

"The students' comments after the shooting serve as a vivid reminder of how strong a role religion plays in the lives of people in Colorado and other parts of the country, but they also suggest why evangelical faith is spreading, particularly among the young: In a society that seems unanchored, it provides certainty."

The reporter then went on to discuss how many have found meaning "in a relationship with Jesus Christ" and in being "born again." She also emphasized how many students considered Cassie Bernall, who was killed after she told one of the gunmen she believed in God, to be a martyr for her faith.

The editors enhanced the reporter's written message with a rather dramatic picture of students kneeling and taking communion. The caption under the picture said that they were "finding solace in prayer groups and their churches, spurning counselors brought in by their school."

In other words, through the work of at least one sensitive and diligent journalist and some supportive editors, the *Times* did get on the record with the spiritual dimensions of the story. But such spiritually oriented stories are few and far between.

Perhaps even more important, the presence of this story illustrates an important feature of the *Times'* overall strategy of news coverage. The paper may endeavor to provide the appearance of balance and fairness with a secondary message (in this case, evangelical Christian spirituality). But simultaneously the primary message conveyed to the reader over time is heavily weighted in the exact opposite, anti-spiritual direction.

If you're trying to influence the minds and beliefs of the news-consuming public, why include the other side of the story at all?

For one thing, any astute editor would know that if he ignored completely the spiritual issues in this situation, the paper might be subject to censure on several levels because faith was clearly an integral part of the story. For example, some might argue that such an omission reflected laziness by the *Times'* reporters and editors in their fact gathering. Others might charge an anti-religious bias.

Still others might suggest that the *Times* really didn't know how to handle a spiritually oriented account.

So for purely journalistic reasons—a need to maintain its good reputation—the *Times* had to "cover its flanks" and fend off potential criticism with at least one story that demonstrated some well-executed spiritual coverage.

At the same time, it's important to recognize that the paper consistently allows extremely limited amounts of space for such accounts. You may find a "token" spiritual story here and there. But the weight of coverage, week after week, is heavily non-spiritual or even anti-spiritual. The reader receives a huge, daily dose of naturalistic, humanistic philosophy and only an occasional article that suggests some possible benefits associated with the spiritual realm, or that goes into depth in such coverage.

By occasionally reporting a spiritual story, the *Times* avoids criticism or even detection of its anti-Christian and anti-spiritual bias and also remains free to engage in under-the-table proselytizing for its own humanistic and naturalistic philosophy.

Note: This use of the "token story" technique—to avoid criticism and appear objective and fair—isn't limited only to stories with a religious or spiritual bent. You'll find the same technique being used in the *Times* coverage of social and political issues, such as homosexuality, abortion, gun control, welfare, and the environment.

The Second Layer of Advocacy: the Editorial Blast

After the paper presents its point of view in important news stories and pictures, the rulers at the *Times* will usually follow up with a strong editorial statement.

That's what happened with the coverage of the Columbine school shooting in Littleton, Colorado, described above. First, the paper's news stories highlighted not only the tragic loss of life but also issues dear to the heart of the *Times*—especially freedom of movement and expression in school, and also gun control. Then, on Tuesday, August 17, the *Times* ran an editorial, "Back

TO COLUMBINE," which commended the high school for taking a moderate approach to beefing up security rather than going overboard with excessive restrictions on student freedom. At the same time, the editors took advantage of the occasion to push for greater gun control—one of the paper's "deadly sins" (described in chapter 10).

This particular editorial shows once again how the *Times* can wield editorials in almost any type of story to promote its articles of faith. The tone may vary from mild, as here, to vitriolic, as was the case when the editors attacked the Catholic League for its criticism of the blasphemous play *Corpus Christi* (see chapters 3 and 5).

Also, remember that the editorial "blast," regardless of its intensity, is often used as part of the devastating one-two punch, consisting of an opinionated news story plus an editorial. The more alert a reader is to this basic technique, the more prepared he or she will be to guard against the impact of Culture Creep and make independent decisions about news reports that may have the power to affect personal beliefs.

The Third Layer of Advocacy: the Op-ed "Hit Person"

As we've already seen in the discussions of Frank Rich and Anna Quindlen, the *Times'* evangelistic effort often relies heavily on support from op-ed pieces, which make explicit arguments in favor of the paper's position. Pontificating from a very prominent position just across from the editorial page, the appropriate op-ed "hit person" can be highly effective in verbally eviscerating or ridiculing opponents. To make matters worse, the victims rarely have an opportunity to respond.

Although these columnists and their op-ed editors may regard their writing as journalism, any pretense of balance or fairness goes out the window when they are dealing with an issue that is absolutely essential to the preservation of their worldview.

Take creationism, for instance. A guest opinion piece on this subject by the physicist Lawrence Krauss was headlined with characteristic open-minded detachment: "EQUAL TIME FOR NONSENSE."

A near-hysterical subhead suggested that even discussing the subject of a God-caused creation would be enough to endanger the future of Western civilization: "OUR TOLERANCE OF FALLACIES LIKE CREATIONISM IMPERILS SOCIETY" (7/29/96, p. A11).

Krauss closed his intemperate attack on creationists—whom he said were motivated by "religious fanaticism, simple ignorance, or personal gain"—with a self-serving reference in his kicker to one of the *Times'* ultimate authorities:

> "We would all be wise to heed the advice passed on by Arthur Hays Sulzberger, the publisher of the *New York Times* from 1935 to 1961: 'I believe in an open mind, but not so open that your brains fall out'" (p. A11).

Such inflammatory op-ed language ignores the fact that the large majority of Americans affirm some version of the belief that God created the earth, life, and human beings. Most likely, few of these believers would expect a secular paper like the *Times* to give equal time to the contention that creation occurred in seven twenty-four-hour days. But perhaps they do have a right to expect some degree of evenhandedness on such an important and complex topic.

Yet the typical story on evolution in the *Times* never explores the nuances or subtleties of different Christian views of creation. Even more shocking, the paper has allotted little space to credible scientists who are raising questions about the validity of evolutionary assumptions (see the discussion in chapter 16). Instead, the *Times* usually promotes the reductionist position reflected in this particular op-ed polemic. There are only two choices: nineteenth century Darwinism or religious "nonsense."

The Fourth Layer of Advocacy: the Bombardment

As the culmination of its overall strategy on a particularly important issue, the *Times* typically barrages readers with feature stories, reviews, and other articles that are designed to give readers the impression that the only reasonable position is the *Times'* position. With an especially fundamental doctrine—such as environmentalism, gun control, abortion, or homosexual rights—the *Times* will reinforce its viewpoint by running subsequent cycles of news stories, editorials, op-ed columns, and features.

When exposed to such journalistic bombardment, it's understandable that many readers, who may lack strong beliefs on a particular topic, eventually conclude that they must either affirm the *Times'* worldview or be relegated to the great, unsophisticated masses who are dismissed as either uninformed or "illiberal." Or such nonconformist readers may find themselves accused of the most serious sin of all: "intolerance."

We'll deal with this particular cultural sin in more depth in the following chapter. But now, let's turn to another red flag that may signal Culture Creep—strategic omissions.

RED FLAG #5: STRATEGIC OMISSION OF FACTS OR OPPOSING VIEWPOINTS

My most excruciating memory of a journalistic omission occurred early in my tenure with the New York *Daily News*, when I was assigned to do a feature on the candidates running for one of the Manhattan seats for the U.S. House of Representatives. Ed Koch, later to become the colorful mayor of New York, was the incumbent who was seeking reelection, and his opponent was Peter Sprague, the millionaire businessman and chairman of National Semiconductor.

As a young reporter with practically no political interviewing under my belt, I was determined to make up for my lack of experience by being extra diligent in gathering the facts and totally fair in presenting them. To this end, I resolved that I would devote approximately equal time to interviewing each candidate. Then, I took pains to give each man mathematically equal space in my article.

Of course, it never entered my mind to favor one candidate over the other or to slant the story so as to give one or the other an edge. In those days—the early 1970s—the main advice I received from editors and more experienced reporters was just to gather and write the facts as accurately and fairly as I could.

More than once, I heard some version of the now-legendary command attributed to Joseph Pulitzer, the founder of the Pulitzer Prizes. Old Joe had reputedly said that the first three rules of good reporting are "accuracy, accuracy, accuracy."

So I spent several hours in the company of each man and put in extra time to organize my notes and write the feature article. Satisfied that my final draft met the basic journalistic tests, I watched the story sail through the city editor and copyeditors with minimal editing.

But when I picked up the paper the next day, I was devastated. Somehow, almost everything I had written about Ed Koch had been dropped from the article!

As well as I could determine, the mistake had occurred during the printing process. Apparently, the last couple of pages of my story had been misplaced, and the final result was a feature focusing almost exclusively on Sprague.

Of course, the Sprague camp was ecstatic. Even as I was trying to run down the source of the problem, I received a call from Sprague's press representative, who complimented me effusively on the great job I had done. That made me feel even worse, and as soon as I had a free moment, I put a call through to Ed Koch to apologize for the error.

Koch was gracious and seemed to understand that neither I nor the *Daily News* was trying to undercut him with a slanted story— and he went on to win the election. But I've never forgotten the principle underlying this excruciating experience: a reporter and his news organization must do everything within their power to ensure that no key facts are omitted, and all sides of the story are covered.

Unfortunately, the *New York Times* sometimes seems uninterested in presenting the complete story—especially when certain facts conflict with particular beliefs or policies that the paper is promoting.

One prominent transgression, which struck me during the National Basketball Association playoffs in 1998, was apparent in an account of how the New York Knicks won a close 3–2 series over the Miami Heat (5/4/98, pp. C13, C16). It seemed that the Knicks would lose, until their guard, Charlie Ward, took charge and hit a 3-pointer to win the game.

The reporter, in recounting Ward's remarkable performance, noted that "Ward found peace" at the very end and later quoted him as explaining that he had "remained calm." But I found myself reading the rather lengthy story over two or three times in an effort to find *why* Ward had stayed so calm and evinced such inner peace.

One reason for my frustration was that I had watched the end of the game on television the night before and had listened to an interview with Ward. In that discussion, he had attributed his lack of nerves and his performance to his religious faith. So I fully anticipated that the *Times*, which had plenty of space to devote to the subject, would expand upon this important factor. Every journalism student and cub reporter knows that a news story should, whenever possible, include answers to the classic who-what-when-where-how/why questions.

In this case, an answer to the "why" query was clearly available. After all, I had heard part of it on TV! Yet the *Times* had ignored it—but why?

Again, a large part of the answer seemed to be the anti-supernatural bias that permeates the paper. In the *Times* newsroom, religious experience simply isn't accorded much of a role in making the world go around. In dealing with the "why" or "how" questions that must be answered in any complete story, no one seems interested in exploring how individuals in a story are responding to the presence of God in their lives.

Also, part of the problem might be traced to impatience among spiritually insensitive reporters who have come to dread what they see as an obligatory, fumbling attempt by athletes to evangelize the audience after a game. Many in the national media—both television and print reporters—have become impatient with the short spiritual acknowledgments (or journalists might call them "advertisements") that many athletes give when asked about the reason for their stellar performances.

In the 1999 NBA playoffs, I was struck by the variety of ways particular players gave credit to their God:

"I just want to thank Jesus."

"God gets the glory."

"Praise be to Allah."

To me, such responses signal that religious faith is playing an important role as top-flight performances occur at the highest levels of sports competition. Yet instead of exploring this issue— and finding out more about how prayer can calm the mind, or how a player may have perceived that God answered certain prayers—most reporters simply roll their eyes or appear uncomfortable when a religious comment arises. Or, as happened in this case with the *Times*, the reporter ignores the issue altogether.

Such omissions make it impossible for a journalist to get at the real story. But perhaps this sacrifice is justified in the minds of certain members of the editorial staff because strategic omissions can be a powerful tool in furthering a news organization's objective to keep genuine religious experience away from public view.

A similar kind of strategic omission can occur with other types of stories—such as those involving politics.

Suppose, for instance, that a certain Democratic paper is breathing a sigh of relief because a sexually promiscuous, impeached Democratic president has just escaped being thrown out of office for his offenses. But suppose further that another, more serious charge has now surfaced—an accusation that the president in question raped a woman years before. Finally, suppose that the full story has been plastered all over competing papers, and a TV interview with the victim convinces most viewers that she is telling the truth—that the president did indeed attack her.

What should be the response to this incident by any "news-paper of record" worth the name?

Clearly, in this case—which involved Juanita Broaddrick's charges against Bill Clinton—the *Times* should have crawled all over the story immediately and marshaled its vast resources to take the lead in coverage. Instead, as a former sex-crimes prose-cutor who followed the sequence of events in detail pointed out in the *Wall Street Journal*, the *Times* waited five days after the story broke to run its first article, and even then played the story far back in the paper, on page A16 (*WSJ*, 3/5/99, p. A14).

The *Times'* story referred to by the *Journal* writer was finally published on February 24, 1999, under the headline, "ON TORTUOUS ROUTE, SEXUAL ASSAULT ACCUSATION AGAINST CLINTON RESURFACES" (p. A16).

The rambling article, which might have been subtitled, "Why We Didn't Publish This Story Any Earlier," was clearly a "house story." In other words, because it dealt with the reporting deci-sions and operations of the *Times* and quoted a high editorial official, Managing Editor Bill Keller, the story was presented with extraordinary care. The writer offered many excuses for the *Times'* failure to report the story—all of which were designed to put the paper in the best possible light.

Why would the *Times* drag its heels in this situation?

The editors may have felt that the credibility of the woman was still questionable. But few who saw her powerful television inter-view on *Dateline NBC* dared to draw that conclusion publicly.

Or they may have rationalized that even if the rape did occur, it deserved to be forgotten because it happened so long ago—more than twenty years in the past. Also, the statute of limitations had expired, and so the president wouldn't be subject to any crim-inal charges.

Such excuses ring hollow. After all, Bill Clinton was no babe in the woods at the time of the incident. He was a fully respon-sible adult in his mid-thirties and also an experienced high state official. A rape is a rape at any age, whether it's an offense that can be prosecuted or not.

Furthermore, the alleged offense was supported by credible evidence—and the accused offender was the highest officeholder in the land. In such circumstances, regardless of the final outcome, the charges should be explored. But the *Times* chose to ignore the issue, apparently hoping Broaddrick would just disappear.

As for the motives for the *Times'* omissions, Managing Editor Bill Keller may have disclosed more than he meant to in the February 24, 1999, article:

> "[W]e talked long and hard about whether to publish anything," he said. "The merits of the allegations are probably unknowable. Legally, it doesn't seem to go anywhere. Congress isn't going to impeach him again. And frankly, we've all got a bit of scandal fatigue" (p. A16).

In other words, Keller revealed, the *Times* had decided to give up before it could even really get started on the Broaddrick allegations.

Also, they abandoned the issue before they could evaluate if subsequent information on the matter would produce other sources. In fact, the *Dateline NBC* interview with the woman didn't even air until the evening after this lone *Times* story ran! Any experienced journalist—including those who work at the *Times*—knows that you often begin to unearth your best sources after an investigative series begins to run. But it's clear that the newspaper of record wasn't interested in pursuing this embarrassing matter any further.

The powers-that-be at the paper, apparently in a maneuver to silence any criticism of their omissions, followed up on February 27, 1999, with a weak editorial, headlined, "The President's Missing Voice" (p. A30).

The editorial writers said that "no one will ever know the complete truth about Juanita Broaddrick's allegation that Bill Clinton raped her in 1978"—a remarkable capitulation for a paper that prides itself on winning Pulitzers through tenacious investigative reporting.

Also, they concluded that "there is no legal or constitutional remedy for the situation"—a statement that reaffirmed their position that apparently nothing short of outright treason could cause them to call for the resignation or impeachment and removal of a Democratic president from office.

The newspaper's oligarchy devoted the last half of the editorial to unsolicited advice. First, they allowed rather gingerly that "it would be nice to hear Mr. Clinton himself address the matter." But then they quickly got off that subject and reverted to basically the same mantra that Clinton and his supporters had been murmuring throughout the scandal and impeachment proceeding— "it's time to move on."

The *Times* did use somewhat different words, talking about the need for Clinton "to re-establish communication with the nation after a traumatic year." But the moving-on message, approved by the Democratic establishment, was basically the same.

Finally, the editorial staff cited one of the paper's anointed cultural authorities, Patricia Ireland, president of the National Organization for Women. Together, Ireland and the *Times* cautioned that it might not be such a good idea for Clinton and his team to trash Broaddrick in the same way they had mistreated previous female accusers of the president.

In taking such a timid and perfunctory approach to such an important issue, the *Times* affirmed once again one of its prime doctrines: Certain important social and political values—such as keeping a Democratic president in office—must sometimes be given precedence over basic justice, good character, and fair play.

In this particular case, the *Times* decided that Bill Clinton had to be saved, even though he was admittedly less than perfect. The controlling consideration that preserved Clinton and his presidency seemed to be that he had become one of the most visible promoters of many of the paper's pet issues, such as abortion and gay rights. To have forced him to accept yet another set of devastating charges might well have ended his presidency. That could have gone a long way toward ensuring the victory of a Republican in the presidential election of 2000—a highly unpalatable and, indeed, totally unacceptable prospect for a staunch Democratic media voice such as the *Times*.

Such decisions often carry serious consequences. The paper's strategic omission of the sordid Broaddrick affair helped subvert one woman's efforts to find some measure of justice for the egregious wrongs that she and many others clearly believed had been committed against her in the past.

RED FLAG #6: A POOL OF LIKE-MINDED PUNDITS

The final red flag that may signal the presence of bias—and the Culture Creep that may insidiously change public attitudes and values—centers on the authorities and pundits that reporters and editors rely upon for quotes and observations. To evaluate a particular pundit, the reader must try to determine just why that person is being put forward as an expert.

One important point to resolve is the ultimate purpose of the writer or editor for giving the person space in the paper. If the expert contributes something new or creative to an issue—and seems not to be serving merely as a tool to spread the *Times'* worldview—then there is no reason to be suspicious.

The legitimacy of a quote or reference becomes even more definite if the expert actually provides an opposing viewpoint in the story. For example, no one would think of criticizing John Noble Wilford's reliance on a California Institute of Technology astronomer, Dr. S. George Djorgovski, who expounded upon a tiny light in the sky that scientists had been unable to explain (8/17/99, p. A1).

On the other hand, if it appears that the paper or reporter is using the pundit merely to back up a preconceived point of view, the reader has reason to be wary. As an illustration, reflect on the *Times'* handling of a series of June 1999 U.S. Supreme Court decisions, which gave new authority to the states and imposed limits on the federal government (6/24/99, p. A1).

To understand how a pundit may be used in such a situation to proclaim the paper's philosophy, it's necessary to take into account the full context and background of the story.

These Court rulings on federalism outraged the *Times*, which is a strong proponent of minimizing states' rights and maximizing the power of the central government. So the paper immediately attacked the Court in an editorial headed, "SUPREME MISCHIEF" (6/24/99, p. A30).

Calling the states' rights decision "alarming," the paper's management accused the Court of "steadily whittling down the legitimate authority of the Federal Government." They also bemoaned the conservative majority's "cramped spirit" and charged that "this was not a worthy exit" and an "unhappy result" for the ending of the Court's 1998–99 term. Overall, the editorial conveyed the message that the Court was out of control and encroaching on the rightful domain of Congress and the president.

Then, using its well-honed bombardment strategy, the paper came out swinging *again* three days later through the voice of the paper's Supreme Court reporter, Linda Greenhouse (6/27/99, pp. 4-1).

In the Sunday Week in Review section—which supposedly involves news wrap-ups, but in fact allows plenty of room for writers to express their opinions in a news-story format—Greenhouse reinforced, in her pithy, potent lead, the notion that the Court had become high-handed:

"The Supreme Court rules," her article began.

Then, after describing to the reader how the Court's decisions had "reconfigured the Federal-state balance of power," she quoted the Acting Solicitor General, who charged, "This is a Court that doesn't *defer* to government at any level" (emphasis added).

The key word in that quotation, which I have emphasized for effect, is *defer*, because Greenhouse used it several times in the story to remind the reader of her dominant theme—which was the Court's imperious arrogance. Or, as she put it herself, what was "most notable" was the court's "*lack of deference* to its ostensibly co-equal branches . . ." (emphasis added).

Finally, having firmly established her viewpoint (which, incidentally, was quite consistent with the *Times'* previous editorial), she was ready to use her main pundit—Harvard Law School Professor Laurence H. Tribe, one of the nation's leading liberal constitutional law experts.

Tribe provided her with a supportive quote that, quite remarkably, used the same "lack of deference" terminology that had popped up elsewhere in the story:

"The Court is telling Congress, 'We think it's not as necessary as you apparently do, so you lose,'" Tribe said. "It's a complete *lack of deference*" (emphasis added).

To sum up, then, the *Times'* editorial, plus the Week in Review article three days later, plus the imprimatur of one of the nation's leading legal experts added up to a powerful impression that the Court had seriously overstepped its rightful bounds in the states' rights arena.

I should mention, by the way, that I recognize that Linda Greenhouse enjoys a reputation as a highly competent court reporter, and I frequently read her stories quite closely—and usually find no reason to criticize her presentation of the facts. Furthermore, I have the greatest respect for the legal abilities of Larry Tribe—who, as it happens, was one of my classmates at Harvard Law School. But in this particular sequence of articles, it's apparent that the facts became much less important than the interpretation of those facts—and the pundit was employed primarily to execute the philosophical coup de grace.

On many occasions, the *Times* calls on experts to support its belief system—and often, as was the case with Tribe, the institutional affiliation of the expert is Ivy League. In fact, a one-year search of the *Times'* Web site for the term "Harvard professor," ending on July 9, 1999, revealed that 742 articles had contained that term, or more than two instances per day.

A total of thirty *Times'* articles referred to "Laurence H. Tribe" for a one-year period ending on August 19, 1999. These included two guest op-ed columns written by the professor, a number of articles relating to the Clinton impeachment proceedings, and letters to the editor responding to Tribe's views.

"Columbia professor" was only a little less popular than the Harvard response, with 657 articles, and "Yale professor" came in a distant third, with 423 articles. "Princeton professor" trailed all the others with 285 articles for the year.

The connection of Ivy League institutions, especially Harvard, with the *Times* is so intimate as to be almost incestuous. The alumni organ of the university, *Harvard Magazine*, is symbolic of the relationship. Replete with deferential *Times'* references and connections, the university organ might on occasion make an unsuspecting reader wonder if he had picked up the *Times'* Sunday magazine by mistake.

The July-August 1999 issue of *Harvard Magazine*, for instance, quoted the economist and Harvard professor, John Kenneth Galbraith, on a discussion he had with President John F. Kennedy about a *Times'* article describing Galbraith's appointment as ambassador to India. Galbraith was rather proud that the paper had called him "arrogant."

In the same issue, an autobiographical blurb revealed that the coauthor of a major article, Bill Kovach, had been Washington Bureau Chief of the *Times* (pp. 35, 97).

Kovach, by the way, is the curator of Harvard's Nieman Foundation, which for many years has brought in specially chosen working journalists, many of whom have worked for the *Times*, for a period of academic study and research.

Also—still in the same issue of *Harvard Magazine*—the only journalist among six participants in the magazine's "roundtable" on the state of democracy in America was Adam Clymer, who had held many *Times'* positions, including Washington editor and correspondent (p. 48).

Finally, two prominently displayed quotes, set apart and highlighted in red—one from the *Times* and the other from the paper's wholly owned sister publication, the *Boston Globe*—adorned an article on the merger of Radcliffe, the women's college, and Harvard (pp. 72-73). Other references to the *Times* punctuate this particular issue of *Harvard Magazine*, and frequent mentions of the paper abound in other issues.

Such institutional back-scratching leads to an inescapable conclusion: The *Times* and the Ivy League, especially Harvard, have become cozy spiritual bedfellows. They work quite naturally in tandem to reinforce a rather consistent worldview—a leftist, humanistic "gospel," if you will—which they have resolved to spread far beyond the bounds of the Northeast.

✣

In wrapping up this discussion, I should note that any one of these six red flags *may* be a signal that points to the presence of Culture Creep—but it's important to marshal all your evidence before you jump to conclusions. Clearly, one isolated editorial, or a slip here or there into editorializing in a news story, doesn't automatically translate into a form of journalism that is designed to affect the way you believe.

But when patterns begin to emerge—such as a series of editorials that push a point of view and are combined with complementary, slanted news stories and back-up op-ed pieces—you can be fairly certain you're not dealing with a publication that is interested only in communicating the facts. It's at this point that you should begin to look for an overall belief system or worldview—and the mechanisms that may be at work to "save" you from your sins of wrong thinking and bad behavior.

CHAPTER 5

THE WEST 43ᴿᴰ STREET PLAN OF SALVATION

or the *New York Times*, salvation has nothing to do with eternity or the supernatural and everything to do with personal self-realization in the here and now. The paper's entire belief system—which may be understood in terms of a rather well-defined secular "theology" or "gospel"—is designed to uphold and enhance the sanctity or holiness of the individual human being.

But this individual self-actualization is not entirely up to the individual. Rules must be followed—rules that the *Times* has outlined quite clearly in its pages.

In your search for truth, it's not acceptable simply to listen for God's voice or even to look within yourself for direction. Through such an independent, unregulated quest, you may become too serious about a particular religious faith. Or you may develop too much enthusiasm for certain questionable political or social views.

Instead, reaching the paper's promised land requires abiding by some basic *Times*-approved beliefs—a set of moral and ethical absolutes that each individual must affirm to progress toward the ultimate goal of self-realization. More specifically, a person can only achieve the *Times'* version of salvation if he or she follows a threefold path toward truth:

- Display "tolerance"—as defined by the *Times*.
- Expose yourself to the proper mental and moral conditioning through a centrally controlled educational and informational environment.
- Engage in culturally correct thinking and action.

In more detail, here is a description of these three basic steps to salvation, which have the power to make you a child of the kingdom on West 43rd Street.

STEP ONE: BECOME "TOLERANT"—AS DEFINED BY THE TIMES

When you enter the special world created by the *New York Times*, you must forget the dictionary's definition of tolerance and related terms, or even what common sense would suggest. Instead, be prepared to enter a world of Alice-in-Wonderland English, where ordinary logic is set aside and words and concepts are given special meanings, as the *Times'* storytellers may choose.

Or as Humpty Dumpty said to Alice in *Through the Looking-Glass and What Alice Found There:* "When I use a word, it means just what I chooe it to mean—neither more nor less" (Carroll, p. 123).

By common definition (*not* by the *Times'* definition), "tolerance" means that you allow free expression to other viewpoints while still affirming your own. Various dictionary entries and etymological analyses of "tolerance" suggest that the most accurate definition involves having a "permissive or liberal attitude"—or showing "sympathy or indulgence" toward beliefs or practices that may differ from or conflict with your own.

The implication according to this standard understanding of the word is that *to be tolerant, you are not expected to give up your own beliefs, nor are you required to place the beliefs of others on the same plane as your own.*

In fact, the Latin root of "tolerate" is the verb *tolero, tolerare*, which means to bear, carry, endure, or just "put up with." So to tolerate another viewpoint in the normal and historic sense of the word, you don't have to agree with that belief, or even like it. True tolerance involves simply a live-and-let-live policy. In our free society, such an understanding of tolerance allows both you, and those with whom you disagree, to affirm your differing world-views within an orderly, non-violent social framework.

But a study of the *Times* reveals that the paper has changed the true meaning of tolerance—primarily to strengthen its position in promoting its distinctive worldview.

The Times' View of Tolerance

First of all, the *Times* defines tolerance with an eye to putting serious religious faith on the defensive. The reason for this is that the paper promotes an absolute set of values—relating to such issues as abortion, marriage, gender roles, and religious educa-tion—that often conflict with the absolute values of traditional or conservative Christians, Jews, and members of other faiths. Charging "intolerance," the *Times* has discovered, can be a potent weapon to neutralize any religious movement that claims—as the paper does—to have a corner on all or most of the truth.

Here's how the paper's "tolerance attack" may work in practice:

A tolerant person—according to the *Times*—must accept all traditional religious beliefs as essentially equal and certainly must not try to proselytize or convert others. After all, can it be mean-ingful or even honest to suggest that another person try your faith if all beliefs are basically the same? Yet any religious person or group who falls into this trap must automatically give up any claim to a special understanding of absolute truth or values.

Even as the paper has enticed many religious leaders of main-line churches and liberal synagogues and their adherents to give up any claim to absolutes, the *Times* continues to insist that it is in possession of Truth, with a capital *T.* In fact, in a strange turn-about in moral leadership, which Alice might have appreciated, many members of the clergy parrot back the same values from the pulpit that they have read during the previous week in the *Times* or one of the many media outlets influenced by the paper.

An old quip that can still be heard in seminaries and among seasoned pulpit orators is that to be relevant, a minister should preach with the Bible in one hand and the newspaper in the other. In our own day, the newspaper is still there, but too often the Bible has been left on the shelf.

Another issue that profoundly disturbs the *Times* about serious or enthusiastic religious movements is that the believers often feel an obligation to spread their spiritual word—and even proselytize or convert nonbelievers. Although that's exactly what the *New York Times* does in its pages every day of the week, members of religious groups don't get the privilege. Instead, the paper discourages the exercise by conservative religious believers of their freedom to spread their particular word or lead others to their understanding of truth. In fact, according to the *Times*, it's downright wrong—or to use a favorite *Times*' term, "intolerant"—to say that your religious faith is the one true way to truth or salvation. Apparently, only the *Times* and its acolytes have that prerogative.

There is also a strange corollary to this understanding of how the *Times*' tolerance rules are expected to work with religious groups. Conservative Christians in particular must refrain from taking a public stand against a film, play, or other artistic creation that denigrates their religion or spiritual leader. If they do, they are no longer tolerant—and may even be deemed bigots. For a case in point, let's consider in a little more detail the controversy surrounding the play *Corpus Christi*, which was mentioned in another context in chapter 3.

An Intolerant Times?

Corpus Christi, a highly controversial 1998 play by Terrence McNally, was widely perceived as so disrespectful toward the Christian faith that many Christians regarded the work as sacrilegious and blasphemous.

According to a front-page story in The Living Arts section of the May 28, 1998, issue (pp. B1, B10), the workshop production of the play featured thirteen men who acted out the life of Jesus in sexually provocative style. Jesus ("Joshua") was portrayed as a young gay man, and other male actors played various male and female characters, including the Virgin Mary.

The play, which was to be staged by the Manhattan Theatre Club in 1998, came under heavy criticism from Catholic protestors and other Christian groups, and was finally cancelled by the Club. But that was just round one in the brouhaha.

Counterprotests mounted in the theater community, with playwrights such as Wendy Wasserstein, Edward Albee, and Tony Kushner signing a petition that called the cancellation "a capitulation to right-wing extremists and religious zealots," according to the *Times*.

Then the *Times*—which is always the eight-hundred-pound gorilla in the room when any cultural fracas erupts in Manhattan—weighed in with its heavy weaponry. In a May 28, 1998, editorial headed, "CENSORING TERRENCE MCNALLY," the paper rightly criticized threats of physical violence that had been leveled at the theater and McNally (p. A28).

Not willing to stop there, the editorial defenders-of-the-faith shifted to their main concern: propounding a virtually unlimited right to freedom of speech for those who support the *Tmes*' positions—but limiting First Amendment rights for those who oppose the *Times*. The paper actually accused the Catholic League for Religious and Civil Rights, which had staged a letter-writing campaign against the production, of suppression of the play. The *Times* then went so far as to equate McNally's play with Christian worship, stating that there "is no essential difference between suppressing the production of a controversial play and suppressing a form of worship."

The *Times* finished off its diatribe with a rather heavy-handed, thinly veiled criticism of conservative Christianity in general, and Catholicism in particular.

"There is a native strain of bigotry, violence and contempt for artistic expression in this country," the paper cautioned darkly.

One result of this confrontation was that those trying to uphold some respect for traditional Christianity lost, and the

Times and its allies won: the Manhattan Theatre Club rescheduled the McNally play for the fall of 1998.

Another significant consequence was that the paper left behind strong anti-Catholic and anti-Christian impressions in the minds of those who had read the editorial and news story. Who could forget the editorial that linked these religious groups to "bigotry" and "contempt for artistic expression"?

Even if the *Times'* tactics produced some semblance of temporary victory over their ideological enemies, a disturbing question raised by the paper's attacks remained unanswered:

How can a newspaper that puts free speech at the top of its list of civic virtues possibly criticize one group (the Catholic League) for exercising its right to free speech against another group (McNally and the Manhattan Theater Club)?

It's hard to fathom how organizing a letter-writing campaign or staging public demonstrations in order to stop or discourage attendance at an offensive play can be deemed "suppression" or "censorship." Rather, such a campaign seems to represent one of the purest expressions of the freedom of speech and assembly that the *Times* claims to defend.

It should be noted, by the way, that there was no evidence whatsoever that the Catholic League was behind any alleged threat of violence. Still, the *Times* attempted to plant this connection in its readers' minds through a couple of old yellow-journalism ploys.

The first involved juxtaposing one sentence, which described the League's letter-writing efforts, with another, highly incriminating sentence that contained a reference to the physical threats. A reader who moved quickly from one sentence to the next would automatically connect the two—even though there actually was no proof of any connection.

The second ploy was the use of an implied slander against traditional Christianity that the *Times* imbedded in the editorial. The editorial writers mentioned some unnamed, twisted misfits who were cursed with a "native strain of bigotry, violence and contempt for artistic expression." Yet it was clear from the context that the main groups they were referring to were the activist Catholics and other Christians who had protested the production of a play as blasphemous and demeaning to their faith.

Such tactics—which amount to little more than cheap smears—are disappointing in a paper that not only purports to be the best in the country, but also is widely accepted as the news organization that sets the agenda for all others.

But Catholics are not always the prime targets for charges of "bigotry" or "intolerance." The paper doesn't hesitate to allow its pages to be used for both subtle and not-so-subtle potshots at other conservative Christian groups, such as Southern Baptists.

Testing Tolerance near Tulsa

A 1998 "student dispatch" described the struggles of three teens to fit into a mostly Protestant community near Tulsa, Oklahoma (4/29/98, p. 4). The teenagers included a young Vietnamese Buddhist, a former Southern Baptist who now eschewed traditional religion, and another student who had also fallen away from the organized church.

The headline encapsulated an important *Times'* assumption about acceptable religious practice: "IN A PROTESTANT COM-MUNITY, DIFFERENT PATHS TO ENLIGHTENMENT."

The implication both in the headline and in the article itself was twofold. First, there are many traditions that can provide the maximum spiritual benefit. Second, no single faith can possibly be the repository of all truth. In a sense, this position suggests a kind of secularized Hinduism, which holds that there are many paths that lead up the mountain of spiritual experience to ultimate truth.

But another, unspoken message is that the *Times* doesn't care what religious tradition a person affirms, so long as that tradition doesn't promulgate views that differ appreciably from those of the paper. Also, it's absolutely *verboten* to claim that your faith is the only source of truth, or even that it contains more truth than other religions. If you dare to affirm a religion that claims all truth, or more truth than other faiths, you are intolerant.

Obviously, such a view of tolerance consigns practically everyone who is serious about his or her faith to the nethermost realm of the intolerant—because most serious believers do assume their particular faith is superior. Otherwise, they wouldn't have committed themselves to that particular one and excluded all the others!

Even many Hindus, who believe that there are multiple paths to truth, believe that their particular Hindu way is the best. In the words of the great Indian philosopher and former president of India, Sarvepalli Radhakrishnan, Hinduism was "Religion" while other faiths were "religions" (Proctor, *Templeton*, p. 168).

The specific theme of this particular *Times'* story centered on how "a few teenagers have chosen their own paths to religious enlightenment"—and how these gallant few had managed to thrive in a largely Christian community, which was presented as narrow and unsophisticated (p. 4).

For example, one of the three featured teens who rejected Christianity was described as saying that he had found "many Christians he knows to be 'conservative and close-minded.'"

In general, the article pictured the Christian students in the community as obsessed with converting nonconformists to Christianity, as disrespectful toward other beliefs, as unloving, or as having "good intentions gone awry."

The final impression that the reader took away from the story was that the Southern Baptists and other conservative Christians in the community occupied a spiritually inferior position to the three "enlightened" teenagers. The reason? The traditionalists weren't "tolerant" enough to abandon their own convictions and acknowledge the *Times'* belief that one way to God is as good as the next.

Tolerant People Must Agree with the Times

A *Times*-tolerant person must also refrain from expressing disagreement with lifestyle choices approved by the paper. So, if you say you have reservations about the morality of homosexual behavior or gay marriage, you are intolerant. Or if you dare to suggest that it's wrong for two unmarried heterosexual people to have sex before marriage, you are also intolerant. Implied in these doctrines is the notion that you are not a truly good or right-thinking person unless you are tolerant by the *Times'* definition.

Assume, for instance, that you find yourself at dinner with a *Times*-believing crowd, which tends to accept at face value practically every report and editorial published by the paper. Now, suppose you express a heterodox view—such as saying you oppose gun control, favor capital punishment, favor school vouchers, favor prayer in public schools, or oppose abortion.

If you try to swim against the intellectual tide of the *Times* in this way, you place yourself at risk of being deemed "intolerant" or even "bigoted" (terrifying terms in the world of Manhattan Fundamentalism). With the scarlet *I* or *B* on your brow, you will most likely be mocked, shunned, or ignored. Certainly, you won't be invited out to dinner again.

So in promoting its peculiar brand of tolerance, the *Times* presents us with a paradox. Those who affirm the values of the paper are by definition tolerant. But the paper encourages extreme intolerance toward many of those who raise questions about the basic West 43rd Street value system.

It may be helpful to put these observations in religious terms because in reality what we are dealing with here is a systematic secular "theology" that has been formulated at the cultural cathedral in midtown Manhattan. According to this theology, certain independent thinkers, especially those with a traditional religious bent, are "lost," at least in terms of fitting into and contributing to social and political programs that will produce progress for all humankind. But "salvation" is still possible—*if* the lost soul repents of his or her independent ways, discards contrary beliefs, and comes around to the *Times'* way of thinking. Through such a personal "conversion," the nonconformist may even become a tolerant person and be invited out to dinner again.

WHAT ABOUT RELATIVISM?

Contrary to what many critics of the paper and proponents of its cultural doctrines have charged, the *Times'* belief in tolerance should not automatically be equated with relativism—or an assumption that knowing absolute truth is impossible because human perception is too limited to grasp reality beyond each individual mind. Nor does the *Times'* philosophy necessarily translate into relativistic ethics, or a belief that right behavior is defined entirely according to what an individual or society believes is right.

It's quite acceptable from a relativistic viewpoint for one person to believe and act according to one set of standards and for another person to operate by an entirely contradictory set of standards. Yet the relativist would say that it's impossible to determine which set of moral rules is correct and which is not, and so the search for absolute values is futile.

Ethical relativism—which can be traced back at least to the thought of the Greek Sophist Protagoras in the fifth century B.C.—now permeates much grassroots thinking and morality in the United States and other Western nations. Protagoras summed up his thinking in the famous sentence, "Man is the measure of all things." In other words, truth is whatever a person believes to be true. Furthermore, it's not possible to find absolute truth beyond individual perceptions.

Today, Protagoras's spiritual heirs express their radical subjectivism and ethical relativism in somewhat different terms:

- "One person's beliefs are as good as the next."
- "Anything is acceptable—so long as you don't hurt another person."
- "If it feels good, do it—again, so long as you don't hurt somebody else."
- "Truth for you lies inside yourself."
- "Truth may be different for you than it is for me—but both of us can still be right."

Many in our Western society—perhaps a majority—hold to some form of such relativism, but there are exceptions, including:

- Orthodox Jews
- Evangelical Christians
- Fundamentalist Muslims and
- The *New York Times*.

Unlike many relativists, the powers-that-be at the *Times* have developed a worldview that they assume should be affirmed by everyone. In other words, they really do believe that there are absolute truths—one of the foremost being tolerance—which every right-thinking person should follow.

Furthermore, these *Times'* truths appear to apply not only to citizens of the United States and Western nations, but also to those of disadvantaged countries and cultures. Imposing Western principles or morality and behavior on the Third World isn't always easy, however.

Limits on Tolerance?

A lead article in the March 6, 1999, Arts & Ideas section—which was considered so important that it was given half of the top of the first page and half of the top of the jump page—reflects the paper's basic beliefs on tolerance. Also, the piece suggested the struggles the *Times* faces in applying this principle to those of radically non-Western nations (p. A15).

The story was entitled, rather tellingly, "TESTING THE LIMITS OF TOLERANCE AS CULTURES MIX—DOES FREEDOM MEAN ACCEPTING RITUALS THAT REPEL THE WEST?" The implication of this headline—and the message of the article—strongly suggest that there are definite limits to tolerance when the practices of other cultures conflict with the absolutes espoused by the *Times*.

In this article, the writer, Barbara Crossette, highlighted Third-World practices deplored by the *Times*, such as female circumcision, and explored whether Somali parents who live in the United States should be free to follow such practices.

The basic question Crossette asked was this: "How do democratic, pluralistic societies like the United States, based on religious and cultural tolerance, respond to customs and rituals that may be repellent to the majority?" (p. A16).

She then described the conflicts that may arise as American doors are opened to immigrants—a particularly appropriate group, since fostering the rights of immigrants is an important *Times'* belief (see chapter 13). For example, how should our culture deal with such customs as female circumcision, or the ritual cutting of girls' genitals—a tradition that flies directly in the face of the *Times'* feminist and human rights belief system?

In attempting to answer this question, the author explored the dangers of taking a purely relativistic view toward developing societies, or accepting uncritically such abusive practices as genital mutilation. She noted that some experts on such non-Western cultures feel that such relativism may "undermine the very notion of progress"—another important value the *Times* prizes highly.

An official from the United Nations Children's Fund (Unicef) was quoted as saying he believes there is *"a global moral minimum,"* which is consistent with the beliefs of human rights advocates in the United States. In other words, there are absolute rules or principles that should govern individual and social behavior throughout the world as we enter the new millennium (p. A17).

This argument for some sort of bedrock absolute values—such as a belief in tolerance, progress, and human rights—is entirely consistent with the worldview promulgated on the *Times'* editorial pages and elsewhere in the paper. So there is strong evidence that the *Times* is *not* by any measure a hotbed of ethical relativism. Rather, the paper is perhaps the strongest media bastion of absolute beliefs and values, which attempt to dictate how the ordinary person should think and behave.

The Mortal Sin of Intolerance

The flip side of tolerance is "intolerance" and also "bigotry"—both words that the *Times* likes to bandy about.

A 365-day search of the *Times'* Web site archives, running from August 1998 to August 1999 revealed that the paper ran 119 articles on intolerance that year—or almost one every third day. A search for the word "bigotry" turned up even more—122 articles.

According to the usual meaning, intolerance refers to an unwillingness to endure another person or grant equal freedom of expression to that person especially with respect to religion. Also, intolerance may be used to describe those who are unwilling to give equal professional, political, or social rights, especially to those of other races.

Ironically, as we have seen, when the *Times* charges "intolerance," the paper's attack may be directed against those who are exercising their rights of free speech or assembly in an effort to oppose some deeply held *Times'* belief. Yet the *Times* in many situations promotes those very same freedoms of free speech and assembly as virtually absolute principles of truth.

Apparently, such freedom of expression is fully available only to those who push the paper's viewpoints—and may be withheld from anyone who is unlucky enough to be classified as a *Times'* cultural reject. This category of outcasts encompasses many conservative Catholics, Protestant evangelicals (especially those who have the highest view of scriptural authority and believe that Jesus Christ is the only way to salvation), "religious fundamentalists" of other faiths, and *certainly* any person or group identified with the "religious right."

Why Bigotry Is So Bad

"Bigotry" may be the most serious offense of all in the listing of the paper's moral offenses. But again the *Times'* understanding of this term diverges from common definitions.

According to the typical dictionary understanding, a bigot is a person who is stubbornly and intolerantly devoted to a particular religious group, party, or belief system. Today's word has been traced back to the Middle French word, *bigot*, meaning a religious hypocrite. Also, one of the most corrupt officials of mid-eighteenth-century France was named, rather appropriately, François Bigot—a circumstance that must have added to the negative connotations of the word. Finally, the derogatory Old French term for the hated Norman invaders of northern France was *bigot*.

In other words, there seems to be nothing in the history of the word to commend it. The overwhelmingly negative associations attached to "bigot" over the years suit the purposes of the *Times* well, as it has fixed on this particular epithet to describe religious groups and social movements that it disagrees with.

Of course, on some occasions when the *Times* describes the actions of a person or organization as "bigoted" or gives an example of "bigotry," the terms may be appropriate. For example, an August 1999 editorial labeled anti-Semitic and anti-white remarks made at a rally in Harlem the previous year as "bigotry."

The editors would be equally justified in applying the same terms to racist speech, and certainly to physical attacks against or killings of homosexuals or members of minority groups. In such cases, the paper may characterize the actions as a "hate crime"— a term that can be found in 190 articles in the one-year period from August 1998 to August 1999. Every reasonable person would agree that the *Times* has correctly mobilized its resources against this kind of intolerance and bigotry.

But problems arise when the paper broadens the definition of "bigotry" or "intolerance" to include those who exercise their right to free expression in speaking against certain practices they see as wrong or sinful, even though the *Times* doesn't. In such a case, the *Times* itself falls into the trap of promoting its own peculiar forms of intolerance and bigotry.

Now, let's move on from this explanation of Step One— becoming "*Times*-tolerant"—to what the *Times'* theology suggests is the second required step to achieve secular salvation, the all-important achievement of a proper education.

STEP TWO: BECOME EDUCATED AND INFORMED—THROUGH CHANNELS THAT PROMOTE THE TIMES' VALUES

For the *New York Times*, a proper education is the ultimate solution to practically every human problem. The paper is so consumed with the subject that more than sixty-three hundred articles dealt with education during the one-year period from August 1998 to August 1999. This translates into an average of more than seventeen articles per day. Of these, by the way, about three articles per day, or more than one thousand, were opinion pieces, such as editorials or op-ed columns.

A Radically Benign View of Human Nature

Some might say that the message conveyed in these news stories, editorials, op-ed pieces, and letters to the editor smacks of grandiosity. In effect, the paper suggests that all intolerance, bigotry, narrow-mindedness, discrimination, wars, poverty—you name it—might be wiped out if only all the ignorant, uninformed, or wrong-thinking people of the world could know what the executives and editors at the *Times* know.

Taking the paper's belief system to its logical conclusion, we might still have the occasional mentally unbalanced assassin or terrorist to create isolated disruptions of the general welfare. But in the world of the well-educated, these would be the exception, not the rule.

Most likely, according to *Times*-think, the most evil political leaders who have caused so much pain for so many millions— those such as the Hitlers and the Stalins—would never have risen to power if only their subjects had been as well informed and well educated as regular *Times'* readers.

> *Note:* The *Times* hasn't always practiced what it preaches. A 1999 book, *The Trust: The Private and Powerful Family Behind The New York Times*, by Susan E. Tifft and Alex S. Jones (a former *Times* reporter), pointed out that the *Times* itself fell short in the face of the Nazi threat. In particular, according to the book, the paper hardly noted the Holocaust when it was first revealed and didn't even use the word "Jew" when concentration camp prisoners were freed. Also, the paper neglected to run an editorial calling for the unconditional surrender of the Germans (9/22/99, p. B8).

But these missteps notwithstanding, the paper's generally benign view of human nature has caused it to operate on the assumption that normal humans can overcome their flaws and foibles and approach moral perfection through the education process. There is no original sin in this scenario. If the *Times* sees one dominant human fault, it is a failure to gain enough knowledge and information to enable an individual to operate without major mistakes.

The Main Education Message

Perhaps the primary message about education conveyed by the paper is that it's best to have some sort of centralized control over curriculum and financing—control that must be exercised according to standards affirmed by the *Times*. Otherwise, local school boards or regional commissions may begin to establish their own standards about such issues as affirmative action, teaching evolution, hiring teachers, experimenting with vouchers, and choosing other ways they spend their money.

In general, the *Times* pushes for producing better qualified teachers and hiring more of them for the existing public school systems. Needless to say, such a policy is music to the ears of one of the *Times'* favorite organizations, the American Federation of Teachers, the union that battles for higher pay and better benefits for public school teachers.

On the other hand, the paper is suspicious of creative private alternatives to the high-priced public school system. The voucher issue, which involves giving families public funds to pay for private and parochial school tuition, provides an instructive case in point.

Why the Times Won't Vouch for Vouchers

The *Times* has made its opposition to vouchers clear both in news stories and editorials. The underlying reason for the paper's opposition seems to be twofold:

First, vouchers tend to promote religious schools and education—a consequence that flies directly into the face of the paper's opposition to conservative religious groups, and especially conservative Christian groups.

Second, vouchers cause decentralization of school control—a tendency that makes it practically impossible for one philosophical voice, such as that of the *Times*, to exert significant influence over public culture.

The shrewd implementation of Culture Creep in the *Times* is evident in a series of articles beginning with two news stories in the August 25, 1999, issue, both of which carried negative messages concerning vouchers.

One article, which was headlined "CLEVELAND VOUCHER PROGRAM IS BLOCKED AT START OF SCHOOL," said that a federal judge had ruled that a Cleveland school voucher program "violated the constitutional separation of church and state" (p. A12).

The story placed a heavy emphasis on speculation—usually without linking the speculation to named legal authorities—that the decision would have a wide national impact against vouchers.

The kicker, or final paragraph in the story, which helps fix the main point in the reader's mind, consisted of a quotation from the president of the American Federation of Teachers:

"The Cleveland voucher program was bad law, bad policy, bad education for the kids. . . . Now we can make sure the money will be in the public schools, where there is a real school improvement effort going on."

A *Times* editorial writer couldn't have said it better.

Another story in the same issue (p. A24) highlighted a 1999 Gallup survey on vouchers—commissioned by a professional association of educators—with this negative headline: "AID PREFERRED TO VOUCHERS IN NEW SURVEY."

Both the headline and the organization of the story were weighted heavily against the voucher concept. First of all, the second paragraph reported that 70 percent of respondents favored the government's involvement in improving public schools, while 28 percent preferred vouchers. But nothing was said about how the questions were framed, an essential bit of information for anyone who wanted to evaluate survey statistics.

A more serious objection is that the reader had to plow through more than half the story before he learned that a majority of Americans favored allowing parents to send their children to a public, private, or church-related school if government pays all or part of the tuition. In other words, most Americans supported the concept of vouchers!

Even more significant, you had to read almost to the end of the story before you discovered the dramatic reversal of opinion on vouchers since 1996. At that time, only 43 percent favored vouchers, while 54 percent opposed them. By contrast, in 1999, 51 percent favored vouchers and 47 percent opposed them.

The kicker in this second August 25 article promoted another important *Times'* belief about education: a commitment to a monolithic set of standards for all students, whether in public school, home schools, or other quasi-public venues.

Specifically, the final paragraph noted that the public overwhelmingly supported providing public school services to children who were being home-schooled. But the concluding sentence stated that most of the respondents "expressed a strong desire to see the students adhere to the same standards as public school students."

The underlying message: It's all right to exercise a little discretion and freedom with your children's home education. But don't wander too far from the paper's set of approved, centrally imposed educational standards! From the paper's editorial history, it seems rather likely that a *Times*-anointed home-schooling curriculum would omit Bible instruction, reject religious practices such as prayer, and feature liberal sex and gender education.

An astute, careful reader might have been disconcerted by the negative slant of these two voucher stories. Also, a person with an activist bent might have prepared to shoot off a critical letter to the paper, berating the editors for not delivering a fair, balanced account. But in an adroit move to provide the appearance of fairness, a *Times* article the very next day could have blunted any outrage.

The paper carried a front-page tearjerker on August 26, 1999, describing how several parents who had been planning on sending their kids to parochial schools had become frantic about the judge's ruling against vouchers and were preparing to take on extra jobs to pay for the tuition.

"Please don't take this away from us," one mother, a house cleaner whose ten-year-old son had been attending a Roman Catholic grammar school, pleaded in the story (p. A1).

"I'll work 10 jobs before I send him to the public schools," she declared later.

Even the kicker showed opposition to the judge's ruling against the voucher program. A truck driver with three children in religious schools, said, "I'll work two jobs."

The reaction was so heart-wrenching that even my own wife was ready to mail a check to one of the parents to help her keep her kids in a private school.

What had happened with the *Times*' coverage in this instance?

On the most obvious level, it's clear that the federal judge's decision had provoked outrage among the Cleveland parents. The *Times* was just reporting the public response. In other words, in this report the *Times* was operating as an ordinary news organ that was following the movement of a controversial issue and was telling both sides of the story.

That's fine so far. But now, let's move to a deeper level of analysis.

A basic principle of Culture Creep is that *to influence public opinion and values, media moguls can't get too far ahead of the public*.

In another context, that's a major reason that politicians these days live and die by the polls. Even if they have an agenda they are pushing, they know that to move the public they must stay within an acceptable range of public opinion. If you move too far in advance of what the public is ready to hear, you may acquire a reputation of being too radical, or even irrelevant. But if you move more gradually and stay ahead, but not too far ahead of what most people believe, you will be in a much stronger position to guide the public over time to an entirely new set of values and beliefs.

That is what has happened with abortion. That is what is happening with the gay rights agenda. And that is what the *Times* hopes will happen with public education issues like school vouchers.

What subliminal message, if any, was the *Times* trying to get across in its story on the emotional responses of the Cleveland parents?

For one thing, the *Times* suggested strongly that the parents were ready to work for the money to send their kids to private schools. And that's exactly what the *Times* would like to see happen. Public tax money should stay in public schools, and yet parents who wanted another choice were to be commended for being willing to sacrifice to send their children elsewhere.

A front-page story two days later put the *Times* back squarely on its anti-voucher track in its news coverage (8/28/99, pp. A1, A26).

The federal judge revised his order and allowed vouchers until the legal issues could be resolved. The American Federation of Teachers also got into the act with a spokesman spinning the idea that the judge's new ruling wasn't a reversal or a case of "the judge backing off."

Finally, as it almost always does on an important issue, the *Times* made its position on vouchers quite plain in an editorial that very same day (8/29/99, p. 14). The editorial called on the U.S. Supreme Court to resolve the "national controversy" on school vouchers—and reminded its readers that "it's likely that the Cleveland program violates the constitutional mandate of separation of church and state."

The *Times* concluded with this declaration: "The Supreme Court should reaffirm its earlier ruling [a 1973 decision banning a New York program giving reimbursements to low-income parochial school students] and declare voucher plans supporting religious education unconstitutional."

This editorial clarified the *Times'* overall strategy on vouchers. The paper's skewed news accounts on vouchers, which at first blush might have seemed puzzling, could now be understood as part of a broader plan for the education of all Americans—a plan that could be summed up quite neatly in three words: *anti-voucher, pro-centralization, anti-religion.*

Did the U.S. Supreme Court Get the Times' Message?

Is there any chance that this message in the pages of the *Times* was communicated to the members of the U.S. Supreme Court?

You can bet it was. Such members of the Court as Associate Justice Ruth Bader Ginsberg not only read the *Times*, but regard it as sufficiently reliable and authoritative to be quoted along with landmark court cases and law review articles.

Consider, for instance, Justice Ginsburg's Benjamin N. Cardozo Lecture on affirmative action and human rights, which was published in *The Record* of the Association of the Bar of the City of New York (May/June 1999). In that article, she footnoted the *Times* several times as factual authority for her arguments, along with the usual heavy legal citations (pp. 298, 299, 306).

But the *Times*' heavy emphasis on influencing formal education is only one component in an overall strategy designed to control the dissemination of public information. The general public represents a far larger "classroom," from which the *Times* can enlist disciples for its worldview. Furthermore, converting the "lost" has become much easier for a savvy paper such as the *Times* because of a recent tendency to relax reporting standards.

Relaxed Reporting Standards: A Chance to Educate on the Grand Scale

In contrast to the situation a few decades ago, it has become increasingly acceptable and even fashionable for reporters to inject statements of opinion into news stories. Even top journalists—including those at the *Times*—can get away with more editorializing in their news stories today than was acceptable even twenty or thirty years ago.

For example, a study by the Committee of Concerned Journalists analyzed more than fifteen hundred statements and allegations reported by the news media during the week after the Clinton-Lewinsky scandal broke early in 1998 *(www.journalism.org/ Clintonreport.htm)*.

The Committee—which was established in June 1997 by Harvard's Nieman Foundation and the Project for Excellence in

Journalism, a Washington think tank—found that 41 percent of the reporting on the scandal wasn't factual—but was based on analysis, opinion, speculation, or judgments by the reporters. Furthermore, 40 percent of the reporting that was based on anonymous sources came from only one source; only one statement in a hundred was based on two or more named sources. Also, one of every three statements was based on no sources whatsoever.

To its credit, the *New York Times* behaved somewhat more responsibly in following traditional reporting standards than the other newspapers surveyed. During the one-week period of the study, 53 percent of the *Times'* reporting was based on named sources—as compared with only 16 percent in the *Washington Post*. Still, a paper such as the *Times*, which cites named sources for barely half of its reporting on a major national story, is not turning in a particularly impressive performance.

Even more discouraging, the *Times'* performance on naming its sources deteriorated in a later survey, which was conducted by the committee in March 1998. In that study, only 41 percent of the *Times'* reports on the Clinton-Lewinsky scandal were based on named sources. Furthermore, in 21 percent of the cases, the *Times* cited other media as the main source for its "facts." The *Washington Post* did much better here, with other media cited only 7 percent of the time *(www.journalism.org/Dcreport2g.htm)*.

Yet these two tests are particularly important to ensure credibility and accuracy—for a couple of reasons. First of all, when a reporter names a source, anyone can double-check the facts. With a sensitive story, it may be necessary to promise anonymity to a source, perhaps to protect the person's safety or job. But a publication that relies heavily on unidentified people has more freedom to fudge the facts or even make them up.

Second, the reporter who cites other media reports as the source of his facts is usually betraying hasty, lazy, or even sloppy newsgathering. A reader might legitimately ask: If the *Times* is just going to copy what other papers produce, why read the *Times* at all?

But it's unlikely that these lapses in relaxing reporting standards will have a lasting or fatal effect on the *Times'* preeminence in the world of journalism. After all, practically every influential paper is now injecting opinion in news stories. So the particular sins of the *Times* will probably just be excused as part of a larger journalistic trend.

Also, the *Times* has undoubtedly learned from the Clinton-Lewinsky experience that to protect its image, it must be more careful than other news outlets. Those who run the show at the paper know that despite the general deterioration in journalistic standards, news media experts still give lip service to the idea that news reports are supposed to be "fair," "balanced," and perhaps even "objective." Also, most would agree that news stories are supposed to be generally free of editorializing.

So any paper that gets a reputation for playing fast and loose with its sources, or that becomes too blatant in expressing opinion in its news sections, will quickly become vulnerable to charges of bias and advocacy—and be demoted out of the pantheon of elite publications.

It's highly unlikely that the *Times* will allow its image to degenerate that far. Consequently, we can expect continued subtlety and artifice as the paper takes full advantage of the general trend toward relaxed journalistic standards. Given the blurring of lines between news stories and the editorial page, it should become increasingly easy for the *Times* to promote its worldview through specially presented news stories, combined with supporting editorials and op-ed columns.

Up to now, we have covered the first two steps in the West 43rd Street plan of salvation: displaying tolerance (as defined by the *Times*) and exposing as many people as possible to a centrally controlled educational and informational environment. The final step required for advancing to a *Times'* nirvana is to engage in culturally correct thinking and action.

STEP THREE: ENGAGE IN CULTURALLY CORRECT THOUGHT AND ACTION

According to the *New York Times*, anyone can work his or her way into heaven on earth. The basic requirement, after you have become acceptably tolerant and properly educated or informed, is simply to have faith. That means buying into the paper's belief system lock, stock, and barrel.

Once you become a true believer, you are expected to avoid certain types of bad behavior, such as raising embarrassing questions that may call into question the veracity of the *Times*' faith. Even more important, you must not fall prey to one or more of the *Times*' "seven deadly sins"—or the most threatening contrary values and behaviors that are regularly attacked in the paper.

Another way of thinking of these sins is in terms of seven "Thou Shalt Not's." Imagine, if you will, a booming voice emanating from the inner editorial sanctum off Times Square and commanding:

- *Thou Shalt Not Be Certain About the Truth of One Religion.*
- *Thou Shalt Not Be Too Conservative.*
- *Thou Shalt Not Support Capital Punishment.*
- *Thou Shalt Not Break the Public Trust.*
- *Thou Shalt Not Bear Arms.*
- *Thou Shalt Not Engage in Censorship.*
- *Thou Shalt Not Limit Abortion.*

Now let's move on to Part II and take a closer look at how the *Times* can help you avoid the wages of these sins—and how your entire belief system might begin to look if you allow the paper's values to seep into your mind and heart.

PART II

THE SEVEN DEADLY SINS—ACCORDING TO THE TIMES

CHAPTER 6

THE SIN OF RELIGIOUS CERTAINTY

Perhaps the greatest threat to the social and political agenda of the *New York Times* is conservative religion—especially evangelical Christianity.

The reason for the perceived danger? Traditional religious groups are often the source of activist movements against many of the *Times*' pet causes—including abortion rights, the gay agenda, and the freedom (often supported by government grants) to engage in "artistic" expressions of blasphemy or sacrilege.

Danger signals that may trigger warning alarms at the *Times* include:

- Public statements, gatherings, or other exercises of free speech or assembly by religious groups that question or contradict principles that the paper holds dear.
- Any claim to absolute truth or morality that challenges what the *Times* regards as its own absolute values.
- Attempts to spread religious faith to non-believers or members of other faiths—even when such attempts are

non-coercive and exercised within legally acceptable limits of free speech and persuasion.

In other words, if you claim certainty or assurance in your faith, you're on thin ice with the *Times*. The paper is much more comfortable with church and synagogue members who say they are still searching for truth, or who express some skepticism or doubt about traditional religious doctrines.

In contrast, those who say they are certain about their beliefs are likely to be dismissed by the paper as "fundamentalists," or biblical "literalists"—or even "zealots," or "bigots."

THE CURIOUS FEAR OF CERTAINTY

As we saw in the previous chapter, the favored term of opprobrium by the *Times* is "intolerance"—which the paper doesn't employ according the normal or historical meaning. Rather, "intolerant," in the peculiar *Times'* sense, usually refers to a religious person who is quite sure about what he believes—and who implicitly assumes that his faith is superior or more complete in some way to other belief systems.

Such religious certainty is unacceptable to the *Times* for several reasons. First, those who are confident about their basic moral and theological values are unlikely to buy into the paper's value system without subjecting it to some careful thought and analysis. Once a reader begins to think seriously about what the paper is saying—and becomes aware of how the writers and editors are trying to change his thinking—any possibility of easy journalistic proselytizing evaporates.

Second, when there is a conflict between religious doctrine and the *Times'* belief system, committed religious people are more likely to rely on their historical creeds, documents, and scriptures for guidance than on the daily newspaper.

Third, those who assume that God answers prayer and speaks through fellow believers and trusted clergy are more likely than non-believers to receive independent messages that are contrary to the teachings of the *Times*.

Conversely, you are "tolerant" —and acceptable to the *Times*— if you deny that your faith is the repository of ultimate truth and concede that all other faiths are as true as your own. Or to put this another way, being "tolerant" is synonymous with being in sync with the *Times'* gospel, and being "intolerant" is the same as identifying with a religious viewpoint that is seriously in conflict with the belief system of the *Times*.

Now, keeping in mind this basic orientation of the *Times* toward traditional religion, let's turn to some of the specifics of the paper's coverage of religion and spirituality.

THE TIMES' BASIC TACTICS FOR COVERING RELIGION

The *Times* relies on five main tactics in its coverage of religion:
1. Highlight the bizarre
2. Puff mainline or liberal theology and clergy
3. Give an occasional token nod to fair coverage (to keep the journalistic watchdogs away from your door)
4. When advantageous, co-opt traditional religious principles and practices
5. Wage constant war against the dark forces of "fundamentalism."

In more detail, here's how the *Times* employs each of these tactics in practice:

Tactic #1: Highlight the Bizarre.

When editors at most news organizations are trying to determine whether or not an event is "newsworthy," and thus worth publishing and reading, they will consciously or subconsciously go down a mental checklist to see if the facts measure up. To be newsworthy, a story must demonstrate such qualities as "significance," or "timeliness," or "conflict."

Another common feature of many newsworthy stories is that they are unusual or that they involve events, people, or movements that are out of the ordinary or bizarre. As far as its religious coverage is concerned, the *Times* frequently favors the bizarre or the unusual—to the point that weird spiritual splinter movements or happenings may receive comparable attention to broad-based grassroots spiritual movements, or even pronouncements by the Pope.

For example, as the year 2000 approached, some editors seemed to become virtually obsessed with accounts of strange apocalyptic interpretations of the end times. At one point, they became particularly fascinated by a book by Alex Heard, *Apocalypse Pretty Soon*, which catalogued theories of religious cults about the end times, UFO predictions, and a host of fringe spiritual movements and strange biblical interpretations. One four-page, full-color feature in the Sunday magazine was entitled provocatively, "APOCALYPSE NOW. NO, REALLY NOW! A COAST-TO-COAST GUIDE TO AMERICA'S MILLENNIAL CHICKEN LITTLES" (12/27,98, pp. 40–43). Very valuable space in the Book Review was also devoted to the same book (3/7/99, pp. 11–12).

The occult, witches, and Satanism are also a favorite topic. In fact, in the one-year period from July 9, 1998, through July 9, 1999, the paper ran fifty-five articles on "satanic" movements and topics (and none of these included Salmon Rushdie's controversial book, *Satanic Verses*). The word "witch" did even better, with 303 articles—or an average of almost one per day.

On August 22, 1999, the film *The Blair Witch Project* became an excuse to run a major Sunday Week in Review feature on the occult and the views of "wiccas," which is the name that American witches like to go by (p. 2). In effect, the witches were given a high-profile forum to express their anger at the film and respond to what they regarded as distortions of their image by the national entertainment media. (Incidentally, I failed to find an instance when a conservative Christian group was given such an opportunity.)

Even the obituary page has been used in an effort to bring witches into America's spiritual mainstream. On October 3, 1999, for instance, the *Times* ran an obituary on Coreen Valiente, who "ADVOCATED POSITIVE WITCHCRAFT," according to the banner headline (p. 55). In an unusual tribute, the paper even ran a two-column picture of the woman in full occult regalia, calling her in the caption, "the mother of modern paganism."

Why should a newspaper like the *Times* give such prominent coverage to witches?

Part of the answer emerges in the article on Valiente, which was published as a six-column spread in the Sunday paper. A sub-heading declared in boldface that the witch inspired "A CREED THAT GREW TO EMBRACE FEMINISM, ENVIRONMENTALISM AND THE NEW AGE." Clearly, the witch's belief system coincided in many ways with that of the *Times*, which is enamored of radical feminism, environmentalism, and much New Age spiritual thinking, especially the assumption that one belief system is as good as the next so long as there isn't any promotion of religious certainty.

On a related note, how does the *Times* treat Satan?

An instructive illustration involved a profile of a female poet in the Living Arts section of September 9, 1999 (pp. B1–2). The writer explored in sympathetic depth the poet's psyche, revealing that the woman, who had come out of a middle-class Episcopalian family, had become disturbed by her exposure to teachings about God, hell, and "doing evil." As a result of this upbringing, she found herself referring often in conversations to Satan and God, and writing poetry that imitated hymns she sang as a child.

Finally, the poet revealed, she found her own voice when she experienced an epiphany that came to her as a "vow to Satan" (p. B2). She determined that she would give up everything she had learned before and focus in her writing on ordinary experiences such as childbirth, mothering, and sex.

Why should a person inspired by a "vow to Satan" be high-lighted in a positive profile in the pages of the *Times?* One obvious answer to this question seems to be that the paper's news hole is skewed more toward bizarre and marginal spirituality.

Tactic #2: Puff Mainline or Liberal Theology and Clergy.

We encounter a different tactic entirely when it comes to the "mainline" or liberal religious groups and clergy. This segment of the spiritual spectrum—which includes the northeastern branches of the Episcopal Church, the United Church of Christ, and the United Methodist Church, finds favor with the *Times* because, in general, their clergy and parishioners agree with the paper's social and political positions.

Also—though certainly there are exceptions—these groups would avoid like the plague any suggestion that they might have something in common with the "fundamentalists" or "evangelicals." Scratch a mainline or liberal church person, and you're likely to find someone who has serious questions about the virgin birth, the physical resurrection of Christ, or the authority of the Bible. And expect unmitigated horror if you suggest that maybe it's a good idea for a Christian to share his faith with a nonbeliever.

For a typical illustration of how the *Times* puffs and encourages this liberal religious orientation, consider three articles that appeared in one three-week period during the end of August and beginning of September 1999:

- One story was headlined "RELIGIOUS COALITION PLANS GAY RIGHTS STRATEGY—A MOVE AMONG THE FAITHFUL TO COUNTER THE RELIGIOUS RIGHT" (8/24/99, p. A9).

  The "coalition" consisted of the liberal wings of various Protestant, Catholic, Jewish, Mormon, and Muslim groups.

  The article, which explained none of the reasoning against gay rights, gave plenty of space to the pro-gay arguments. Among other things, the writer linked the gay rights movement to the civil rights movement of the 1960s, and he also included strategic quotes connecting the gay activists to Gandhi and Martin Luther King Jr.

  Toward the end of the story, one gay activist was quoted as saying, "God has given us the courage of strength."

- A second story on September 6 (p. A8) emphasized the Roman Catholic faith of Democratic Labor Secretary

Alexis M. Herman, the first black woman to hold this position.

Although traditional Catholicism is often suspect or under attack in the pages of the *Times*, in this case the Catholic connection was apparently acceptable since Herman's career had been devoted to "Democratic politics." In general, her goals were to support the Clinton agenda, including expanded health care rights, welfare reform, and government-sponsored training programs for the unskilled.

- The third article, which appeared on September 10, was headlined "Religion Leaders Call Housing a Sacred Right" (p. A21).

    The focus of this story was on how a broad group of religious leaders, including Roman Catholics, Protestants, Jews, Buddhists, and Muslims, had signed a letter calling on President Clinton to allot more money for housing for the poor.

    One of the signers who was accorded sympathetic coverage was Rabbi Eric Yoffie, president of the liberal Reform Judaism's synagogue organization. Another was the Episcopal bishop Richard Grein of the New York diocese—one of the nation's main hotbeds of left-wing Episcopalianism.

In citing these three stories, I don't want to be understood as rendering a blanket condemnation of all the issues involved. For example, reasonable people on the left or right side of the political spectrum might agree that something should be done to help the poor or train the unskilled.

Instead, the point I want to get across is this: The *Times* provides regular, broad, and sympathetic coverage to those religious devotees whom the paper perceives as being "in its camp" and advocates of its gospel. But spiritual groups that don't fall into this category may have to wait until Times Square freezes over permanently before they receive such kind treatment.

Tactic #3: Give an Occasional Nod to Fair Coverage.

You'll recall in our discussion of the Columbine High School tragedy in the previous chapter that one effective way the *Times* may try to give the illusion of balanced coverage is by throwing in token reports to tell the other side of the story. These occasional nods to fair coverage also help keep journalistic watchdogs and ombudsmen at bay. But the overwhelming weight of news stories, editorials, and columns on certain extremely important issues and policies will continue to promote a *Times* "doctrine" or special belief.

Here are a few illustrations of how the paper keeps its reputation as the "newspaper of record" that publishes "all the news that's fit to print"—even including a few pieces sympathetic to traditional Christianity:

- A cover story in the Sunday magazine on April 4, 1999, centered on the struggles and ideals of young Catholic seminarians who were studying to become priests (pp. 28ff).

In general, the writer, Jennifer Egan, portrayed the priests-in-training sympathetically as committed to traditional Catholic doctrines and values and to personal spiritual disciplines such as prayer. Even though they opposed abortion, affirmed celibacy, and believed in evangelism, the writer treated their views seriously.

A quote by one seminarian near the end of the story reflected the overall tone: "God will triumph. The church will triumph. . . . The essentials will never change. How do we know that? Because Christ said so" (p. 59).

- Christians on the New York Yankees were accorded sensitive coverage in a prominent Sports Pages story, headlined: "THE YANKEES IN PRAYER GROUP BELIEVE, QUIETLY, THAT SUCCESS IS HEAVEN SENT—SHARING OF FAITH IS NOT UNCOMMON IN SPORTS, BUT YANKEES MEET EVERY DAY" (8/23/98, pp. 27, 29).

An emphasis was placed not only on the inner strength the players received from prayer and fellowship, but also on the religious tolerance on the team.

- Occasional op-ed articles give a positive picture of conservative religious faith.

Michael Novak, a theologian at the conservative American Enterprise Institute who generally provides an intellectual slant to his religious punditry, is one of the *Times'* favorites for this role (see 5/24/98, p. 11).

- The "Beliefs" column, authored by religion writers Gustav Niebuhr and Peter Steinfels, can provide stimulating, in-depth treatment of current events that raise spiritual issues.

For example, at the height of the Clinton-Lewinsky scandal, Steinfels wrote a provocative article drawing an analogy between the president's sexual travails and the challenges facing King David after his adulterous encounter with Bathsheba (10/3/98, p. A12).

- On very rare occasions, a writer will provide an exceptionally deep and subtle analysis of the spiritual forces that drive a particular individual.

One example was a reflective study in the Sunday Arts section by Nancy Raabe of how personal faith influenced Austrian composer Gustav Mahler in creating his *Third Symphony* (8/1/99, pp. 27, 28).

Raabe offered new insights into how Mahler's developing Christian faith—after his conversion from Judaism in 1897—had shaped the symphony's portrayal of such motifs as the search for God and the power of divine love. Having obviously engaged in considerable research, she referred to the frequent biblical references that "dot Mahler's letters after 1892" and cited in some detail the composer's written jottings in German on his manuscript, which expressed his spiritual exhilaration (p. 28).

Clearly, the *Times* has the potential to publish meaningful articles on classic or historic Christianity. But such features are extremely rare. Also, it's rather interesting that the writer of this particular article, Nancy Raabe, didn't work for the *New York Times* at all. She was the music critic for the *Birmingham News* in Alabama.

Tactic #4: When It Seems Advantageous, Co-opt Traditional Religious Principles and Practices.

Like any other made-up belief system—including many of the eclectic New Age cults and creeds—the *Times'* worldview results from a pick-and-choose process, which involves grazing among various philosophies of life and selecting those features that best fit one's personal preconceptions about what is good and true. Sometimes the *Times* even assimilates some traditional Christian practices and values, though the paper is careful to distance itself from the underlying Christian theology.

One of the *Times'* most dearly held convictions, for instance, involves the importance of helping the poor and downtrodden. The paper's regular, and commendable, support of the "Neediest" campaign in its pages, which is designed to provide sustenance for the poor, is one illustration of this commitment.

The *New York Times* Neediest Cases Fund was established by Adolph S. Ochs in 1912. In 1998 the fund raised a record $6.5 million for a number of charities that help the poor in various ways. Every year the paper intensifies its campaign for donations during November and December (11/28/99, p. 10).

Of course, this commitment to help the needy isn't original with the *Times*. The way the principle is often stated and advocated in the paper has strong echoes in the Old and New Testaments and especially in the words of Jesus:

- "For I was hungry, and you gave Me something to eat; I was thirsty, and you gave Me drink; . . ." (Matt. 25:35).

- "He who shuts his ear to the cry of the poor will also cry himself and not be answered" (Prov. 21:13).

- "Blessed are you who are poor, for yours is the kingdom of God" (Luke 6:20).
- "God loves a cheerful giver" (2 Cor. 9:7).

To be sure, the *Times'* versions of these charitable imperatives omit all references to God and Jesus. Furthermore, the paper sometimes runs articles that explicitly distance the *Times'* gospel from the Christian gospel.

One op-ed piece, for instance, was headlined, "IT TAKES MORE THAN FAITH TO SAVE THE POOR" (8/29/99, p. 15). The message was multifaceted. For one thing, the writer contended, it's far better to rely on government than on religious groups for largesse to the poor because the religious organizations are too likely to follow "exclusionary policies" by "employing only born-again Christians." Also, according to this op-ed argument, giving by churches raises the specter of church-state violations. The writer finally concluded that the government does a better job than private organizations of providing for the poor.

This article was loaded with *Times* doctrines. First, actions by religious groups are automatically suspect because they believe too profoundly in their faith. Also, these groups set up their organizations so that "born-again" workers tend to get involved in quasi-governmental aid projects—a practice that poses a constant threat to the separation of church and state. So the best solution is pure government-sponsored welfare (an important *Times'* belief) or perhaps non-religious private charitable help, such as what the *Times* promotes through its Neediest Cases Fund program.

Another variation on this secular substitute for religious giving emerged in a *Times'* Sunday magazine article by the Australian philosopher Peter Singer—who, incidentally, also advocates such practices as euthanasia of severely disabled infants and treating humans and animals as morally equal (9/5/99, pp. 60–63).

Singer, a philosophical favorite of the paper who was also featured in an earlier article, has advocated sacrificial giving of one-fifth of one's income to famine-relief agencies. In his magazine piece, "THE SINGER SOLUTION TO WORLD POVERTY," he went even further by challenging well-to-do readers to give most of their wealth surplus, over and above essential needs, to the poor.

Without referring to any biblical source, he even commented on the tithe concept—which is stated powerfully in Malachi 3:10 and elsewhere in the Old Testament—by saying that those who tithe should not only give their tenth, but "should be doing much more" (p. 63).

Again, we have a strong echo of Jesus' words in Luke 11:42 where he criticizes the Pharisees not for tithing but for neglecting other matters of justice. He concludes: "these are things you should have done without neglecting the others [i.e., the tithes]."

In short, some of the *Times'* most commendable values come directly from the Bible. But as might be expected from a faith that opposes traditional biblical faith, references to the Scriptures, the Hebrew prophets, or Jesus are left out.

Tactic #5: Wage Constant War against the Dark Forces of "Fundamentalism."

The terms "fundamentalism" and "fundamentalist" are used by the *Times*, as well as by other media organizations that follow its lead, to describe in a derogatory way adherents of conservative religious groups and especially Christian Protestant conservatives. A one-year search of the *Times'* Web site turned up 178 articles dealing with the term "fundamentalist" and 73 on "fundamentalism" (7/9/98–7/9/99).

Unfortunately, the *Times* has redefined these words to give them a wider and more negative meaning than originally intended. Historically, "fundamentalist" was first used to refer to members of a Protestant movement in the early twentieth century who were reacting to "modernist" influences by more liberal theologians and church leaders. The fundamentalists criticized the liberals for watering down or undercutting the basics, or "fundamentals," of the faith.

According to various historical sources, the "fundamentals" included a belief in at least five basic doctrines: the inerrancy of the Bible; the imminent and bodily return of Christ; the Virgin Birth; the physical Resurrection; and the substitutionary atonement for all human sins by Christ on the cross. As the twentieth century unfolded, however, the term "fundamentalist" was applied more and more to conservative Christians who opposed evolution, abstained from alcohol, refrained from dancing, avoided movies, and in general, attempted to separate themselves from the sinful influences of the world.

In the 1950s, some conservative Christian leaders, such as the Rev. Harold J. Ockenga, pastor of the Park Street Church in Boston, chose to rename the more intellectual and less separatist wing of the movement as "evangelical," or "new evangelical." But the old "fundamentalist" term still stuck to those superconservatives who were more separatist and more restrictive in their social practices.

The *Times* has capitalized on the pejorative connotations of the term "fundamentalist" in an effort to dismiss as irrelevant or anti-intellectual most conservative Christians—as well as conservatives of other faiths—because they advocate social, moral, or political views opposed by the paper. In other words, the paper has departed from the rather specific and narrow historical roots of the word "fundamentalist." Instead, the word has become a verbal weapon that the *Times* wields in an attempt to slash and bludgeon its mortal religious enemies, whether they are violent right-wing extremists or quite rational biblical conservatives.

The same use has been made of "literal" and "literalist," which are meant to denigrate or marginalize those who hold a serious or high view of the Scripture. (A certain irony attaches to this attitude because the *Times* does expect its readers to be "literalists" in reading the paper's daily reports and opinions. In other words, they want people to accept what they write and report at face value, as a true and honest presentation of the facts.)

The term "religious right" is another label that the *Times* uses as a put-down for conservative Christians and their cohorts who have entered the lists of cultural combat as political activists who oppose the paper's pet beliefs, such as abortion. You may recall that a search of the *Times'* archives for a full year ending in July

1999 showed that 936 articles in the paper used the term "religious right." That translates to an average of about three articles per day.

In general, the paper pictures the "religious right" in negative terms. Two front-page stories, one in June 1998 and another in March 1999, are illustrative.

The first, headlined "RELIGIOUS RIGHT'S TACTICIAN ON WIDER CRUSADE," featured the former Christian Coalition head and prominent conservative political consultant Ralph Reed—but also focused on the "widening schism" between different factions of "American's religious right" (6/12/98, p. 1). Toward the end of the article, the reporter took a shot at Reed with a strategically placed reference to a murky conflict of interest charge and then quoted a Reed opponent as saying, "It's a pitiful shame that Ralph Reed is willing to prostitute himself like this" (p. A16).

In the second article, "UNITY IS ELUSIVE AS RELIGIOUS RIGHT PONDERS 2000 VOTE," the emphasis was again on the negative. This time, the writers focused on internal arguments among conservative Christian political activists about their mission.

The problem with such articles is not simply that they are negative but that there is no significant counterweight of positive stories about the "religious right." Instead, the *Times* has labored rather successfully to turn the term into a label that connotes all that is narrow-minded, divisive, and meanspirited.

The use of "fundamentalist" and "fundamentalism" represents a somewhat different linguistic strategy. Because these words begin with negative connotations for many people, the *Times* merely has to attach them to its religious opponents in as many different contexts as possible.

In a front-page 1996 story on former President Jimmy Carter, for instance, the writer emphasized that Carter, who is known for his identification with "born-again" Christians, had apparently turned on some of his conservative supporters with a "blistering critique of fundamentalism" (12/15/96, p. A1).

Although this story acknowledged that Carter opposed abortion, he was also pictured as practically a poster boy for many points in the *Times'* belief system. Specifically, the article reported that Carter was against the death penalty, against the creationist position that the world was created in six days, sympathetic to special homosexual rights, and generally opposed to the idea that those who don't accept Christ are lost or going to hell.

He was also presented as a regular guy who could tell an off-color joke in his Sunday school class in Plains, Georgia, and not as an uptight fundamentalist. In this instance, the joke was about President Bill Clinton and one of Clinton's accusers, Paula Jones, who had charged the president with indecent acts in her presence.

The *Times* employs the term "fundamentalist" liberally in many different contexts and sections in the paper, apparently in an attempt to fix in the reader's mind the negative connection between the word and certain groups and beliefs the paper dislikes.

For example, the "Letters" section, which is situated next to the editorials, is often used to promote the paper's beliefs, both through the selection of letters and the headlines attached to them. One reader's letter published on November 25, 1998, was headlined, "'CHRISTIAN' VALUES." Note the quotation marks around "Christian," signaling that what was about to come didn't fall within the paper's or the writer's special definition of the term "Christian."

The writer of the letter went on to say that she was "of the Christian faith" but was angry because "small, right-wing denominations have usurped the word 'Christian' to be their own." She also rejected what she said was the "rigid, self-righteous view of the world now being espoused by this group of fundamentalists."

In addition, the writer argued that "most" American Christians were Episcopalians, Methodists, Lutherans, and the like—in other words, were in liberal mainline denominations that generally support the *Times'* worldview. She conveniently overlooked the fact that the conservative Southern Baptist Convention is far larger today than any of the mainline Protestant denominations.

And if you add the millions of members of other conservative denominations and independent Bible and Pentecostal churches to the Baptists, the liberal Protestants shrink to a small minority.

Another subliminal point that the paper likes to embed in the reader's mind is that those who fall into the category of "fundamentalist" are violent or potentially violent. In other words, fundamentalists are not the kind of people you can tolerate in a *Times'* world because they are too threatening to the social fabric. They may even become terrorists.

A film review of the movie *Destiny* is a case in point (10/16/98, p. B20). The film, which focused on such issues as free speech in twelfth-century Spain, dealt with the excesses of Christian and Muslim "zealots" in that earlier era. The reviewer, in his last-sentence kicker, made it clear that he had the present in mind: "The movie isn't so much a reappraisal of religious strife eight centuries ago as it is a warning against the dangers of fundamentalist intolerance now."

Using these five tactics, *Times* writers fire away at religious conservatives from multiple vantage points—much as a military force might do in an attempt to pummel a dangerous enemy into submission.

Here's an overview of how the broad-based attacks can be employed against evangelical Christians.

A TASTE OF THE TIMES' ANTI-CHRISTIAN FIREPOWER

Suppose you had provoked the *Times'* wrath and found yourself on the receiving end of an extensive campaign designed to bring you to your knees. That's precisely the challenge that conservative Christians have faced since they dared to enter American politics.

Abuse from the Op-ed Page

The most intemperate, bare-knuckled attacks against evangelical conservative Christians often come from the regular columnists on the op-ed page. Here are two illustrations—one from
Frank Rich, whom we have met before, and the other from
Anthony Lewis, a longtime *Times'* writer who hasn't hesitated to
identify himself as an opponent of conservative believers.

Frank Rich, again. Frank Rich, tarring conservative Christians
with his usual broad, sarcastic brush, went after practically every
major "religious-right" figure on the public scene during the 1996
presidential campaign in a column headed, "PAT ROBERTSON AND
BOB DOLE, FRIENDS AGAIN." He also managed to execute his attack
by using virtually every low blow in the journalist's arsenal.
(Remember, don't assume that only people who read the *New York
Times* had access to this attack. Quotes from this column are taken
from a reprint on the Web site of the *Standard-Times*, a
Massachusetts paper serving several communities on the state's
south coast.)

Here are some of Rich's not-so-subtle calumnies, which were
intended both to denigrate conservative Christians and their
moral and social beliefs and also to strike another blow against the
Republican Party and the Dole-Kemp ticket. The occasion was a
convention of the Christian Coalition, which was supportive of
the Dole-Kemp presidential ticket.

Rich made sure that he published his enemies list for the day,
a conservative *Who's Who* that included Bob Dole, Jack Kemp, Pat
Robertson, Ralph Reed, and GOP leaders Dick Armey and J. C.
Watts. By naming plenty of names, he apparently hoped to establish a negative link in readers' minds with as broad an array of his
opponents as possible.

Then he devoted the first four paragraphs of his column—or
nearly one-third of the entire article—to unsubstantiated insinuations that the Christian conservatives were anti-Semitic. Among
other things, he implied strongly that the only Jews this group of
Christians liked were those who were far away in Israel. He also

complained that because the Christians were holding their meeting on Rosh Hashanah, he had been forced to miss his family's religious New Year celebrations.

Rich's objections came across more as left-wing whining than as a substantive, reasoned critique. Part of his problem was that the facts confronting him flew in the face of his suggestions of anti-Semitism. For one thing, Rich had to try, rather unsuccessfully, to downplay the fact that two rabbis were featured speakers on the program. He also had trouble dealing with the presence of another speaker, the prominent Jewish-Christian attorney Jay Sekulow, who delivered a spellbinding address about his battles in the courts against abortion and for the First Amendment rights of Christian activists.

Facing a dearth of factual ammunition, Rich fell back on ploys that have made him the premier supermarket-tabloid stylist for the *Times*. For one thing, he pressed as many hot buttons as he could find that were associated with issues that the *Times* supported and Christian conservatives opposed. The main issues he singled out in this article were abortion, special rights for homosexuals, and public prayer.

Perhaps most important of all, Rich's tone was designed to inspire fear and hostility toward Christian conservatives and anyone sympathetic to them. To this end, he made dark references to:

- The Christians' "ominous agenda";
- Senator Dole's alleged decision to "pander to the religious right";
- Dole's alleged support of some "gay-bashing rally";
- The specter that if the conservative Christians had their way, the line separating church and state would be "blurred if not obliterated."

Clearly, Frank Rich operates at the margins of social and political commentary. His intemperate language, artless rhetoric, and open hostility to evangelical Christians may offend those conservatives and moderates who bother to read him. Although few bother to respond to him, one exception is the conservative political scientist, Professor Hadley Arkes of Amherst College, who has acknowledged Rich's presence by deigning to exchange verbal jousts with him in print. Arkes typically takes his shots from the opinion pages of the *Wall Street Journal*, and Rich, of course, blasts away from the *Times* op-ed page (see the discussion on pp. 232 ff.).

But Rich is only the most extreme op-ed weapon the *Times* employs against Christians who claim to be certain about their faith and morality. Other columnists also periodically go on the attack, including the generally respected Anthony Lewis, who has enjoyed a long and varied career on the *Times*, including the award of the Pulitzer Prize for national reporting in 1963.

Good Cop, Bad Cop

When comparing Anthony Lewis and Frank Rich, the "good cop, bad cop" analogy may fit. Rich is the police interrogator who shouts in your face and maybe even swats you around a few times with a rubber hose. Lewis, in contrast, comes across as a little gentler and more reasonable on the surface—but nevertheless doesn't have your best interests in mind.

In a September 29, 1998, column, when the impeachment of President Clinton seemed imminent, Lewis issued a last-ditch warning that impeachment would be such a monumental victory for the "Christian right" that the face of the nation's culture would change radically (p. A31).

Lewis said he was desperately worried that the "religious conservatives" would become still more influential in the Republican Party. That might mean more restrictions on abortion; legislation to suspend international U.S. aid for population control; less government support for "'indecent' art"; and "punitive moralism" in the criminal law, such as putting more criminal minors in prison.

Lewis then began to incorporate some of Rich's alarmist rhetoric as he raised the specter of a possible "coup d'etat" by the religious right, which he said had engaged in "a right-wing conspiracy of sorts to bring down this President." In his last paragraph, he said that those who disagreed with the religious right wanted "an open and tolerant society"—the obvious implication being that those who *did* agree with the conservatives were closed-minded and intolerant.

Lewis's attacks on religious conservatives, which have continued regularly for years, have ranged over a wide variety of issues. On October 12, 1999, for instance, he ventured well off his customary turf with a rather disdainful attack on the majority of Americans who favor teaching creationism along with evolution in the public schools (p. A31).

Lewis acknowledged a Gallup poll showing that 68 percent of Americans favored teaching creationism along with evolution and 40 percent favored dropping the teaching of evolution completely. But then he referred to this huge segment of people as "an America locked in rigid certainties and shibboleths."

Rather condescendingly, he suggested further that because this misled majority had become despondent over the deterioration of our society, they might be lashing out blindly at the nearest secular target—in this case, the evolutionists. In the end, he dismissed as hopelessly ignorant any soul who would dare suggest that perhaps God had a hand in creation.

Overall, then, the op-ed columns in the *Times* tend to be staunchly opposed to those Christians who are confident and sure of their salvation and the moral principles that arise from their faith. But this antagonism is also evident in other parts of the paper, especially when Christians who are certain of their beliefs begin to exercise their right to free speech to evangelize, pray, and study in public.

The Times as Opponent of Free Exercise of Religion

The *Times* supports free speech so long as such freedom enhances the paper's worldview. On the other hand, if freedom begins to turn the tables on the *Times*—if the paper's beliefs can't prevail in an environment that features an unfettered exchange of ideas—then freedom must be curtailed.

A frequent alarm sounded by the paper as it prepares to restrict some aspect of religious freedom is that the lines between church and state are being "blurred" or "crossed" or "breached." Also, in the face of too much effective communication from religious conservatives, the paper's writers may talk about the dangers of "proselytizing" or "intolerance."

On June 12, 1998, for instance, a lead editorial headlined, "BREACHING THE CHURCH-STATE WALL" tore into a Wisconsin Supreme Court decision that upheld the use of public funds for parochial school tuition. The paper charged that the school program had "religious indoctrination" as its "core purpose" (p. A20).

Similarly, in a July 3, 1998, editorial headed, "PRAYER IN A BRONX SCHOOL," the *Times* adamantly supported the dismissal of a sixth-grade public school teacher for leading her class in prayer. In arguing its case, the paper denounced the "Christian right" and Christian "proselytizing" and concluded: ". . . it is right to keep the classroom free of prayer."

Also, in an apparent attempt to link the Republican presidential front-runner, Gov. George W. Bush, to political and religious extremism, the *Times* Sunday magazine ran an article on Marvin Olasky, the guiding light behind the governor's philosophy of "compassionate conservatism."

In this article, Olasky wasn't pictured as the political theoretician and scholar that he is; nor was he identified as the founder of the influential evangelical political and social affairs journal, *World* magazine. Instead, the writer tried to pigeonhole Olasky as an eccentric who was a kind of spiritual Svengali for Bush. Most of the emphasis of the article was on Olasky's "compassionate conservatism" brainchild—a faith-based, anti-poverty program for the inner city called "New Start."

But the article didn't place Olasky in any standard contemporary category for social activism. Instead, apparently solely because he was a conservative Christian, he was labeled a "zealot" and "perennial convert" who had been at various times a "Jew, atheist, Communist, evangelical Christian."

To further the far-out stereotype, the article showed Olasky standing next to Bush in a photo captioned, "THE ZEALOT AND THE

CANDIDATE" (pp. 62–63). In the end, the *Times'* writer seemed less impressed by the potential for good that might come from Olasky's efforts than by the danger that he and his followers might "proselytize their faith" and violate the "increasingly blurred line between church and state." But the *Times'* effort to restrict the advocacy of traditional Christianity isn't limited to the political arena. The art world has also been targeted by the paper.

Blasphemy in Brooklyn

In the *Times'* worldview, whenever traditional Christian values and symbols come into conflict with free artistic expression—including expression that is funded by public taxes—art should always win over Christian faith and sensitivities.

A case in point is the controversy that arose over the display of an excrement-smeared "portrait" of the Virgin Mary, which was part of a fall 1999 exhibition in the Brooklyn Museum of Art. The picture—by an artist named Chris Ofili who used elephant dung as part of his palette—provoked outrage from New York Mayor Rudy Giuliani, according to a story published on September 23, 1999.

The mayor called the art "sick" and a "desecration" of Christianity and threatened to cut off public funding to the museum. The *Times* and its allies weighed in on the other side, and according to the *Times* Web site, the report generated seventy *Times* articles during the next three weeks!

The main issues boiled down to First Amendment freedom of artistic expression versus respect for a particular religion. In such a showdown, according to the *Times'* gospel, religion must lose.

An evaluation of the seventy articles that had appeared by October 13 (an average of more than three per day) showed that thirty-seven were mostly in favor of the exhibit and against the mayor and religious critics. Also, the editorials were extremely negative. Only nine articles clearly supported the Christian position. The other twenty-four articles were generally neutral in their presentation of the controversy.

The steamroller strategy of the *Times* in supporting the exhibition of the controversial painting—and in opposing the Christian protestors—emerged in stark relief in two editorials published during this three-week period. An editorial headline on September 24, 1999, one day after the mayor's protest, established the *Times'* basic position, "THE MAYOR AS ART CENSOR" (p. A26).

This statement by the paper's top editors and management was replete with buzzwords designed to stir up indignation among the pro-*Times* cognoscenti: "censor," "First Amendment," "perpetual human struggle with the limits of perception," "autonomy and artistic freedom of the city's museums."

The last sentence leveled the most devastating charge of all, at least for anyone who might want to conform to the *Times'* belief system: "This week he [the mayor] is failing dramatically . . . in a fashion that makes him and the city look ridiculous."

The paper followed up on October 2 with another editorial, "THE BATTLE OF BROOKLYN," which once again attacked the mayor and extolled the Brooklyn museum as an institution "that dared to defend artistic freedom" (p. A24).

In the meantime, the editors were marshaling other journalistic weapons to take potshots at the mayor and traditional Christianity. First of all, the "Letters" section next to the editorials reinforced the paper's basic position. One headline made the *Times'* position clear: "DOES THE MAYOR KNOW ANYTHING ABOUT ART?"

Perhaps the most powerful assault against the mayor and the Christian opponents of the art exhibit came from the op-ed page.

- Regular columnist Bob Herbert: "A CHILL GROWS IN BROOKLYN" (9/27/99, p. A23).

In a sarcastic tone, he derided "more mayoral hysteria" and his "tyrannical, puritanical and political tendencies." Again using favorite, if hackneyed, *Times'* buzzwords, he implied that Guiliani was ignoring "artistic freedom" and "intellectual freedom." He also summarily dismissed the fact that Cardinal O'Connor and the activist Catholic League were "upset" over the exhibition.

- Regular columnist Frank Rich: "PULL THE PLUG ON BROOKLYN—AND WHY NOT LINCOLN CENTER TOO?—TIME FOR A REAL CULTURE WAR" (10/9/99, p. A27).

The sarcastic headlines and subheads, which Rich is authorized to write himself, would have been enough to get his not-so-subtle points across. But Rich is rarely content to deliver a reasoned argument and then stop. Instead, he proceeded to heat up the rhetoric to a white-hot pitch by drawing thinly veined comparisons linking the actions of the elephant-dung critics in Brooklyn to efforts by the Nazis to suppress art.

- On the op-ed page in the Sunday Week in Review, guest columnist Jon Robin Baitz lambasted leaders of other New York museums for not being more decisive in standing up to the mayor's pro-Christian position.

The headline of his op-ed piece was full of buzzwords: "A SHAMEFUL APPEASEMENT—WHERE IS THE CITY'S PASSION FOR ARTISTIC FREEDOM?" (10/3/99, p. 17).

- Apparently in response to such criticisms, the director of the Museum of Modern Art decided to get on the bandwagon with his own guest op-ed column: "THE ART THAT DARES—FEAR OF 'SENSATION' IS FEAR OF THE NEW" (10/13/99, p. A31).

In line with the *Times'* generally accepted rules of cultural correctness, he said that "artists reviled" in one era were likely to be revered in another. This was a convincing reason, he contended, for giving artists our "moral, intellectual and financial support, as well as a fundamental belief in their importance." (With such one-sided rhetoric, some might wonder if his column was actually a fund-raising letter.)

In any event, the director argued, critics of the dung-stained depiction of Mary should avoid being "intolerant" and should not condemn that which they "do not understand."

Apparently in an effort to ward off charges that its barrage against the mayor and the church was far too one-sided, the *Times* did publish a few opposing viewpoints. One of the best crafted was "MANICHAEAN MADNESS—CULTURAL ELITE ASSAILS 'YAHOOS'" by regular op-ed columnist William Safire (9/30/99, p. A31).

Safire, making some of the most telling points of the entire three-week debate, began with the description of an imaginary and absurd art show. He fantasized that the exhibit might contain such "art" as a statue of Moses wearing a Nazi swastika; a painting of Martin Luther King Jr. having his way with the nineteenth-century feminist and suffragette Elizabeth Cady Stanton; or a collage depicting a homosexual torturing a puppy.

Then he asked, "Is there anybody I haven't offended?" and answered his own question: "Yes. Christians."

The rest of the article deplored the stupidity of the elite New York art world for going out of its way to offend the sensibilities of most American Christians and probably jeopardizing public support for museums, both in New York and in the U.S. Congress.

"The art world is thoughtlessly flirting with a democratic public's pre-emptive censorship," he warned.

But this voice of reason—a voice crying in a wilderness of anti-American-majority, anti-Christian rhetoric—was ultimately out-shouted by the mass of pro-dung articles, which placed unswerving faith in the rectitude of their version of "artistic freedom." Perhaps the biggest beneficiary of the brouhaha was the artist, Chris Ofili. Described by the *Wall Street Journal* as the artist "who uses dung in his art," Ofili sold five paintings for prices ranging between forty thousand and fifty thousand dollars at an October 1999 Manhattan art show.

This short but intense cultural battle highlighted not only the solid alliance between the *Times* and the elite cultural leadership of New York City but also the speed with which the paper could mobilize its formidable media arsenal to attack religious enemies. But often in its attempts to minimize the cultural influence of traditional religion—especially traditional Christianity—the *Times* employs more subtle tactics.

How the Times Attempts to Corrupt Christianity Through Culture Creep

A well-established method of persuasion—and a formidable weapon in the process of Culture Creep—is to concede or acknowledge part of what your opponent believes or contends, but then to attack ferociously in those areas that are most important to you. In this way, you can project a reasonable and fair-minded image and have the best shot at changing minds on key issues.

Using this technique, many articles in the *New York Times* that deal with Christian thought and belief may acknowledge the truth of some portion of the classic, traditional understanding of the faith. Then at some strategic point they throw in a zinger that is designed to nudge the reader toward the paper's worldview and away from the faith.

This powerful method of persuasion can be seen in an obituary of the popular Roman Catholic novelist Morris West (10/12/99, p. C25). The article discussed how the author's strong, traditional, doctrinal positions were evident in many of his books, such as *The Shoes of the Fisherman*. But the kicker—the final two paragraphs that left the reader with the strongest impression of the writer—ended like this:

> "Toward the end of his life, Mr. West acknowledged his unhappiness with religion.
>
> "'Christian belief is not always a comfort but a bleak acceptance of a dark mystery,'" he said."

The message in this article was that Christianity is okay up to a point. But in the end, the faith will never satisfy.

With a slightly different twist, a front-page article headlined, "WHITE HOUSE SEEKERS WEAR FAITH ON SLEEVE AND STUMP," purported to be a roundup on the role of public professions of faith in national political campaigns (8/31/99, p. A1). Reference was made to Gov. George W. Bush's decision to "recommit my

life to Jesus Christ" and Elizabeth Dole's discussion of her conversations with God.

Occasionally the story betrayed a cynical tone, with references
by the reporter herself to "God talk" and quotations from
"experts" who interpreted the religious language of the candidates
in mostly pragmatic terms. For example, one "senior fellow" at a
Washington think tank observed that "a little bit of religiosity can
cover . . . a multitude of political sins" (p. A14).

The article ended with the inevitable kicker-with-a-message.
In the final paragraphs, a historian was quoted as saying,
"Wouldn't it be wonderful if you saw a candidate come along now
who said, 'I'm an atheist,' just for a change of pace?"

Then the reporter asked rhetorically: "And what chance would
that candidate have of winning?" and turned to the historian for
the answer:

"'None,' he said."

An underlying assumption throughout the article was that
while some politicians may have a genuine faith, in almost every
case those beliefs are rather superficial and are expressed in public mainly to get votes. Furthermore, if a non-believer wants to
hold high public office, he had better cover up his religious
views or be prepared to lose the election.

Certainly, there is some truth in this assessment. But when a
reporter has an opportunity to explore the real nature of a politician's religious beliefs, it's rather unsatisfying for the reader to
have to read generalizations by historians and pundits rather than
in-depth reports of the convictions of the individual candidates.

Most important of all, such reporting is likely to reinforce in
readers the view expressed by Minnesota governor Jesse Ventura
that religion is for the "weak-minded." But then again, maybe
that's the attitude toward religion that the *Times* wants to foster.

A Nudge toward New Beliefs

In its religion coverage, the *Times* also nudges readers
toward its novel views on various social issues, such as same-sex

marriages, feminism, biblical authority, evangelism and conversion, and specific doctrines like hell and salvation.

A basic technique to achieve a change in belief is to chip away at "undesirable" religious certainty by presenting favorably certain controversies or doctrinal disputes promoted by factions or splinter groups. The more a reader is exposed to such slanted coverage, the more likely he or she is to get the impression that the insurgents represent the most intelligent or desirable viewpoint. If enough readers from a particular denomination begin to buy into the *Times'* position on a particular issue, an entire religious group or denomination could become more likely to change its doctrines on that issue.

Here are a few illustrations:

The Drive to Change Traditional Moral and Social Doctrines. A huge six-column article led off the "National Report" section on June 11, 1999, with this headline and subheads: "68 CLERICS DEFY CHURCH OVER A SAME-SEX UNION—METHODISTS LEADERS MUST WEIGH PENALTIES—CHURCH TENSIONS RISE OVER DEAL WITH GAY AND LESBIAN MEMBERS" (p. A18).

A picture of one of the rebel preachers and two lesbians, whose union he had blessed, dominated the visual layout of the article. The final paragraph stated the *Times'* position and the viewpoint the paper wanted the reader to carry away:

> "[A Methodist bishop] said he did not believe that the church needed to have a position on every issue. In some cases, he said, judgment should be left to God."

In effect, no room was allotted for opposing viewpoints—or the "other side of the story" that is supposed to characterize a balanced report. Only two short paragraphs dealt with comments by the leader of an evangelical wing of Methodism—and the quotes attributed to him focused mainly on the impact that the proponents of pro-gay marriage were likely to have on the broader church.

As such media influences intensify, the United Methodist Church and other mainline denominations edge further away from their historic social and moral doctrines.

The Drive to Undermine the Authority of the Bible. When Southern Baptists were criticized for taking a strong stand on husband-wife relationships in the 1998 annual convention, the *Times* presented the issue as primarily an attack on the rights and dignity of women—and a misguided attempt to return to some outmoded principles of family relationships. But in reality, the primary attack was aimed at the authority of the Scriptures.

A front-page story on June 10, 1998, under the headline, "SOUTHERN BAPTISTS DECLARE WIFE SHOULD 'SUBMIT' TO HER HUSBAND," emphasized that even though the denomination had sixteen million members, its view of the role of women was at the extreme edge of Christian thinking and practice (p. A1, A20).

Note the quotation marks around "Submit" in the headline— a telltale signal of the paper's disdain for this traditional religious language. The paper reinforced this negative image with the use of various condescending, anti-evangelical buzzwords and descriptions, such as the Baptists' "literal interpretation of Scripture" and their affirmation of "some of the most conservative positions."

One problem is that such articles never define what a "literal" interpretation of Scripture means. Instead, "literal," like "fundamentalist," has become a weapon word to attack evangelical Christians and others who believe they can discover some measure of spiritual certainty by treating the Scripture seriously and authoritatively.

Yet if "literal" is understood in its normal etymological sense, reading or interpreting something "literally" means taking it at face value. That is, the words, phrases, and any figures of speech are accepted for what they purport to be. So that which purports to be history is interpreted as history; that which purports to be journalism is interpreted according to the rules of journalism; that which purports to be poetry is read as poetry, and so on. But in this particular front-page "news" story, "literal" was used rather artfully to marginalize and ridicule one of the greatest conservative religious threats to the *Times'* worldview, the huge Southern Baptist denomination.

Predictably, the attack continued in more explicit terms on the op-ed page six days later. In a guest column, written under the clear, anti-biblical headline, "THE GOOD BOOK OF FEW ANSWERS," author A. N. Wilson made no bones about his contempt for the Baptists and his doubt about the historical authenticity of the Bible.

At the outset, for instance, he referred to the Letter to the Ephesians as "a text that may or may not have been written by Saint Paul." Later, he dismissed a key passage on women in the church as "obviously an interpolation by a later, misogynist Christian Scribe."

Touching base with the *Times'* most loyal constituencies, Wilson bemoaned the "dismay" expressed by "women's groups, liberal Christians and those who have noticed that social and familial conditions in modern America differ somewhat from those of first-century Asia Minor."

But as his polemic progressed, the tone degenerated to rank name-calling and verbal abuse. As might be expected, he fell back on the usual buzzwords—making charges of "intolerance," associating Christianity with "self-mutilators" and "desert dropouts," and disparaging "fundamentalists" and the like who are trying to recapture the "vanished age" of the Bible.

His most pathetic efforts were reserved for a half-baked Tom-Paine-wannabe assault on traditional Bible interpretation. For example, he suggested that if "Christian fundamentalists" today are so serious about the Bible, why don't they keep Jewish dietary laws, or engage in "stoning adulteresses"?

Wilson's attempts at anti-Christian apologetics can easily be answered, but they are too silly to dignify with a serious response.

The only truly thoughtful points Wilson made in his article didn't come until his final paragraph, when he said: "A true biblical faith recognizes that the Bible is not a book of answers. It's the story of the human race getting it wrong over and over and over again. Even Saint Paul frequently contradicts himself, rebuking his own folly, harshness and intolerance. Like us, he lived in a time of social and moral dissolution. The imaginative freedom that he sought from the bonds of 'Law' is something truly exciting, if one could begin to grasp its meaning."

Granted, a person with an evangelical orientation might take issue with several of his observations here. But at least there are some insights worth talking about.

Still, the thoughtful part comes too late to salvage the article. In the inimitable style of Frank Rich, Wilson has staked out his claim on the far, loony edge of the *Times'* anti-evangelical turf. But as Rich once said, if there's a dirty job, somebody's got to do it.

In somewhat more temperate terms, the *Times* has also worked to reinforce its opposition to biblical authority in other sections of the paper. One approach is to give high-profile publicity to theological fashions, such as the perennially favorite argument that the authors of the Bible were not really who tradition says they were. A common liberal corollary to such contentions is that many parts of the Bible were written and edited (or "redacted," to use the technical term) at much later dates than tradition holds.

For example, a story in the January 23, 1999, Arts & Ideas section (p. A19) was headlined, "Is THERE A BOOK HIDDEN WITHIN THE BIBLE?"

The article presented a variation on the well-worn premise that if you pick and choose your Bible verses creatively, you'll find a hidden narrative—especially in the first five books, the Pentateuch, of which Moses has traditionally been accorded authorship. But in this case, the scholar suggested that substantial parts of the Pentateuch, as well as later books, may have been written by an unknown woman (surprise!). Most likely, the argument goes, she lived twenty-eight centuries ago, or well after Moses lived and wrote.

Instead of being presented as a somewhat intriguing but essentially odd deviation from mainstream biblical studies, this speculative theory was presented as a serious advance in biblical scholarship. For those in the general public with little or no biblical background, such reporting can be misleading and contributes to a general weakening of historic biblical authority. But of course, such a result is consistent with the *Times'* aversion to religious certainty and its opposition to use of the Bible as a standard for faith and practice.

Other articles may attack biblical authority and authenticity more directly—and disrespectfully. In a 1995 Sunday magazine article, which was published on Christmas Eve in a remarkably tacky anti-Christian stroke, the author, Jack Miles, gave his personal version of the nativity account:

"Jesus was born in Palestine sometime near the turn of the era. That much is historical. The rest—the census, 'no room at the inn,' the manger, the shepherds, the wise men, the slaughter of the innocents and the flight into Egypt—is not historical" (12/24/95, pp. 28ff.).

He retold the Christmas story through a mishmash of allusions to pop culture and Greek mythology and finally concluded with this rather puzzling piece of claptrap: "The Christmas story didn't happen, in sum, and it need not be believed, but it still matters, and it still works" (p. 33).

Miles's short bio, which accompanied the story, listed him as "a former Jesuit and now a practicing Episcopal layman." As I discovered from being a New York Episcopalian for several years, the Episcopal church can encompass a broad range of parishioners—from agnostics to passive pew warmers to devout believers. In light of his theological predilections, it seems obvious that Miles would not feel comfortable placing himself in the third category.

His identity as a "former" Jesuit suggested that for some reason he was now in a state of spiritual or theological reaction or rebellion against his background.

Finally, Miles's bio said that he "holds a doctorate in the Old Testament from Harvard"—again, a revealing tidbit. Having taken courses at Harvard Divinity School myself, I have become particularly sensitive to the powerful, anti-Christian influences of Cambridge "theology."

As suggested in chapter 3, Harvard and the *New York Times* are so closely linked in worldview that they might be described as philosophically incestuous. In particular, the anti-evangelical-Christian bias at the *Times* today is not that different from that at Harvard, including the Divinity School, when I was an undergraduate and law student there.

During my sophomore and junior years, I took classes from and even engaged in head-to-head arguments at dinner with the liberal theologian Paul Tillich. I still recall challenging Tillich during a dinner at Kirkland House after he made a derogatory remark about Billy Graham. Yet I learned in Tillich's rather sheepish response that he had been pronouncing his opinions without any real understanding of Graham's ministry or his role in the American Christian tradition.

Even though Tillich has been dead for years, his anti-evangelical biases continue to infect the thinking of many liberal ministers and churchmen who were influenced by this thinking at Harvard and elsewhere. And it's to those same non-orthodox clergy and church leaders and members—such as Jack Miles—that the *Times* looks when it seeks an authority on spiritual issues.

Overall, then, the *Times* presents a formidable, solid front of opposition to the classic Christian worldview—and the insistence of traditional Christians that they, not a New York newspaper, are the true guardians of absolute spiritual values and certainties.

But even the *Times* can't always impose perfect philosophical conformity on its staff or dictate every direction of the human spirit. A refreshing exception to the paper's anti-Christian bias emerged for a brief moment in the writings of the op-ed columnist A. M. Rosenthal, who, despite his paper's foot-dragging, took up the cause of persecuted Christians in far-flung parts of the world.

THE GREAT EXCEPTION:
A. M. ROSENTHAL'S VALIANT BATTLE AGAINST RELIGIOUS PERSECUTION

"A voice of one crying in the wilderness"—that description of the prophet certainly seems to describe A. M. Rosenthal, the former executive editor of the *Times* who eventually wrote for the paper as a regular op-ed columnist.

Despite the sparse coverage given in the *Times'* news hole to persecution of Christians abroad, Rosenthal took up the cause in 1997. After that, he wrote dozens of columns on the topic—most with the fervent, urgent tone he established in 1998:

> If I were Christian I would complain that Christian leaders, political, religious and business, around the world have failed in their obligations to rights oppression of their co-religionists. I am complaining anyway . . .
>
> Organize congregations to pay attention, more and continuously, to co-religionists outside America; make sure every American official meeting any Communist or [Muslim leader] protests and warns about persecuted Christians every time; fight for legislation strengthening the rights of religious refugees and the use of economic refugees (published in 1997 in *NYT* and reprinted in *Explorations*, American Interfaith Institute/World Alliance of Interfaith Organizations, Vol. 11, No. 2, 1997, p. 1).

Rosenthal confessed that his initial column condemning the persecution of Christians was "late" and lamented that "astonishingly few" journalists, legislators, or clergy had spoken out against the persecution of Christians. But in the years that followed, he made up for lost time with hard-hitting attacks against President Bill Clinton and other political leaders, whom he accused of putting international business interests with other nations, such as China, ahead of human rights of Christians, Tibetan Buddhists, and others.

For example, in a 1998 Christmas day column he charged:

"In 1994 Bill Clinton, breaking his pre-election promises, sold to China the American commitment to human rights for Chinese and Tibetans. What he got in return was the permission to continue business with China. . . . And it frees China from Administration action or denunciation for the arrests of more Christians who refuse to worship in government-regulated churches . . . ." (12/25/98, *NYT* Web site, p. 27; 8/13/99, p. A19).

Explaining his reasons for taking up the cause of suffering Christians, Rosenthal wrote on October 1, 1999 (p. A29):

"I am asked why I write often about religious persecution of Christians, since I am a Jew, and not even religiously educated. One simple reason is sufficient: sufferings of the religious are as painful as of the secular.

"But there is another—neither religious nor secular freedoms will flourish where one is denied."

On at least two occasions, Rosenthal took his cue from Christian activist Nina Shea, the director of the Center for Religious Freedom of Freedom House, whom he called "a human rights army in herself" (12/25/98, *NYT* Web site, p. 27). Among other things, he quoted repeatedly and approvingly her call to action in her book, *In the Lion's Den* (Broadman & Holman, 1997):

"Millions of American Christians pray in their churches each week, oblivious to the fact that Christians in many parts of the world suffer brutal torture, arrest, imprisonment and even death . . . for no other reasons than that they are Christians" (p. 27).

As legislation proceeded through Congress to help in the fight against persecution, Rosenthal kept the heat on an unenthusiastic U.S. president, a complacent public, and his own paper. For the most part, however, the *Times'* news accounts have been filled with qualifications and biased nuances.

One illustration is a front-page 1998 story on the passage of a U.S. House bill against religious persecution abroad. The second paragraph editorialized against the bill by raising a host of possible objections by unnamed "critics":

> "The lopsided vote . . . masked many lawmakers' ambivalence toward a popular bill that aims to champion religious liberties worldwide, but which critics say will imperil religious minorities, create a hierarchy of human rights violations and hurt United States foreign policy" (5/15/98. p. A1, A8).

A major emphasis of the story was not on the views of the 375 legislators who voted for the bill, but on the 41 who voted against. Yet the objections cited in the above quoted second paragraph—which set the tone for the entire article—were backed up only by short quoted remarks from a few legislative opponents and a general, negative observation from a missionary who was not quoted directly.

When the Senate finally passed a watered-down version of the bill, the *Times* ran a story filled with sighs of relief. A boldfaced subheading in effect dismissed the final measure as a necessary sop to evangelical Christian pressure groups: "FULFILLING A PROMISE TO CONSERVATIVE RELIGIOUS GROUPS" (10/10/98, p. A3).

To check the level of interest in the persecution of Christians, I ran a one-year survey of articles listed in the *Times'* archives on its Web site, from October 19, 1998, through October 19, 1999. The term "persecution of Christians" turned up only seven articles, and the separate terms "persecution" and "Christians" appeared in only twenty-eight articles. Seven of the latter twenty-eight references were from Rosenthal's "On My Mind" column, and none were from the paper's editorials.

Despite the generally sparse and one-sided news reports elsewhere in the paper, Rosenthal remained committed to this cause until he was fired in 1999 (see *Overseas Press Club Bulletin,* Dec. 1999, p. 7).

Unfortunately, his columns stand virtually alone as one finger in a media dike that is overflowing with anti-Christian sentiment.

Still, his call to complacent Christians and the public at large should serve not only as a warning about religious persecution abroad, but also as a general alarm about the media threat to all matters dear to traditional Christianity.

A Warning to Traditional Believers

As we have seen in this chapter, as well as in earlier chapters, the main religious targets of the *Times* tend to be evangelical Christians and traditional Roman Catholics. These groups typically espouse philosophical, social, and political positions that conflict with the *Times'* worldview. So from the paper's viewpoint, it is imperative that their influence be neutralized.

Liberal Protestant denominations and leaders, as well as liberal Roman Catholic institutions and clergy, usually escape the wrath of the *Times*—for the opposite reason. That is, they tend to dismiss as irrelevant to the contemporary world the spiritual authority of the Bible, of the historic creeds, and of traditional church leaders.

In short, because of the inordinate power of the *Times* and the many media voices that follow its lead, traditional Christians—as well as traditional followers of other faiths, such as Orthodox Jews—are being pushed steadily into the role of a not-so-loyal opposition. Traditional believers are, in effect, becoming part of a spiritual counterculture, which stands in opposition to almost every important moral and philosophical belief that is espoused and promoted through the *Times* and reflected increasingly in the culture at large.

Those who feel certain about the truth of traditional religious doctrines will of necessity find themselves on a direct collision course with the *New York Times*. It's impossible to serve two masters—two worldviews that claim access to opposite sets of absolutes.

CHAPTER 7

THE SIN OF CONSERVATISM

The *New York Times* is a liberal Democratic paper—in fact, the leading voice of liberalism in the United States. Few would dispute the paper's liberal credentials, which include support of such issues as:

- Centralized government over states' rights.
- Federal influence, or control over primary and secondary education—including support of national teachers' groups and unions.
- Use of public funds for public education, but not for education provided by private or religious schools, such as through a voucher system.
- An impenetrable wall of separation between church and state, including opposition to prayer in public schools or other open expressions of faith in formal public forums.
- Labor unions.

- Protection of American labor interests in international trade agreements and policies. A corollary: opposition to the North American Free Trade Agreement (NAFTA).
- A naturalistic, anti-supernatural, hyper-scientific view of the world, with no respect for traditional religious explanations of creation, the physical universe, or the appearance of human beings.
- Total freedom of the press.
- More government regulation of firearms.
- Complete, government-enforced freedom of a woman to have an abortion—with no rights at all bestowed upon the fetus.
- Virtually total government-enforced and publicly financed freedom of speech and artistic expression, including the use of profane, sexually explicit, scatological, or blasphemous language and depictions—but with definite limits placed on the rights of free speech and assembly of religious groups.
- Government support of entitlements, including national health care and health insurance, day care, and various forms of welfare. Emphasis on increasing the range of interest groups that can claim such entitlements.
- Extensive government involvement in controlling the environment.
- A globalistic philosophy, which promotes increased power of the United Nations and other international organizations that promote the *Times'* version of human rights and economic progress. A corollary: support for gradual lessening of the power of nations, including a weakening of the international dominance of the United States.
- Elimination of the death penalty.
- Approval and promotion—through favorable *Times'* publicity, governmental fiat, and other means—of a broad range of rights upholding various debatable sexual practices. Traditional family values, such as stable marriages,

are downplayed in favor of new laws and customs that support various forms of premarital, extramarital, and homosexual sex.

- Multiculturalism, with expansion of rights for immigrants, refugees, and other groups that represent increased "diversity" in society.

A Litmus Test for Liberalism

Other specific issues might be included in addition to the above "liberal doctrines," which the *Times* promotes and most true liberals affirm.

In fact, this list can provide a fairly clear litmus test to indicate where a person stands on the American political spectrum. Of course, not every liberal would agree with all of these points, nor would every conservative reject them all. But it seems fair to suggest that anyone who would support five to ten of these positions would be at least a "moderate liberal." Those who support eleven or more of these issues would be heading toward an "extreme liberal" or "far left" designation.

Although the word *liberal* comes from the Latin root, *liber*, meaning "free, independent, or unrestrained," contemporary political liberalism—as suggested in the above listing—involves plenty of limits and constraints. But anyone familiar with American history knows that this current understanding of liberalism—which emphasizes the use of the powers of central government to enforce certain "rights"—is a relatively recent phenomenon. Not too long ago, a "liberal" could easily have been confused with what many would call a "conservative" today.

The Real Meaning of "Liberalism"

As late as the 1960s, most scholars, even those from Harvard and other elite, left-leaning universities, understood the term "liberal" in the classic terms of traditional American political philosophy.

These mid-twentieth-century thinkers—who represented the mainstream of American political philosophy, both liberal and conservative—began by emphasizing that American society was not established on the feudal base of European civilization. Europe's clearly defined hierarchy of serfs, bourgeoisie, and aristocrats was totally foreign to the new culture.

Rather, those who settled the American colonies and later created the American Republic threw off their European social and political heritage and affirmed decisively the assumptions of John Locke, the seventeenth-century English Enlightenment philosopher. Among other things, Locke believed that everyone is born with a non-negotiable package of natural, God-given "rights." Or, as he put it in his classic second *Treatise on Civil Government*, "we are born free as we are born rational. . . ." (reprinted in *Man & State: The Political Philosophers*, New York: Washington Square Press, Inc., 1966, p. 90).

Locke's logic is instructive as we reflect today on the true meanings of such terms as "human rights," "liberal," and "conservative." Relying heavily on biblical authority, with many specific references to Old and New Testament passages and concepts, Locke built his argument for the existence of human rights this way:

> "The state of nature has a law of nature to govern it, which obliges everyone; and reason, which is that law, teaches all mankind who will but consult it, that, being all equal and independent, no one ought to harm another in his life, health, liberty, or possessions" (p. 60).

What was the ultimate source, or guide, that enabled human reason to discover these basic human rights of "life, liberty, and property"?

Locke answered that human beings are, in their totality, "the workmanship of one omnipotent and infinitely wise Maker—all the servants of one sovereign Master, sent into the world by His order, and about His business" (p. 60).

He also wrote:

- "'God has given us all things richly' (1 Tim. 6:17), is the voice of reason confirmed by inspiration" (p. 74).

- "God and his reason commanded [man] to subdue the earth, i.e., improve it for the benefit of life . . . He that, in obedience to this command of God, subdued, tilled and sowed any part of it, thereby annexed to it something that was his property" (p. 74).
- "God gave the world to men in common. . . . He gave it to the use of the industrious and rational" (p. 75).

In other words, Locke believed that natural law and fundamental human rights could be discovered by reason. But God was the ultimate source of human reason and everything else. So reason could only be exercised effectively in accordance with the will and guidance of God.

Thomas Jefferson, who was profoundly influenced by Locke, incorporated the same basic ideas—in practically the same language—in his final draft of the Declaration of Independence:

"We hold these truths to be self-evident, that all men are created equal, that they are endowed by their Creator with certain unalienable Rights, that among these are Life, Liberty and the pursuit of Happiness."

This classic statement of American "liberal" philosophy lies at the heart of a consensus that has characterized American society since its founding. To be sure, the Founding Fathers of the United States failed to provide the benefits of human rights to certain important groups, such as African-Americans and women. But over time—as a result of such events as the Civil War, the suffrage movement, and the civil rights movement of the 1960s—many of these sins of omission were recognized and corrected. Increasingly, the practical American expressions of Locke's original understanding of human rights began to be more consistent with the spiritual foundations he had honored.

For many years, as these necessary changes were occurring in our specific understanding of human rights, Americans in general assumed with Locke that God and his transcendent principles were the ultimate source of their liberty and other rights. These fundamental spiritual assumptions were clearly part of what historians have called the great "American consensus," or our common belief in equality and human rights. There has been little dispute that this belief in basic human rights is what helps make our political system unique and empowers us to excel both at home and on the world stage.

The Great American Consensus

As an American history "concentrator" at Harvard College in the 1960s, I was told by one of my astute tutors that Louis Hartz's *Liberal Tradition in America* was an absolute "must" read for anyone who wanted to understand American history at Harvard.

Hartz, as well as anyone, described the nature of the liberal consensus that had developed in the United States since its founding. Relying on Locke's essays, Alexis de Tocqueville's *Democracy in America*, and other classics, Hartz concluded that the "master assumption of American political thought" was "the reality of atomistic social freedom" (Hartz, p. 63). By this, he meant that, in the classic Lockean sense, the American public assumed without serious question that each individual was "born free," or endowed with a set of natural rights (p. 66).

Even as Hartz wrote during the mid-twentieth century—almost two centuries after Jefferson penned the Declaration of Independence—a common assumption still prevailed among the general public that the ultimate source of spiritual authority for the American belief in rights was the God of the Bible.

The average person could speak with assurance about our "God-given rights." Furthermore, almost everyone was comfortable with Jefferson's words in the Declaration of Independence that "all men are created equal, that they are endowed by their Creator with certain unalienable Rights. . . ."

But as the twentieth century drew to a close, the foundations of the traditional American consensus came under increasing attack—with the *New York Times* acting as the spearhead for a false liberalism devoid of an authoritative spiritual base.

THE TIMES ATTACKS LOCKE—AND TRUE AMERICAN LIBERALISM

The liberalism of the *Times* is fundamentally a set of beliefs rooted in shallow soil and consisting primarily of the intellectual fashions of the moment.

Ask a *Times*-liberal, "Why do you support rights or entitlements for this particular group, or deny them for that group, or affirm this or that political philosophy?"

Even the best-educated reader will almost certainly appeal ultimately to human reason. Yet if you probe deeper, the shallowness of this appeal becomes evident.

In a strange and radical twist on Francis Bacon's philosophy of progress and the perfectibility of man, the *Times*' reliance on reason goes only as deep as the human knowledge and understanding that are available at any particular moment. In effect, the paper dismisses the notion of plumbing the possibilities of eternal verities—because God doesn't exist. Or if he does exist, he remains the impotent God of the most radical deist, largely irrelevant and uninvolved in human affairs.

Of course, John Locke and his philosophical heirs, including Thomas Jefferson, understood the concept of liberalism quite differently. For them, the personal liberty and other human rights inherent in *true* liberalism had to be derived from the universal truths established by the God of the Old and New Testaments, and not from human reason functioning in a spiritual vacuum. Even Jefferson, who had deistic tendencies, never came close to the anti-Christian, human-centered extremes of some modern-day liberals, such as those at the helm of the *Times*.

For the classic liberal, reason apart from valid spiritual moorings would inevitably give rise to "freedoms" and "rights" that careened out of moral control. Or as Locke described authentic, spiritually rooted human freedom, "though this be a state of liberty, yet it is not a state of license" (p. 60).

The original understanding in Locke's time and in the early American Republic was that government was necessary to keep order and protect the free exercise of inherent human rights, untrammeled by the constraints of an overbearing central government. The Bill of Rights, the first ten amendments to the U.S. Constitution, became the practical, institutional embodiment of this concept of personal rights and freedom from state control.

Yet the more recent reinterpretation of "liberal," "liberalism," "human rights," and similar terms—as espoused by the *New York Times*—turns this original, classic understanding of freedom on its ear. On the one hand, the *Times* promotes some traditional rights to new extremes—especially freedom of the press, apparently because such freedom reinforces the paper's own position of influence and power.

Also, the *Times* has worked hard to expand a novel group of "rights," which would most certainly have puzzled Locke or Jefferson, and which continue to puzzle their true heirs in our own day. The most prominent of these include the rights of those with unusual sexual orientations and preferences. One of the paper's great crusades has been an effort to create a status for activist gays and lesbians that will place them on a constitutional and legal plane equal to that of racial minorities and women.

Also, the *Times* views with some suspicion certain well-established rights that Jefferson and his soul mates included in the Bill of Rights and other documents. For example, the rights of free speech and freedom of religion should be restricted, according to the *Times*, especially when the paper's conservative religious opponents are exercising those rights.

In addition, human rights, as the *Times* understands the term, apparently don't extend to any unborn child, even if that child is minutes or seconds away from delivery. The "right" of a woman over her body always prevails over the right of the unborn.

The extent to which the paper may in the future edge gradually into some affirmation of infanticide or euthanasia remains to be seen. One question that presses for an answer is whether the right to live should be denied to seriously deformed infants—even though those infants have already been delivered after a full-term pregnancy, and have the capacity to exist without life support.

As the nation's leading exponent and defender of late twentieth-century anti-theistic liberalism, the *Times* takes seriously its duty to attack the conservative opposition. Ironically, these modern-day "conservatives" quite often fit into the classic understanding of "liberal."

For one thing, many of today's conservatives look back for philosophical guidance to an earlier time, when the central government was weaker and citizens were freer to exercise their natural "rights" of free speech, free assembly, freedom of religion, and the like without significant interference. Also, today's conservatives tend to affirm the laissez-faire economics of Adam Smith and his followers, who have consistently advocated free markets with minimal interference from government.

The *Times* takes the opposite tack. The paper pushes the idea that a strong central government—which paradoxically must take away the freedom to act in certain ways—is necessary to preserve the rights that the paper holds dear.

Primary conservative targets of the *Times* include not just traditional religious groups, as we've seen in the previous chapter, but also political, social, and even economic movements that give individuals too much freedom.

What issues trigger a "*Times*-liberal attack"?

Expect a hostile response if you want the freedom to educate your children with reduced government interference, such as through a voucher system. Or if you think you have the right to own firearms. Or if you want to take other actions that could threaten central government authority. Certainly, the freewheeling views of many libertarians who believe in broad or absolute freedom of thought and action—are ready-made to rattle the paper's sense that all is right with the world.

In a sense, the *Times*' gospel actually promotes the notion that freedom is the enemy of human rights—at least those human rights recognized by the powers-that-be at the paper. In the topsy-turvy world of this new liberalism, some freedoms, such as speech and assembly, may in effect become "selective rights," which must not be made freely available to the paper's enemies.

Two Tactics to Promote the New Liberalism

So how does the *Times* promote its peculiar brand of liberalism?

One tactic is the smear. In other words, use all the standard journalistic weapons—news stories, op-ed pieces, and editorials—to pigeonhole conservatives as right-wing extremists. It's much easier to dismiss someone as a Nazi, religious fanatic, or member of a hate group than it is to deal with a William Buckley or a modern-day version of Edmund Burke.

A second tactic is to turn a guest column over to an influential national leader who can be counted on to parrot support for one of the paper's pet causes.

Here's how these approaches work in practice.

The Extremist Smear. The op-ed page often takes the lead in attempting to push conservatives in general and the Republican opposition in particular out of the realm of social acceptability.

The attacks have ranged from Frank Rich's verbal extremism at one end of the spectrum to more subtle digs by certain guest columnists and the editorial page. Rich's article, "GODZILLA OF THE RIGHT," which has already been mentioned in another context, is a classic of the over-the-top genre (5/20/98, p. A23).

After labeling the conservative and urbane Christian activist and author James Dobson as "Godzilla" and linking him to the Ku Klux Klan, Rich went on to scream in print at other Republicans who seemed to him to be leaning too far to the right. These included Missouri Senator John Ashcroft and presidential candidates Gary Bauer and Steve Forbes, whose main sin, in Rich's eyes, was to "pander to the religious right" on such issues as outlawing abortion.

Rich's parting shot ended with this kicker: "If there's anything that may play worse with voters than the disingenuousness of Clinton Democrats, it just may be the hard right's politics of mean."

Rich, like many other op-ed writers, made it clear through this column and others that he wasn't happy with Clinton's shenanigans in office. But as always, he reserved his most vitriolic attacks for the majority of Republicans who, in his view, comprised the "hard right" and practiced "politics of mean."

In another typical op-ed outburst, Rich continued to slam other Republicans as purveyors of "pure hatred of government" and "anti-establishment barking." He specifically pointed to House Whip Tom DeLay and Bob Barr, who both took a lead role against Bill Clinton in the House impeachment proceedings (2/6/99, p. A29).

Rich also included a curiously irrelevant aside in this particular column in an effort to savage another of his enemies—the traditional evangelical men's movement, the Promise Keepers. He characterized their mass rallies as a "90's music-and-pantheism be-in to rival Woodstock."

Pantheism? Anyone with even a modicum of knowledge about the Promise Keepers' theology would undoubtedly be puzzled by that crack. But as usual, Rich seemed to focus more on sarcastic rhetoric than facts.

Gary Bauer and Steve Forbes again came in for villification, but this time Rich also slapped the label "soldiers of the right" on practically everyone else—George W. Bush, Dan Quayle, Rush Limbaugh. It would seem that, in Rich's two-dimensional philosphical universe, there can be no subtleties in characterizing conservative thought. Consequently, almost no Republican can escape his wild verbal flailing.

But Rich, though he may be the most extreme, isn't alone in leveling intemperate attacks at conservatives. Another op-ed regular, Bob Herbert, picking up on a front-page *Times* headline, "G.O.P.'s Right Talks of Bolting Faithless Party," took left-wing rhetoric to another level.

In a column headlined, "Restless Radicals," Herbert declared, "The Republican Party is already right wing. It's already the party of the mega-corporations and the ultra rich" (7/1/99, p. A21).

Such ravings from regular op-ed page columnists find support in somewhat more rational terms from guest columnists and editorial writers. For example, in a guest op-ed column entitled "THE COURTS' PERILOUS RIGHT TURN," Cass R. Sunstein, an author who has written on the Supreme Court, charged that "judicial activism on the part of conservative judges is a much more serious problem" than activism by liberal judges of the past (6/2/99, p. A29).

Sunstein singled out for criticism the courts' support of such issues as states' rights, laws restricting abortion, and laws regulating pornography. Toward the end of his article, the author even said that "some conservative judges are fighting democracy."

On the editorial page, the top *Times'* editors reinforce the op-ed attacks by constantly sniping at conservatives in Congress. Too often, they use excessive language that questions their opponents' patriotism.

One illustration was an editorial condemning a Senate vote against President Clinton's questionable test ban treaty proposal, in which the paper accused the Senate Republicans of being "reckless" and "armed isolationists." In particularly alarmist language, the editorialists said the majority had "all but abdicated its constitutional responsibility to play a thoughtful and deliberative role in the shaping of American foreign policy" (10/15/99, p. A30).

What the *Times* didn't point out in its highly politicized, divisive editorial were the serious, well-reasoned objections to the bill by both Republicans and Democrats. Democratic Senator Robert C. Byrd, for instance, declared in the same issue of the paper that he had chosen to vote "present" on the treaty because both sides had politicized the process (10/15/99, p. A31).

FEAR OF A SLIPPERY SLOPE

An explicit assumption in the most virulent op-ed pieces—and a strongly implied assumption in many *Times'* editorials and news stories—is that conservatism is dangerous because it's likely to put a person on a slippery slope to a life of hate and "intolerance." The end result, in the view of the paper, may be affiliation with hate groups, Nazism, the Ku Klux Klan, and all manner of far-right extremism.

To be sure, certain prominent conservative and moderate Republicans—such as William Kristol, William Buckley, and former White House counsel Peter Wallison are occasionally accorded space to explain views that may be contrary to those of the *Times*. But the overwhelming weight of opinion pieces and news coverage demonizes conservatism of every stripe.

Unfortunately, such paranoia—on a par with Hillary Clinton's wild charges of a "vast right-wing conspiracy" against husband Bill (before the truth of his dalliance with Monica Lewinsky was established)—makes it impossible for the paper to cover conservatism and conservatives fairly and intelligently. When any news organization elects to become an advocate for a particular political or social viewpoint rather than be a detached observer and reporter, balance becomes impossible—with the result that the organization's credibility may be irreparably damaged.

When a President Becomes a Public Relations Man. The *Times* is also constantly on the lookout for high officials or other national leaders who are willing to support one of the paper's pet anti-conservative positions in print. The greatest prize is a current or former U.S. president, especially one who is a Republican.

The *Times*—by pulling former presidents Gerald Ford and Jimmy Carter into its stable of advocates—achieved a double-barreled blast at Republican opponents of President Clinton during the impeachment proceedings at the end of 1998 and in the early part of 1999. In their December 21, 1998, op-ed piece, entitled "GERALD FORD AND JIMMY CARTER: A TIME TO HEAL OUR NATION," the two issued a joint statement calling for a censure of Clinton on the op-ed page after the Senate impeachment vote.

This position was substantially in line with the *Times'* editorial stance. The paper had originally opposed impeachment. But after the House vote passed, the editors began pushing for censure rather than a Senate trial, which might have ended in the conviction of Clinton, the paper's choice for the presidency in the previous two elections.

The two presidents acknowledged Clinton's "lurid misconduct," his "wrongdoing," and the "very real harm he has caused." But they concluded that a Senate trial might inflict long-lasting wounds on the nation. Instead, they called for a bipartisan censure resolution, which they argued, would "go a long way toward healing our divided nation" (Web site article, pp. 1–2).

Not surprisingly, the position taken by Ford and Carter was almost exactly the same as the view the *Times* was pushing. In other words, the two presidents were used to reinforce the paper's strong editorial stance.

Even President Clinton—who temporarily fell out of favor with the *Times* because of his misconduct in office—was later given space to argue in favor of his controversial bombing in Kosovo (5/23/99, Week in Review, p. 17). In this op-ed piece headlined, "A JUST AND NECESSARY WAR—NOTE TO NAYSAYERS: OUR STRATEGY IS WORKING," Clinton offered various justifications for his decision to collaborate with NATO in the skies over the former Yugoslavia.

Predictably, Clinton's position was substantially the same as the editorial view promoted by the *Times*.

How To Protect an Embarrassing Democratic President?

Despite the *Times'* predictable editorial endorsement of Democratic candidate Clinton at election time and a general agreement with his liberal social and political policies, the paper has engaged in a love-hate relationship with the forty-second president. The ambivalence emerged clearly in the coverage of the scandals and impeachment proceedings of 1998–99.

First of all, support among the ultraliberal bloc of regular op-ed columnists began to disintegrate as it became clear that he really had engaged in "sexual relations with that woman" and lied to his wife, his cabinet, the American public, and everyone else within earshot.

Bob Herbert actually suggested in the late summer of 1998 that resignation might be in order. Maureen Dowd, in a satiric column headlined "KING OF THE WORLD," imagined that Clinton won in the Senate and then "boogied into his victory rally chewing on a Cohiba and beating on bongo drums" (1/24/99, Week in Review, p. 15).

Despite these lapses, the brave liberal front of the *Times* held together for the most part. Herbert, for example, was clearly back on track on December 17, 1998, (p. A31), when he whimpered in his column, "The right wing of the Republican Party clearly is out to destroy Mr. Clinton."

Herbert did express suspicion that Clinton might have bombed Iraq during the impeachment proceedings in a "wag-the-dog" effort to divert attention from his domestic travails. In the end, however, he returned to form by labeling Tom DeLay, the House Republican whip, a "right-wing zealot" and accusing Republican moderates of "lining up like lackeys to follow Mr. DeLay's fanatical lead."

The sharp-tongued Dowd retreated to the liberal camp in a column that ran on December 13, 1998, (Week in Review, p. 15). She still expressed her dissatisfaction with Clinton but was even more horrified that a conservative cadre might impeach and throw him out of office:

"The Republicans are doing something far more ominous than what Bill Clinton did," she concluded in her kicker. "He debased the Presidency, but they are debasing the Constitution."

In a remarkably similar conclusion in his own column on the very same day—a piece he entitled, not too subly, "THE CAPITOL HILL MOB—IS THERE NO ESCAPING THE FANATICS?"—Bob Herbert ended with these words:

"There is no doubt that Bill Clinton has demeaned the Presidency. There is no defense for his actions or his lies. But the voters have chosen him twice by substantial margins and they stand behind him still. It is not up to the hatchet men of the Republican Party to undo that" (p. 15).

During this crucial December period, as the impeachment debate was coming to a head, the *Times* did run an occasional opposing opinion, such as the op-ed piece by the moderate Republican Peter J. Wallison, former Reagan White House counsel (12/17/98, p. A30).

Wallison's main point was that lying in the Clinton manner could be an impeachable offense. Deftly relying on a *Times* editorial that said Clinton had "a mysterious passion for lying," the attorney argued that when such lying destroyed the president's credibility and capacity to lead the nation in international military venture—as had happened during the bombing of Iraq—the lying became an impeachable offense.

Seemingly in rebuttal to Wallison's points, the *Times* printed a contrary editorial across the page on the very same day. The editors declared that it was "unfair" to link the impeachment process and Clinton's desire to rehabilitate his image with the bombing (12/17/98, p. A30). The editorial went on to say that the bombing was "fully justified."

Although such verbal repartee makes for interesting reading, the really important thing to look for in these exchanges is editorial balance. Unfortunately for the *Times'* credibility, such balance in the impeachment reporting was lacking. Over a period of days and weeks, the anti-impeachment stories and rhetoric—with a heavy dose of vitriol directed at any conservatives or moderates in range—far outweighed the pro-impeachment stories.

Editorials Set the Tone

As usual, the backbone of this left-wing campaign against conservative critics of Clinton was the editorial page. In a series of editorials, beginning on September 30, 1998, the *Times* hammered away at the resolution of the Clinton problem, a strategy the editors clearly felt would constitute the best form of damage control.

Their apparent objective with this position was threefold: to uphold their brand of liberalism; to preserve the Democratic president they had supported; and yet to give him enough of a slap on the wrist to enable the paper—and ultraliberalism—to retain some semblance of credibility.

The sequence of the editorials went like this:

- The *Times* staked out its basic position rather early in "THE IMPEACHMENT PICTURE," which ran on September 30, 1998 (p. A22).

   Deathly afraid of impeachment by the House and possible conviction and removal by the Senate, the paper declared: "This page advocates a negotiated settlement that would allow Mr. Clinton to remain in office in exchange for a censure based on his admission of lying under oath."

- Perhaps sensing that momentum was building in favor of impeachment, the *Times* conceded that more than a wrist slap might be required in an October 6, 1998 editorial:

   "From our point of view, [it is essential to] reach a negotiated settlement that involves heavy censure and an unqualified admission of lying by Mr. Clinton."

- As impeachment became more likely, the *Times* took off the gloves in a December 6, 1998 editorial that was headlined rather combatively, "THE IMPEACHMENT BULLY" (Week in Review, p. 18).

   The "bully" in this case was a favorite target of the liberal establishment (and the *Times'* op-ed page), Republican whip Tom DeLay. The news management used such inflammatory language as "ferocious partisan" and "parliamentary trickery" to describe DeLay and his tactics.

- A week later, the *Times*, now apparently becoming frantic about the likelihood of impeachment, employed a similar approach in an editorial entitled, "THE MISUSE OF IMPEACHMENT" (12/13/98, Week in Review, p. 14).

The main thrust of this piece was to charge the Republican majority with "constitutional heresy" for regarding impeachment as a serious censure of the president.

- After impeachment occurred, the *Times* kept the pressure on for the case to be closed with censure, rather than a Senate trial (1/24/99, Week in Review, p. 10). Finally, the paper was able to breathe a sign of relief the day after the Senate acquitted the president on two articles of impeachment (2/13/99, p. A30).

As this editorial battering of Republicans and their conservative allies was going on, the *Times* simultaneously launched assaults in other sections of the paper. In the Week in Review news section, for instance, which supposedly carries news features—the editorializing mounted.

In an evident attempt to influence not only public opinion but also Congressional votes, a high-profile article on December 6, 1998 (Week in Review, p. 3), argued blatantly for censure of Clinton—or the very same position the *Times* was promoting on the editorial page.

The writer led off by implying strongly that the past actions of Congress in other areas provided solid precedent for censure. Then, he attempted to make the opponents of censure seem ignorant or excessively partisan with dismissive statements such as these: "To many politicians, the arguments against censure seem preposterous."

In a remarkably unsubstantiated statement—which apparently was designed to influence the ultimate outcome of the congressional proceedings toward the *Times*' viewpoint—he said: "Ultimately, many politicians agree, censure is the most likely outcome. There may not be enough votes in the House for impeachment."

Obviously, this article didn't succeed in its aim—because the president was impeached and wasn't censured.

But such failures didn't keep the *Times* from continuing to try to impose its anti-impeachment position on the country. An op-ed article in the *Times'* philosophical foe, the *Wall Street Journal*, cataloged a series of other anti-impeachment salvos by the "darlings of the elite liberal culture," including the *Times*.

These included a Magazine piece by Andrew Sullivan, who "lambasted Republicans for 'prurience' and 'puritanism'" . . . a charge by playwright Arthur Miller that the Republicans were guilty of "witchcraft hysteria" . . . and a statement in a news profile that Clinton prosecutor Kenneth Starr "has picked up where Senator Joseph R. McCarthy left off" (see *WSJ*, 10/21/98, p. A22).

Another Vast Right-wing Conspiracy?

During the impeachment controversy, the evidence mounted that liberals were becoming even more paranoid about nefarious conspiracies than some extreme right-wing groups they constantly criticized.

Of course, the parody of the liberals' "vast right-wing conspiracy" theories began after Hillary Clinton's charges against those who were uncovering her husband's infidelities in the Oval Office. The *New York Times* finally succumbed to the temptation of making such charges on its front page—even though the paper couldn't deliver any significant evidence of such machinations.

In the front-page story published on January 24, 1999, the *Times* attempted to impugn the work of prosecutor Kenneth Starr and his staff by linking them in some unethical or underhanded way to "a small secret clique of lawyers in their 30's who share a deep antipathy toward the President" (p. A1).

These attorneys allegedly "KEPT PAULA JONES'S CASE ALIVE," according to the headline, supposedly by feeding Starr tips through a labyrinthine scheme designed to mask their involvement. (A reminder: the Paula Jones case involved charges of sexual misconduct against Clinton, which led to the president's lying under oath during a deposition.)

The story relied mostly on suggestion and innuendo and never really established any solid connections to the prosecutor's office. Instead, the writers relied on breathless potboiler rhetoric, such as saying the lawyers became involved in "cloaking their roles." They also resorted to quotations from Clinton's lawyers to the effect that there was "collusion" between Starr's office and the lawyers for Paul Jones.

Also, the reporters implied Starr had engaged in some sort of cover-up. The reason given for this accusation was that he hadn't mentioned that alleged conservative conspirators were the source of some of his information in the report he delivered to Congress on Clinton.

All these suggestions and insinuations might be dismissed except for two factors: 1) what the story says about the *Times'* bad judgment and 2) the way the article was timed to coincide with and influence political events.

Factor #1: Bad journalistic judgment. First, the documentation for the story was shaky, and solid "conspiracy" connections among the *Times'* conservative opponents, such as Kenneth Starr, were never firmly established. In other words, by playing this weak story in such a prominent position, the paper appears to have subordinated good journalistic judgment to its hatred of the Republicans and its fear of losing a Democratic president.

Of course, this fact didn't prevent other *Times* liberal evangelists from referring to the alleged link between Starr and the supposed cabal of young lawyers as gospel truth. Op-ed pundit Maureen Dowd went the extra self-serving mile in a column on February 7, 1999 (Week in Review, p. 17):

The President behaved terribly. But he was entrapped into lying by his scheming political enemies, a hideous cabal that included New York literary agent Lucianne Goldberg, Ms. [Linda] Tripp, and the lawyers for Paula Jones. It was fortified by a clique of young, conservative lawyers who secretly worked on the Jones lawsuit from its inception and then helped orchestrate Ms. Tripp's fateful call to Mr. Starr.

Despite the prosecutor's denials that his office colluded with the Jones lawyers, those ties have been exposed in the brilliant stories of the *Times's* Don Van Natta and Jill Abramson.

Here, Dowd's acerbic but reasonably controlled anticonservative rhetoric degenerated into irrationality. One hardly knows whether to be amused or embarrassed at her naiveté. She actually railed that Clinton—generally regarded by all sides as one of the most notorious political schemers of all time, and certainly not an easy man to hoodwink—was "entrapped into lying by his scheming political enemies."

Certainly, it must have been disappointing for her that a liberal president would lie and engage in extramarital sexual acts in the Oval Office. But regardless of how the dirty details came to light, there seemed little point for her to offer even a weak defense for the president's actions.

In any event, Dowd's sweeping, artless attack on Clinton's conservative opponents seems beside the point, and her high praise for the conspiracy theory outlined in the article does little to enhance her journalistic credibility. Surely she knew that this article did not represent one of the great peaks of *Times'* journalism.

The editors apparently recognized the shallowness of the attempt to make a case for a dark conspiracy, because after a few murmurs here and there in later stories, they let the issue die a rather quiet and merciful death.

Factor #2: The timing issue. An even more significant factor about the conspiracy article was its timing.

This front-page story appeared the day before Democratic Senator Robert Byrd was scheduled to present a censure resolution—which the *Times* hoped would end the Clinton matter on the paper's terms. Obviously, a prominent article suggesting conspiracies, cover-ups, and tainted tactics by the president's conservative opposition could be useful in achieving this end.

In the conspiracy article, the reporters noted that they had done "nearly two dozen interviews" and combed through "recently filed court documents." Clearly they had spent some time trying to get the goods on the Republicans and were not bound to publish on a particular day. As with most investigative pieces, the paper had some discretion about the publication date. From the date the editors chose, it's abundantly clear that they wanted the story to coincide with Senator Byrd's attempt to push through a censure resolution.

But the conspiracy story seems to have had little impact. Byrd's resolution failed, and the *Times* lost this particular round because there was no censure resolution. As a result, Senate Democrats who were unhappy with Clinton's conduct had no formal way to save face through a formal legislative reprimand.

The Starr Diversion

One of the saddest and most reprehensible chapters in the *Times'* involvement in the impeachment matter involved the character assassination perpetrated by the paper on independent counsel Kenneth Starr.

Granted, Starr made mistakes along the way and failed miserably to give his image a positive spin because he lacked an expert public relations plan. But as I periodically tried to detach myself from the daily insults and counter insults flying back and forth in the press, I could never see any factual justification for the comprehensive strategy followed by the *Times* and other liberal voices to demonize Starr.

Instead, it became clear that the main motives driving the *Times* were political and philosophical. Apparently, the oligarchy that runs the paper decided that the best way to divert attention from Clinton was to go on the offensive against his conservative opponents. Starr, as the independent counsel in charge of the case, was the most visible target. The strategy seemed to be that if you could destroy Starr, you could destroy the impeachment movement—and at the same time, discredit much of the conservative political establishment.

Not one to let such an opportunity slip away, the *Times* published numerous calumnies against Starr over a period of several months in most sections of the paper. Here are just a few of the countless insults levied against the man during late 1998 and early 1999:

- Columnist Frank Rich referred to the prosecutor as "weirdly prurient" (12/16/98, p. A31).
- An editorial, headlined "KEN STARR'S MEDDLING," called him "an obsessive personality" and a "narcissistic legal crank." Also, in this same editorial, the paper's pooh-bahs charged Starr with "legal mischief," "flapping around," "meddling," "customary blundering," and in need of a "slap" by the U.S. Senate (2/2/99, p. A24).
- In an apparently vindictive effort to begin the tarring and feathering of Starr in the history books, the *Times* opened its widely read Sunday op-ed page to Alan Brinkley, a professor of history at Columbia University (2/7/99, p. 17).

In an extremely clever essay, Brinkley first catalogued the possible ways that Starr might be remembered: "the personification of a harsh, puritanical trend in American politics . . . 'Sexual McCarthyism' . . . puritanical zealot . . . Heavy-handed uses of official power."

Brinkley concluded that the best comparison was to the worst prosecutorial excesses of the late U.S. attorney general Robert Kennedy, whose admirers "found his relentless assault on a single man [Jimmy Hoffa] even frightening."

Years in the future, historians who are combing the pages of the *Times* to understand this period of history and establish a permanent record will undoubtedly focus on Brinkley's final paragraph:

". . . Kenneth Starr will be remembered by history—to the limited degree he is remembered at all—as a strange, aberrant and ultimately ineffectual figure, most notable for his repudiation by the American public."

Such is the influence of the *New York Times* that it's almost certain that Ivy League historians like Brinkley—who will write definitive works in the future on the Clinton impeachment and its major players, such as Kenneth Starr—will follow the slanted views of the "newspaper of record" in lockstep.

Furthermore, the writings of these historians will set the tone for future public opinion about what our times were like and who the "bad guys" and "good guys" were in our political and social events. Yet unlike us, they won't have the firsthand experience to be able to read between the lines. They won't be able to see that the most powerful news media organization on earth has shrewdly orchestrated its editorial, op-ed, and news pages to promote a powerful public bias against conservatism and against those prominent figures on the national and world stage who represent various conservative causes.

CHAPTER 8

THE SIN OF CAPITAL PUNISHMENT

The previous chapters have set the philosophical stage for the *Times'* peculiar belief system—and have covered in some detail the potent, though often intricate, techniques the paper employs to proselytize fence-sitters and unbelievers in the culture at large.

Admittedly, we've encountered some complexities in our exploration of the way that the *Times'* corporate culture envelops thought processes both at the paper and in the public. But now our task becomes simpler as we consider a series of relatively clear-cut, straightforward cultural "sins" that the *Times* expects every culturally correct, well-educated person to reject.

The first of these mortal offenses is the sin of capital punishment.

THE TIMES' DOCTRINE ON THE DEATH PENALTY

An editorial entitled "INNOCENTS ON DEATH ROW" summed up the paper's unequivocal, long-standing opposition to the death penalty:

175

"This page has long opposed the death penalty in all cases" (5/23/99, Week in Review, p. 16).

But the *Times* has consistently moved well beyond just stating its conclusions about capital punishment. Whenever an opportunity arises, the editors and reporters attempt to shore up their case with well-crafted arguments based on solid facts and the exploitation of holes in the pro-execution position.

For example, in the above May 23 editorial, the paper focused on a heart-rending issue that could easily turn readers with borderline beliefs on capital punishment to the *Times*' camp—the fact that many people sentenced to death are, in fact, innocent.

Knowing the emotional power of the human interest illustration in persuading the public, the paper led with a detailed description of one Ronald Jones, who had been exonerated and saved from execution in Illinois as a result of new evidence that had been uncovered.

Then the editorial gurus used another effective technique to promote their cause. They tried to chip away at laws supporting the death penalty by proposing the adoption of cumbersome legal procedures. These included giving every person accused of a capital crime a specially trained lawyer, providing access to DNA testing for every death-row inmate, and providing an opportunity for the defense to introduce new evidence whenever it was uncovered.

Finally, they used what might be called a "shame-the-opposition" ploy in their final sentence: ". . . even [the death penalty's] most ardent supporters should be troubled by the likelihood that people are being executed for crimes they did not commit" (5/23/99, Week in Review, p. 16).

The *Times* continued to emphasize these themes in a powerful follow-up article, which was presented in a huge Sunday spread in the Week in Review section on August 22, 1999 (8/22/99, pp. 1, 4).

The main thrust of the story focused on the mistakes in sentencing innocent people to die. To highlight this issue, the paper pointed out that since the U.S. Supreme Court reinstated capital punishment in 1976, 566 people had been executed—but during the same period, 82 death-row inmates had been exonerated. Playing the numbers game for all it was worth, the paper noted "a ratio of 1 freed for every 7 put to death."

But perhaps the strongest part of the article was a full-page spread with pictures and short case histories of inmates who had been sentenced to death—but later freed. Again, considerable space was devoted to how DNA testing and other techniques were unveiling the flaws in the current criminal justice system.

A Lesson in Times-speak

Whenever the *Times* picks a fight over a fundamental issue, you can automatically expect to witness plenty of polemics. In an editorial published on June 26, 1999, the *Times*' managers signaled the pending sarcastic attack against the U.S. Supreme Court with this macabre headline: "THE SUPREME COURT TIGHTENS THE NOOSE" (p. A24).

The image was picturesque, like something out of a Clint Eastwood western, with black-robed, white-haired justices working diligently on a hangman's rope to be sure that the neck of the condemned man didn't slip out.

A lot of finger-wagging language followed as the paper described the Court's decisions as a "distressing trend" that reflected an "increasing willingness to overlook unfair procedures in death penalty cases." The writers referred to "two miserable decisions" by the Court characterized by "cavalier" conclusions.

The *Times*' final "kicker" sentence summed up the paper's contempt for the court: "Given the majority's casual approach to due process, the case also marked another low moment for the nation's highest court."

In such editorials, it's fairly easy for the reader to identify the tone just by looking at telltale words and phrases, such as those quoted above. Because the majority justices were conservatives whose views differed significantly from those of the *Times*, the editors felt no compunction about relying heavily on words that projected contempt and sarcasm toward the highest Court of the land.

All the News That's Fit to Slant

News stories in the *Times* on the death penalty also frequently contain a definite point of view, even if the editorializing is less obvious than the hot rhetoric on the editorial page. In a story headlined "SUPREME COURT TO REVIEW USE OF ELECTRIC CHAIR," the paper focused on an upcoming U.S. Supreme Court case dealing with whether electrocution was a violation of the constitutional prohibition against "cruel and unusual punishment" (10/28/99, p. A16).

Among other atrocities, the article described in gruesome detail the process of electrocution with all its gory details: nosebleeds, blood seeping through the clothing, and burned flesh, which filled the witness room with stench. The narrative also included a macabre historical overview of hangings and other modes of execution.

In the kicker paragraph that concluded the story, a professor was quoted as saying, "the Court has never seen pictures of an inmate sitting on a chair with blood on his face." To emphasize the inflammatory message, a stark picture was included of the electric chair in one of Florida's "death chambers."

Such accounts, though not as explicitly polemic as editorials on the subject, are still clearly slanted against the death penalty. In this particular article, as well as in most others that the paper runs on the topic, no cogent arguments were included in support of the death penalty. In fact, anyone reading the *Times'* coverage on a regular basis would automatically assume there is only one side to this story.

Of course, that's exactly what the *Times'* firmly entrenched corporate and philosophical culture is all about: establishing an atmosphere that allows for only one point of view on important issues.

There are plenty of analogues to this blinders-on approach in other fields. The typical lawyer who has been trained as an

American attorney and practiced in the system for a while never questions the adversarial system. In other words, there is no doubt in the lawyer's mind that even the most vicious criminal deserves the best representation possible, and if he gets off by cunning advocacy, so be it.

Similarly, if you've become enmeshed in a religious cult, you never question the values of the group or the directions of your cult leader. Or if you've been trained as a U.S. Marine, you obey the orders of a superior, even if such obedience seems illogical or puts your life in jeopardy.

In the same vein, it never dawns on many of those caught up in the *Times'* culture that perhaps there is another point of view on the death penalty, or political liberalism, or abortion, or some other key topic. Slanted stories seem quite reasonable and satisfactory, so long as they are slanted in the direction that *Times'* disciples, who are conditioned by Culture Creep, expect and accept.

THE GREAT INCONSISTENCY

Some reflection on the *Times'* opposition to the death penalty might cause even the most fervent believer in the paper's gospel to take pause. Consider, for example, how other *Times'* beliefs—such as abortion or assisted suicide—give rise to tensions or even conflicts with the paper's position on capital punishment.

Here are two sample questions that may trigger further thought:

Question #1: "If humane treatment of human beings and an affirmation of the sanctity of human life are primary reasons for the *Times'* opposition to the death penalty, why not apply the same rationale to abortion?"

This question becomes particularly disturbing when a viable fetus is involved—an unborn child who could survive outside the womb. As we'll see in chapter 12, the *Times* argues that in such a situation the total freedom of the mother to choose the unborn child's fate should prevail. But in a free, democratic society, to give one person complete control over another is singular and without real precedent.

Granted, the *Times* can take the line that the fetus, even if viable, isn't a real "person" and therefore should be treated differently from an individual outside the womb. But sophistry rather than solid reason seems to underlie any attempt to distinguish between a viable six-, seven-, or eight-month-old unborn child, and a one-day-old newborn.

Also, sophistry seems at work in the attempts to deny that a viable unborn child must surely feel some pain during the controversial "partial-birth abortion" procedure. It would seem that those who lament the pain experienced by a convicted killer during an execution should be more than horrified at the potential for pain by an unborn child during a violent abortion procedure.

There is absolutely no chance that the *Times* or those who follow its belief system would condone the execution of even the most vicious and clearly guilty convicted killer through the "dilation and extraction" (partial-birth abortion) technique. (This method involves puncturing the brain, sucking out the contents, and collapsing the skull.) Yet the inconsistency in the respective rationales for abortion versus capital punishment seems to escape those who affirm the *Times*' gospel.

> *Question #2:* "Suppose a mistake in the judicial process has resulted in the conviction of the wrong person—and new evidence might be presented to exonerate the condemned inmate. If preserving human life to avoid any possibility of such a mistake is a reason to oppose capital punishment, why not apply the same reasoning to eliminate the practice in some jurisdictions of giving drugs to the terminally ill to enable them to commit suicide? After all, a new cure—like new evidence—might appear shortly after death."

The *Times* ran a strong editorial on October 30, 1999 (p. A26), condemning attempts by the U.S. House to change an Oregon law that gave doctors the right to prescribe lethal drugs to terminally ill patients so that these patients could kill themselves.

The paper ridiculed the legislators as "a bad-tempered elephant, stomping and trumpeting to overturn an assisted-suicide law." (Of course, with the reference to "elephant," it takes little imagination to surmise that the paper's finger-pointing was directed toward its Republican enemies in Congress.)

Let's be clear about one thing: the issues involved here aren't limited merely to relieving pain during a terminal illness or medicating patients who have already entered a coma. Rather, this Oregon law allowed those who were judged to be terminally ill, with up to six months to live, to agree to be killed by a doctor through a drug overdose.

The paper didn't go quite so far as to condone the philosophy of the Michigan "angel of death," Dr. Jack Kervorkian, who was responsible for the deaths of more than one hundred patients and actually killed one person on a nationally aired videotape. But any distinction between Kervorkian and the *Times'* position in this editorial seems to turn as much on style as on substance.

The editorial chiefs seemed to leave the door open to all sorts of newly sanctioned legalized killing in their final sentence: "The Senate or, failing that, President Clinton should kill this bill, and let people deal with their own issues of life and death, in states that permit it" (p. A26).

These views raise serious moral and legal questions.

For example, suppose that a person dies with the assistance and encouragement of physicians and family members. But then a month or so later, a cure is found for the illness. Or even less dramatically, suppose some new technique or medication is developed that will allow the patient to live for a couple of years instead of a few weeks or months.

Such circumstances seem disturbingly similar to the situation in death penalty cases when new evidence is uncovered that points to the innocence of the condemned prisoners. So on reflection, isn't it possible that the extremely positive view the *Times* has of active euthanasia is somewhat inconsistent with the paper's stance on the death penalty?

The paper, of course, would deny any inconsistency and point to what the management regards as the superior, controlling principle: the absolute right of the individual to control his or her own destiny.

The problem with this position, of course, if that when the sick person is depressed or has lost hope—and physicians and family members are solid in their support of a quick death—the medical deck is unfairly stacked against the patient. He or she may *seem* to choose death. But in such coercive circumstances, is the choice really informed and independent? Is the impaired will of the patient really free?

The *Times* and its followers seem overly eager to get rid of gravely ill people, perhaps because their presence appears to be too much of a burden on the caregivers. But their rationale has echoes of the pro-abortion arguments.

In other words, the desires and emotional well-being of the pregnant woman (or with euthanasia, the caregiver or potential survivor of the sick person) should be given precedence, according to this reasoning. The life of the weaker must be sacrificed for the self-interest of the stronger.

On balance, then, the problem with the *Times*' position on capital punishment is not so much that the paper opposes executions. Rather, the editors are far too aggressive in trying to select who should live and who should die. Perhaps even more troublesome from an ethical and moral perspective, they are too aggressive in favoring the healthy and the strong over the weak and defenseless.

It might make some sense if the *Times* opposed capital punishment *and* abortion *and* the aggressive use of drugs by doctors to kill a person who may actually have as long as six months to live. But such is not the case. Consequently, a thoughtful observer might question whether the paper's selective morality on these issues amounts, in the end, to no morality at all.

CHAPTER 9

THE SIN OF BROKEN PUBLIC TRUST

A major contribution the *New York Times* has made to American society over the years is the crusading spirit it has followed in ferreting out many of the corrupt, fraudulent, and other shady practices that suggest a violation of the public trust.

In most cases, it doesn't matter whether the offender bilking the public is a private individual, an elected official, or the head of a private charity or public corporation. If there is an injustice and the *Times* gets wind of it, the paper is usually capable of mobilizing the most formidable investigative journalism machinery in the world to right the perceived wrong.

CRUSADING JOURNALISM, TIMES STYLE

The *Times* can respond like a media pit pull in assailing the offenses of tobacco companies, corporate polluters, nonprofit scams, or other obvious violators of the public trust. But the editors and reporters are also on the lookout for less obvious civic sins, both in the United States and abroad.

The paper's response may take the form of a regular news story, as happened in the aftermath of the massive 1999 earthquake in Turkey. Under the headline "THE TURKISH QUAKE'S SECRET ACCOMPLICE: CORRUPTION," reporter Stephen Kinzer unmasked how "unscrupulous building contractors" had erected homes and other buildings with cheap materials, which violated basic standards of safety. The result was that many innocent people who might have been spared died in the collapse of defectively built structures (9/29/99, Week in Review, p. 3).

The *Times* was also on the case when word surfaced from the Federal Trade Commission that hundreds of Web sites were promoting phony cures for many health problems, including AIDS, multiple sclerosis, liver disease, and cancer (6/25/99, p. A16). In an article with a biting headline that would have made my old *Daily News* editors proud—"TRADE AGENCY FINDS WEB SLIPPERY WITH SNAKE OIL"—reporter Sheryl Gay Stolberg helped alert the Web-surfing public to the danger.

Such reporting is one of the reasons I will always read the *Times*, regardless of its other deficiencies. In a paper with a smaller news hole or less concerned editors, such a threat to the public welfare could easily be overlooked.

The editors are also quick to report charges of violation of the public trust in non-government organizations—such as the scandals that plagued the International Olympic Committee (I.O.C.) in 1999. A one-year search of the *Times*' Web archives from November 1, 1998, through November 1, 1999, turned up 186 articles on the IOC and eight editorials on the evidence of bribery of Olympic officials so that sites like Salt Lake City could secure a favored status.

A typical news headline, which ran across almost the entire top of the SportsFriday section on January 22, 1999, said: "CORRUPTION IS EXTENSIVE, I.O.C. OFFICIAL FINDS" (p. C21). In similar fashion, the headlines of many editorials provided such solid condemnations that it almost wasn't necessary to read the accompanying articles to get the point:

"HIGH NOON FOR THE IOC" (3/15/99)

"THE WIDENING OLYMPIC SCANDAL" (2/11/99)

"FIRE THE OLYMPIC PATRIARCH" (2/26/99)

There is no question that the *Times* has been quick to respond to signs of broken trust when non-governmental organizations and agencies are involved. But the situation becomes a little stickier when politics enter the picture.

Is the Times Too Cozy with the Political Establishment?

Over the years the *Times* has been criticized for being too close to the political establishment and thus unable to provide truly detached and critical coverage of political issues. For example, some have charged that the coziness has caused the organization to respond too slowly to questionable international policies, such as the Vietnam War and other foreign military ventures.

With a free press, there is always going to be a tension between being close enough to the government establishment to develop authoritative sources and encourage news leaks, and yet not so close as to cause the news organization's independence to be totally preempted. To its credit, the *Times* has regularly run articles calling for government reforms and accountability when it seemed that the public trust was in jeopardy.

One illustration is the paper's ongoing effort to secure campaign finance reform in national elections. In a typical nagging editorial on this issue, entitled "CRUNCH TIME FOR REFORM," the top editors railed against the "corruption of the political system by special interests using an alleged loophole in the campaign laws" (5/22/99, p. A26).

The main targets of the *Times'* attack were congressional leaders who were dragging their heels for reform because they were benefiting from big money from oil, tobacco, gambling, and other interests. Predictably, the paper focused mainly on Republican offenders. Still, in a backhanded complement, they grudgingly acknowledged that "the grumpy Republican majority leader and no fan of clean up campaign laws," Dick Armey, was also on board with the reform effort.

But too often, partisan carping and posturing—when the favored Democratic Party is involved in dirty dealings—has at various times tended to compromise the paper's crusading image. Again, the *Times'* treatment of the scandal-ridden Clinton White House provides a ready illustration.

CLINTON JUST WON'T GO AWAY!

As we've already seen, the *Times* found itself in something of a quandary with the antics of Bill Clinton. The management couldn't bring itself to call for the Democratic president's resignation. Yet at the same time, they couldn't condone his most egregious breaches of the public trust—nor would they agree to compromise institutions and procedures that they felt were still bulwarks to protect the public trust.

For example, the paper condemned the president's attempts to shield his misconduct from public scrutiny by misusing the executive privilege doctrine (see editorial, 5/4/98, p. A22).

Of course, critics of the paper could argue that the *Times* was just operating in its own self-interest here because the precedent of hiding behind executive privilege could have worked against free news gathering in other situations in the future. In fact, the *Times* admitted its motives quite openly in the editorial: "News organizations, including The New York Times, have been actively fighting the secrecy rules."

But the *Times* was capable of looking mainly to the public's interest, and not just to its own self interest—on at least one occasion, after the dust from the impeachment battle had settled. In a rather remarkable editorial, "FIXING THE INDEPENDENT COUNSEL ACT," the paper went against prevailing opinion across the entire political spectrum and actually advocated that the independent counsel law, under which the dreaded Kenneth Starr had operated, be retained with modifications (6/28/99, p. A20).

After blaming both Clinton and Starr for "[undermining] public confidence in the independent counsel law," the *Times* concluded on a higher note:

> "It would be a disservice to the nation if Congress used their conduct as an excuse to scrap an important mechanism that can hold top leaders accountable for wrongdoing."

The *Times* is at its best when acting as self-appointed watchdog to guard the public welfare. In this role, the paper has helped define the highest standards for what is sometimes called the "fourth branch of government," or the "Fourth Estate"—the free and fair public press.

The crusading efforts of the *Times* might by themselves justify the paper's claims to preeminence, fairness, and even impartiality in covering all the news that's fit to print. Indeed, there might even be reason to agree with the self-serving jacket copy on the 1999 *Times'* style and usage manual, which immodestly describes the media leader as the "World's Most Authoritative Newspaper" (see review in the *New York Times Book Review*, p. 17, on the *New York Times Manual of Style and Usage* [New York: Times Books/Random House, 1999]).

Unfortunately, at the very moment when the *Times* may seem to be scaling some sort of journalistic Olympus, the paper's strong cultural advocacy and attempts at proselytism always bring it right back down to earth. This tendency toward bias and imbalance becomes even more evident as we consider the methods used by the paper to conduct witch-hunts against those who are suspected of other "deadly sins" condemned by the paper.

CHAPTER 10

THE SIN OF THE SECOND AMENDMENT

The fifth deadly sin according to the *New York Times* is free access to firearms.

If the *Times* had its way, draconian limits would be placed on the right to possess guns in the United States. Still, in its play of news stories, op-ed pieces, and editorials, the paper has shown strong signs of political realism in outlining the preliminary steps that our society might take to move us finally to a weaponless state.

In other words, even though it seems that the *Times* would have no objections if somehow every gun in America could be registered or even confiscated, it's equally clear to those who run the paper that this is not going to happen overnight. Consequently, the *Times* seems content to pursue a relatively low-key strategy of moving American public opinion toward an anti-gun position.

Even as the paper maneuvers to chip away at the freedom of individual citizens to own firearms, the ultimate objective remains the promotion of a basic "gun control doctrine," which would severely restrict the right of any private person to own or use firearms.

THE BASIC GUN CONTROL DOCTRINE

Any position on gun control must begin with an interpretation of the Second Amendment to the U.S. Constitution. The amendment reads this way:

> "A well-regulated Militia being necessary to the security of a free State, the right of the people to keep and bear Arms shall not be infringed."

Generally speaking, those who advocate placing no limits on the rights of the individual American citizen to own firearms—such as the National Rifle Association (NRA)—would emphasize the "right of the people" provision in the last part of the amendment.

In contrast, those who believe that the government should control the individual use and possession of guns would stress the "well-regulated Militia" phrase at the beginning of the Amendment.

The *Times*—which falls into the latter category of strict control advocates—summed up its basic gun control doctrine rather well in a 1999 editorial entitled, "BREAKING A GUN-CONTROL BARRIER" (6/17/99, p. A24).

The occasion for the editorial was the response of the Democratic presidential candidates, Vice President Al Gore and former Senator Bill Bradley, to an appeal for gun control by a group of Colorado teenagers. As part of the aftermath of the Columbine High School shooting, the teens had visited the Capitol to call for strict regulations on firearms, and Gore and Bradley didn't disappoint.

The *Times'* editorial writers cited with special approval Bradley's program. He called for a complete ban on cheap handguns

("Saturday night specials"); a rule that all prospective gun buyers would have to pass a safety course and secure a license; and a requirement that all guns would have to be registered with governmental authorities.

The top editors and management expressed some reservations about Gore's views because they felt he didn't go quite far enough with his proposal. Also, they dismissed the leading Republican presidential candidate, George W. Bush, for backing a "watered down gun-show provision" and for signing a Texas law that banned lawsuits against gun manufacturers for their marketing practices.

The editorial concluded with this kicker: "Mr. Gore and Mr. Bradley have added something new to the Democratic race. They have also made it harder for Mr. Bush to ignore the strong popular support for strict gun control."

But as might be expected, the *Times*' position on gun control is more detailed than this. For example, after a 1998 shooting at an Oregon public school, the paper ran an editorial emphasizing the need for laws that would prevent children from "getting their hands on loaded guns" (5/22/98, p. A24).

The editors cited approvingly a bill proposed by a New York legislator, which would have imposed criminal sanctions on adults who failed to lock up their firearms and required gun makers to produce safer, childproof weapons.

A perusal of the news stories over a period of several months reveals many other nuances in the *Times*' gun-control position. Even more importantly, these articles show how the paper has orchestrated coverage of this issue to move politicians and the public toward stricter regulation of firearms.

WATCHING THE TIMES WORK THE CROWD

To illustrate how the *Times* manipulates the gun control debate by implanting certain ideas in the mind of the reading public, consider this sequence of stories, spanning the period from May through October of 1999.

The stories began with the deep public concern generated by the school shootings at Columbine High School in Colorado and elsewhere. The *Times* obviously saw these tragedies as an opportunity to push its belief in strict control of firearms. But the outcome was not quite what the paper had hoped for or expected.

In the wake of the Columbine High School shooting tragedy, another boy was charged in Georgia with the non-fatal shooting of several high-school classmates. In reporting the story, the *Times* emphasized in a headline, "BOY TOOK PARENT'S GUNS FOR ATTACK, SHERIFF SAYS" (5/22/99, p. A8).

The implied message: laws should be passed to punish adults whose guns get into the hands of children.

On the same day, the paper ran a front-page story with headlines that were designed to generate enthusiasm for reform. The headline on the front page read:

HOUSE DEMOCRATS PRESS EARLY VOTE ON FIREARMS BILL— G.O.P. BACKS SOME LIMITS—GUN CONTROL GAINS MOMENTUM, EVEN AS SOME REPUBLICANS COMPLAIN OF THEATRICS (5/22/99, p. A1).

An implied message: Reform is a real possibility, but if anything happens to derail the momentum, the Republicans will be at fault.

On the jump page, the *Times* continued to hammer away with two sidebar stories. One dealt with special "small-print" provisions of the gun bill, which would help stanch the flow of illegal guns to criminals and children. Another focused on how Democratic Senator Max Cleland of Georgia had, in effect, been "converted" from a pro-gun position to a belief closer to the *Times'* doctrine of strict background checks for those who buy weapons at gun shows (5/22/99, p. A10).

The message: There is hope for change in even the worst sinners who believe in a broad right to bear arms.

The very next day the paper ran a high-profile feature in the Sunday Week in Review suggesting that even though the gun-control measures that had passed in the Senate the previous week were inadequate, at least some progress was being made (5/22/99, p. 3).

In the Week in Review section one week later, two major stories on gun control suggested that "the earth finally moved, at least politically speaking," after the tragic Columbine High School shootings in Littleton, Colorado (5/30/99, p. 3). In one of these reports, the paper suggested that the power of the National Rifle Association had been undercut by the series of school shootings.

In the other story, the *Times* conceded the possible validity of new legal interpretations of the Second Amendment by liberal scholars, such as Harvard's Laurence H. Tribe—interpretations that the paper said were a "nightmare for gun-control advocates." The story did quote Tribe as saying that most existing and proposed gun-control measures would probably be ruled constitutional, however (5/30/99, p. 3).

The *Times* even opened its op-ed page to Tribe a few months later to let him explain his position, which turned out to occupy a middle road between confiscation of all private firearms and an absolute right to private ownership. Tribe argued that gun-control advocates might gain the confidence of many Second Amendment supporters if they moved more to the center. But he ended by saying:

> "Conversely, gun control critics would have greater credibility if they dropped their insistence that virtually no restrictions are permissible. Sometimes, the truth—both constitutionally and democratically—lies at neither extreme" (10/28/99, p. A25).

Overall, Tribe's position appeared to be less extreme than that of the *Times*. The messages in the paper's editorials and editorialized news story showed that the *Times* preferred a stricter gun control position than either Tribe or the U.S. Constitution would allow.

But in the *Times'* view, Tribe's opinions evidently represented some movement in the right direction—i.e., toward greater restrictions on gun ownership. So the paper acknowledged Tribe's viewpoint and then continued to highlight stories on the broader movement to restrict firearm possession and use.

On May 31, 1999, the paper ran a front-page piece that proclaimed, "GUN CONTROL LAWS GAINING SUPPORT IN MANY STATES—PRO-FIREARMS BILLS FADE—FRESH RESOLVE IN LEGISLATURES AS MEASURES WIN CONVERTS IN LITTLETON'S AFTERMATH" (p. A1). Positioned on the far right column on page one, this was the lead article in the paper that day.

The jump page headline for this story continued to hammer away at the anti-gun message: "ACROSS THE U.S., THE STATES PRESS HARD FOR GUN CONTROLS—BACKGROUND CHECKS, LOCKS AND 'SMART GUNS' ARE CONSIDERED IN STATEHOUSES—FRESH RESOLVE BACKS A VARIETY OF NEW AND OLD GUN-CONTROL MEASURES" (p. A9). The tremendous power of headlines is evident in this story. A reader could easily get the main message in the story just by reading the heads and subheads.

In a sidebar on how gun owners and the NRA were afraid of a gun-control movement in Connecticut, the opponents of gun control were pictured as on the defensive. Also, the final two paragraphs referred to a Republican governor who had, in effect, "converted" to the gun-control side and a Democratic representative who was also a strong gun-control advocate.

An article in the *Times* Sunday Magazine on June 13, 1999, entitled "PLAYING WITH FIREARMS," made fun of best-selling novelist Tom Clancy's conservative, anti-gun-control views. Then a series of news stories over the next few months kept the issue in the public spotlight.

One story linked gun flow to criminals to a tiny fraction of firearms dealers (7/1/99, p. A12). Another report described a movement to require "smart-gun" technology in New Jersey, which would make guns unusable by anyone other than the authorized owner (7/2/99, p. A16). On the same day, the paper ran a front-page story on a California measure that restricted the purchase of handguns to one per month (p. A1).

Also, resorting to a favorite *Times'* theme of how the usually conservative Republicans were doing an about-face on their firearms philosophy, the paper featured a story on September 4, 1999, headlined: "MANY G.O.P. GOVERNORS NOW PUSHING FOR GREATER GUN CONTROL" (p. A7).

The apparent message: A movement against unrestricted gun ownership is building! Even the Republicans are caving in!

❖

The *Times'* views on the "deadly sin" of the Second Amendment provide an excellent lesson about the complexity that's involved as any institution—even the most powerful news organization in the world—attempts to shape and change the attitudes of an entire culture.

In a free society, monolithic views on important or "hot" cultural issues rarely exist, and that principle holds true for gun control. It's simply not realistic to expect everyone who considers himself a conservative to think exactly the same way as all other conservatives. The same principle goes for those who call themselves liberals.

So on the conservative side we should expect that at one end of the spectrum some people would oppose any effort to control individual ownership of firearms. But other conservatives, such as some of the Republican politicians cited by the *Times*, might go along with some restrictions.

Similarly, some liberals—such as a number of the scholars and Ivy League professors cited regularly by the *Times*—would interpret the Second Amendment to eliminate practically every right to individual ownership of firearms. But other liberals, such as Harvard Law Professor Laurence Tribe, would take a more moderate stance.

Where does the *Times* stand in this debate?

The paper is clearly in the far-left gun-control camp—and as the *Times* goes, so goes the rest of the national news media. What you hear about gun control on your television news and what you read about in your local paper will probably be influenced in some way by the position that the *New York Times* has staked out in its pages in recent months.

Currently, this position seems to involve two distinct strategies: 1) the confiscation of Saturday night specials and probably other handguns, and 2) mass, unlimited registration of all other weapons.

In the *Times* worldview, one of the deadliest of sins is to interpret the Second Amendment in such a way that the individual citizen retains any significant right to bear arms. Only the federal government can be trusted with this responsibility. Moreover, through the process of Culture Creep, you can expect this message to seep into your consciousness through other news sources—whether you happen to be a *Times* reader or not.

CHAPTER 11

THE SIN OF CENSORSHIP

In the worldview propounded by the *New York Times*, one of the greatest cultural sins is censorship—an offense that especially focuses on any interference with the exercise of freedom of the press.

The term "censorship" is derived from the title of certain early Roman officials called *censores*, whose many duties included monitoring and shaping public morals and conduct. For the *Times*, the most flagrant expression of this activity today would be any attempt to influence or discourage what a news organization plans to print or broadcast. After all, only the *Times* and those who follow its lead have the right and duty to influence public morality!

Secondary censorship violations include any effort to discourage social activists, writers, artists, or others from spreading beliefs espoused by the *Times*.

The paper regards the sin of censorship to be so important that articles on the subject appear on average nearly once a day. (A search of the paper's Web site archives showed that "censorship" was featured in 267 articles during the year ending November 8, 1999.)

But paradoxically, the paper doesn't hesitate to act as censor itself. For example, the *Times* is more than ready to serve as self-appointed guardian of American values when certain religious groups, such as evangelical Christians, attempt to exercise their rights to free expression in the "wrong" way. As we have already seen, the *Times* will not tolerate Christian groups that speak out against plays, art exhibits, or other events that those groups regard as immoral or blasphemous.

The spiritual authority to which the *Times* appeals in condemning this mortal sin of censorship involves a peculiar, absolutist view of part of the First Amendment.

ABSOLUTE FAITH IN THE PRESS

The *New York Times* believes that the First Amendment right to freedom of the press is virtually absolute. In other words, in the best of all possible worlds, no restrictions should be placed on the right of journalists to report the news and comment upon it.

To understand the full implications of the paper's absolutist position, it's important to consider the press provision in its constitutional context. The entire First Amendment reads this way:

"Congress shall make no law respecting an establishment of religion, or prohibiting the free exercise thereof; *or abridging the freedom of speech, or of the press;* of the right of the people peaceably to assemble, and to petition the Government for a redress of grievances" (emphasis added).

This amendment, which has been applied to the states through the Fourteenth Amendment, establishes six distinct freedoms:

1. Freedom from governmental establishment of any religion
2. Freedom to exercise one's religious beliefs
3. Freedom of speech
4. Freedom of the press
5. Freedom to assemble peaceably, and

6. Freedom to petition the government for redress of grievances

Of course, many U.S. Supreme Court decisions over the years have interpreted and fleshed out the meaning of these freedoms. Furthermore, from a constitutional viewpoint, the six First Amendment freedoms are generally equal in the sense that one isn't more important than the others.

But the *Times* has devised its own version of the Constitution when it comes to freedom of the press. The paper seems to regard that right as practically absolute, and, in effect, superior to the other freedoms.

It's evident, for instance, that the *Times* wouldn't make absolutist claims for the other First Amendment rights, such as freedom of religion, speech, or assembly (see the discussion in chapters 3 and 5 about how the *Times* pushed for restriction of the exercise of these rights when religious groups protested the *Corpus Christi* play).

If you asked a typical *Times* reporter or editor why this free-press principle is so important and even superior to the freedom of religion and other First Amendment freedoms, the answer might go something like this:

- "A free press is the cornerstone of a free society."
- "Independent journalists are our only insurance policy for keeping politicians and bureaucrats honest."
- Relying on the usual Ivy League authority, *Times* reporter Nina Bernstein said in a feature on pornographer Larry Flynt: "If America has a civic religion, as the Harvard scholar Henry Louis Gates, Jr. has observed, the First Amendment is its central article of faith" (12/22/96, Sec. 2, p. 1).
- If they did a little digging, true *Times*' believers might wind up quoting Alexis de Tocqueville, the French observer of American life in the 1830s, who wrote: ". . . the press is the chief democratic instrument of freedom" (Toqueville, 2:343).

Apart from these high-flown principles and ideals, there are more mundane, pocketbook reasons for the *Times'* affirmation of a virtually absolute press freedom. After all, without a broad right to publish whatever they please—short of clearly actionable libel—the profit potential of even so august a news organization as the *Times* would shrink.

So publishing "all the news that's fit to print" must include the right to gather and disseminate as much news as consumers are willing to buy. This money motive dictates that the paper retain extremely wide powers for choosing what goes into its pages. Censorship of any type could easily mean fewer interesting and marketable (and sometimes salacious) stories—and fewer reporters and editors who would go home with a full paycheck.

But what exactly constitutes a true "reporter," "editor," or "journalist"—a legitimate news gatherer who qualifies for broad rights and privileges under the First Amendment? And just how far would the *Times* go to bestow power on these revered news representatives—and shelter them from outside regulation or control?

WHAT'S A "JOURNALIST"?

Legitimate press membership—or those whom the *Times* would admit into its approved, elite news club of "real journalists"—is relatively limited under the paper's standards.

First of all, the "established media," according to the *Times*, consists of other traditional newspapers and selected electronic news organizations, such as network and public broadcasting news divisions. Most other purveyors of information don't qualify.

In an editorial headlined "FIGHTING OFF THE FLYNT VIRUS," the *Times* said that "smut" magazines—such as Larry Flynt's *Hustler*—should not be regarded as "just another branch of the established media." Nevertheless, the paper's management went on to concede in a rather snooty tone that the "First Amendment offers protection to all varieties of the media, even Matt Drudge, who shovels raw gossip onto the Internet."

Granted, the iconoclastic Matt Drudge may have pushed the outside of the envelope in his rush to get news snippets out into the public arena before the more sluggish *Times*. But it seems a mite hypocritical for the *Times* to look down its nose at Drudge. After all, Drudge was, on occasion, at the forefront of breaking news during the Clinton-Lewinsky scandal. In contrast, the *Times* often trailed well behind.

Yet even as the *Times* was struggling along back in the pack, it didn't always observe the highest journalistic standards. For example, according to the Committee of Concerned Journalists— an independent watchdog group with many representatives from the mainstream secular news media—the *Times* based almost 50 percent of its early coverage of the scandal on anonymous sources (see *www.journalis.org/Clintonreport2.htm.*, p. 2).

Not Quite a Profession

The *Times* has acknowledged in its own reporting that the line between news and entertainment has become blurry. Also, the paper has had to admit that the U.S. courts haven't defined what a journalist is (10/24/98, p. A10).

Furthermore, there is no real consensus among news organizations, legal experts, or anyone else about the definition of a reporter or journalist. In fact, journalism isn't really even a profession, at least not in the normal sense of the word. To get into the news business, you don't have to pass a professional test or be licensed by a government or other official body, as lawyers, doctors, and certified public accountants must do. You don't have to go to graduate school in the field or even take any college courses in journalism.

For that matter, you don't have to go to college at all! You can just set up an Internet site that puts out information, start circulating a newsletter, or just pass out some news releases. If you decide to call yourself a journalist, bingo, you become a journalist.

If you are part of a new or fly-by-night operation, old-line papers such as the *Times* might not regard you as being on their level. They might even argue that you are not really a journalist, and you might have trouble getting a police press pass. But as long as you're acting like a reporter, you have as many legal and constitutional protections as more established or conventional news gatherers do.

The Ultimate Goal: Greed or Power?

In the last analysis—as much as the *Times* or other traditional news organizations might like to think otherwise—journalism consists largely of a combination of entertainment and muckraking with some public service stories sprinkled in for good measure. The reason for this is that the ultimate objective of the press is as much to secure and retain paying customers as it is to fulfill some higher civic purpose.

For a news organization to succeed, the bottom line must always be linked directly to the deadline. If reporters and editors are late delivering their material, or if the material is dull or uninteresting, circulation and ad revenues will decline.

By definition, news is "new" or fresh material for which readers, viewers, or listeners are willing to pay. Advertising dollars follow increased paid circulation, especially when that circulation is comprised of elite or well-heeled patrons. Needless to say, a news organization that doesn't maintain healthy circulation won't be in business very long.

But even though profits may come first with the "newspaper of record," power—the ability to influence minds and opinions—is a close second. The *Times*, probably more than any other news organization, is driven by the desire to shape individual and societal standards through Culture Creep. We have witnessed the range of this raging ambition clearly in the previous pages.

Thus, the paper's obsession with upholding the freedom of the press as an absolute social and moral virtue is firmly rooted in self-interest. Freedom to operate means freedom to maximize income, and to wield the greatest possible cultural power.

Is the Times Above the Law?

In upholding a virtually absolute principle of press freedom, the *Times* expects reporters to be so intrepid in their news gathering that they will go to practically any length to do their jobs, even to the point of breaking the law.

The *Times* may not be above the law—but sometimes the paper's managers seem to think they are. At least that was the basic message conveyed in a *Times* editorial about a Cincinnati *Enquirer* reporter who "proceeded to reveal to the court the name of one of his major sources" (4/7/99, p. A22).

Although many murky, labyrinthine issues were involved in the case, the *Times* came down hardest on the reporter's decision to comply with a legitimate court order to disclose the names of those who had given him information for a story.

The *Times* declared that the reporter "certainly has every right to mount a vigorous defense, but his decision to disclose sources betrays the most basic code of what is undoubtedly now his former profession. The contract between a source and a journalist is one of the sacred bonds, and many a reporter has promised to go to jail to protect such an agreement."

In other words, the message from the *Times* to the Cincinnati reporter was this: break the law rather than disclose your sources.

Again, we have a clear affirmation of freedom of the press as an absolute moral and cultural principle—which should prevail even over the law of the land.

Standards of the "Profession"

There are some limits the *Times* would place on reporters and editors. First of all, reporters are required to get their basic facts right. At the same time, there is an unspoken assumption that it is acceptable to slant the facts, or select and arrange them to promote the paper's worldview. But still, the facts that are chosen, and the quotations that are used, must be correct.

Over the years, a number of reporters have gotten into trouble and even lost their jobs because they concocted facts for their stories. For example, a spate of reports in 1998 charged that certain columns at the *Times*-owned *Boston Globe* contained fabricated material, including fictitious people and quotations. The reporter at the center of the controversy resigned (6/22/98, p. C7; *WSJ*, 6/22,98, p. B6).

The *Times* certainly did not approve of the practice of trying to pass off fiction as fact. But the paper's executive editor, Joseph Lelyveld, noted, "We operate from a position of trust in our reporters" (6/22/98, p. C7).

❖

On the whole, then, the *Times* sees its mission as the highest, most sacred endeavor known to humankind. The freedom of the press occupies a position as an absolute principle of faith in the *Times'* gospel. Attempting to censor what the paper publishes is a mortal sin—almost like censoring revelation from God would be reprehensible for a believing Christian, Muslim, or Jew.

But the paper has indicated that it may be appropriate to limit the rights to free speech and assembly when those rights threaten the values held dear by the *Times*. In the next chapter, we'll see that dissent doesn't sit well with the *Times* when one of those values—the unlimited right to an abortion—is called into question.

CHAPTER 12

THE SIN OF LIMITING ABORTION

The *New York Times* favors a broad, apparently unlimited right of a woman to have an abortion. A brief survey of the paper's editorials and play of news stories shows not only the remarkable range of the *Times'* far-reaching beliefs in abortion, but also its strategy for spreading those beliefs.

THE TIMES' ABORTION BELIEFS— A STATEMENT OF FAITH IN THE PAPER'S OWN WORDS

To begin with, the paper has staked out its position at the far edge of the abortion debate by supporting unequivocally the extreme procedure known as "partial birth abortion."

This operation—known technically as "dilation and extraction" ("D&X") or "intact dilation and evacuation" ("intact D&E")—may be performed in a late-term pregnancy (second or third trimester) on a "viable" fetus, or an unborn child who could survive outside the womb.

It works like this: The doctor induces delivery of the fetus, with the feet exiting the birth canal first. Then, with about a quarter of the upper body, including the head, still in the birth canal, the physician punctures the unborn child's head, sucks out the brain, and removes the body "intact" (hence, the medical name for the operation).

Many have cautioned that the line between this partial-birth procedure and outright infanticide can easily become blurred. For one thing, most premature babies born after eight months or even a shorter period in the womb are well enough developed to go directly home after birth without special treatment or hospitalization.

Even more ominous, most avid abortion supporters—such as the *Times* and Planned Parenthood—fail to deal seriously or consistently with important philosophical questions. For example, how are we to draw biological, emotional, or spiritual distinctions between the infant who has just been born and the viable unborn infant who still has a few seconds, hours, or days to go before normal delivery?

In fact, some evidence suggests that the *Times* may be testing the waters for public support in the near future for certain forms of infanticide. As indicated in chapter 6, for instance, the staff has become enamoured with featuring the Australian philosopher, Peter Singer, who supports euthanasia of severely disabled infants and the notion that humans and animals are to be treated as morally equal (Sunday Magazine, 9/5/99, pp. 60–63).

In the meantime—until the public is ready for the next step—the *Times* is pushing the limits of abortion acceptability as hard as it dares. For example, in a May 16, 1998, editorial entitled rather provocatively, "THE PARTIAL-BIRTH STRATAGEM," the paper came out swinging against a Wisconsin law banning partial-birth abortions (p. A26). Among other things, the editorial management charged that the law is "a direct assault on the right to choose abortion as a medical decision."

By December of that year, the Seventh Circuit Court of Appeals had overturned the law, and federal courts had also thrown out similar laws in Kentucky, Arkansas, and Florida. The court decisions, like the *Times*, typically focused on the rights of the pregnant woman and assumed that the unborn child had no rights at all (see Hadley Arkes's article, *WSJ*, December 7, 1998, p. A31).

In an apparently concerted and well-orchestrated effort to chip away at the pro-life opposition, the paper has led the pro-abortion forces on other fronts through its editorials.

On one level, the *Times* has consistently attacked the motives of anti-abortion legislators as being entirely politically motivated. In "'PARTIAL BIRTH' DECEPTIONS," the editorial writers said that the "real goal" of the Republicans who supported a bill banning partial-birth abortion was "to gain an edge in next year's election" (10/20/99, p. A30).

The paper has also waged its pro-abortion war in other ways. For example, an editorial entitled "A DUBIOUS CHOICE AS HEALTH CHIEF," criticized the appointment of Antonia Novello as New York State's health commissioner solely because she was an opponent of abortion. Specifically, Novello had taken the relatively moderate position of opposing abortion, except when rape, incest, or a threat to the health of the mother was involved (6/8/99, p. A30).

The *Times* has also published editorials that favor charging anti-abortion activists as racketeers (4/23/98, p. A20) and opposed a federal bill imposing criminal penalties on anyone other than a parent who accompanied a minor who sought an abortion across state lines (6/30/99, p. A28). Predictably, the paper has also made clear its position that abortion should be a part of international family planning programs (10/13/99, p. A30).

Other commentators have noted the incredibly far-reaching nature of the *Times'* pro-abortion position. Thomas Sowell, in a column published on August 2, 1993, in *Forbes*, criticized the *Times'* ideological opposition to adoption as a compassionate alternative to abortion. He even cited approvingly another study that charged the *Times*, along with *Playboy*, with waging a media campaign against adoption (p. 67).

In a *U.S. News & World Report* article entitled "ALL THE NEWS THAT FITS OUR BIASES," John Leo highlighted the failure of the *Times* to give play to significant stories that were critical of the partial-birth abortion legislation. Specifically, he noted that on May 2, 1996, the Rev. Billy Graham had told columnist Cal Thomas that he had met with President Clinton and criticized him for vetoing the Partial-Birth Abortion Ban Act. According to Leo, a computer search "failed to turn up any mention of it in the *New York Times* and the *Boston Globe*," both of which are owned by the *Times* (June 10, 1996, p. 26).

As if that weren't enough, on the very same day the *Times* failed to report a statement by New York Senator Daniel Patrick Moynihan that he opposed Clinton's veto because partial birth abortions are "too close to infanticide." (The *New York Post* did report this quote, while the *Times* finally referred to it indirectly three weeks later in the context of another story.)

Clearly, the *Times* has a deep commitment to abortion in its many forms and stands ready to omit important anti-abortion stories and to savage pro-life advocates who would dare to push for any restrictions. But the question remains, Why is the paper such an abortion advocate?

WHY IS THE TIMES SUCH AN AVID SUPPORTER OF ABORTION?

The stated reason for the paper's strong belief in abortion rights is a woman's "right to choose" or exercise complete control over her reproductive functions and her life as a whole. Hence, the "pro-choice" label favored by pro-abortion advocates.

Here's how the editorial writers expressed their position in a March 22, 1999, editorial called "THE NEW ABORTION RHETORIC" (p. A24).

". . . the abortion debate, no matter how it is presented, is always about each woman's right to make her own intensely personal decisions relating to pregnancy."

In other variations on this theme, the paper has emphasized that each woman should be able to make her decisions in consultation with her doctor and no one else. In this view, pregnancy is a medical matter that relates only to the pregnant female.

There are serious problems with this rather reductionistic and simplistic line of reasoning. One major difficulty, of course, is that focusing only on the woman fails to take into account any rights of the unborn child.

Abortion supporters have fought long and hard to keep courts, pundits—and shapers of public opinion like the *Times*—from conceding that the fetus has anything to do with humanity. Heaven forbid that at any point, even moments before a full-term birth, an unborn child could be regarded as a "person"!

If that ever happens, Locke and Jefferson's rights to "life, liberty, and property," "due process of law," and other constitutional mandates will automatically come into play. The unborn child with a minute to go before birth will become the equal of the newborn one minute after birth—and of the pregnant mother as well. In one fell swoop, the entire house of cards erected by abortion supporters to keep the unborn child out of the human community will collapse.

Another extremely serious flaw in the *Times'* abortion logic is the subtle assumption that pregnancy is not really that serious a business. The idea seems to be that no broader responsibilities should be attached to conception because an embryo, a fetus, or an unborn child moments before birth is essentially a cipher. It's nothing, except perhaps it is a piece of flesh. A growth. According to this view, animals and pets have more rights that protect them against cruel treatment than a developing human being in the womb.

The underlying objective of this kind of reasoning appears to be essentially political. In a radical and seriously distorted extension of principles of basic human rights and equality, the *Times* would bestow upon the pregnant woman an absolute right to privacy over everything that is going on inside her.

According to this view, she must be given total control *not* just over her body, but *also* over her pregnancy and the life she carries in her womb, without reference to any outside impact her decisions may have. The wishes and whims of the mother must ultimately sweep away any claim to rights by the father of the unborn infant, or the unborn infant itself.

So it doesn't matter if a woman has chosen to become pregnant or engage in relationships that could carry a high risk of pregnancy. Personal responsibility isn't a consideration in the *Times'* belief system—at least not when the personal wishes of the pregnant woman are at issue.

In essence, these assumptions lie at the heart of much contemporary feminist thinking, including the brand of feminism that has been affirmed by the *Times*. The destiny and desires of the adult woman are the only considerations during pregnancy. Moral and religious principles must be bent and molded to accommodate these feminist beliefs.

A necessary casualty of this philosophy has been the unborn child. As illogical as it may seem, he or she must be defined out of existence in order to eliminate any threat to a woman's absolute dominion over her destiny. In many respects, then, the paper's crusade against the "sin" of limiting abortion stands as a distressing symbol of spiritually rootless human rights gone haywire.

As much as the *Times* rails against "fundamentalism" and traditional religious beliefs that rely heavily on Scripture, the paper is itself incapable of supplanting time-tested religion and spirituality. As hard as it may try, the organization simply lacks the philosophical horsepower or depth to create a credible and comprehensive new faith. Yet without solid moral and ethical underpinnings—such as the biblical principles that guided John Locke—any attempt to establish an authentic and balanced set of individual rights must fail.

On the other hand, when the idea of rights is sown in fertile philosophical and spiritual soil, the concept can grow and blossom. And in the end, everyone—men and women, the born and the unborn—will have the opportunity to benefit and flourish.

In Part II, we have focused primarily on certain major "sins"—beliefs or activities that the *New York Times* opposes. Now, in Part III we'll turn to what, for want of a better word, I've called the cultural "spirits" that rule the paper's corporate culture.

PART III

THE CULTURAL SPIRITS
OF THE TIMES

CHAPTER 13

THE SPIRITS OF GLOBALISM AND MULTICULTURALISM

Globalism and multiculturalism—like the other *Times*' beliefs discussed in this third section—are "cultural spirits" in the sense that they really are active, invisible forces that guide and influence the paper's approach to news coverage.

On occasion, they almost seem to take on a life of their own as they shape and influence the *Times*' corporate culture. And as we have already seen, this corporate culture plays a major role in determining how individual editors and reporters—acting both consciously and subconsciously—gather, write, and present the news and help transform public attitudes and beliefs, including your own.

THE FOREIGN CONNECTION

The *New York Times* prides itself as being an international newspaper, and rightly so. The paper's coverage of foreign affairs, both in news stories and columns, is comprehensive and incisive and often worthy of the many journalism prizes that the reporting has generated.

But the *Times'* international coverage shouldn't be viewed just as the product of the isolated activities of a separate foreign affairs desk or division. Rather, this foreign reporting must be placed in the broader context of an attempt to promote on a global scale a comprehensive package of *Times*-certified values.

These values include the paper's affirmation of an approved international policy as well as a package of human rights, which mirrors many of the domestic rights we've already discussed. The driving force in spreading the gospel of the *Times* abroad is specially related to two important processes known as *globalism* and *globalization*.

What's the Difference between Globalization and Globalism?

Globalization refers to the tendency of ideas, products, and technologies to spread around the earth without any special centralized help or guidance from those who promote a particular, overarching philosophy or national policy. The proliferation of computerized technology and American fast-food restaurant chains over practically every part of the earth are examples of the globalization of particular types of American businesses.

In these situations, a specific corporate strategy to "go international" may be operative. But such plans usually focus on relatively limited interests and goals—such as making money by opening new markets for a particular consumer product.

On the other hand, *globalism* involves a more comprehensively planned strategy or policy, designed to affect most of the international scene—or to achieve globalization according to a broad, preconceived worldview. Many, if not most, of the *Times'* news articles on foreign events have been coordinated with editorials and columns to promote the paper's special philosophy of *globalism*—which includes the promotion of the *Times'* gospel on an international scale.

An Overview of the Times Brand of Globalism

In a nutshell, the *Times'* philosophy of globalism stands for such principles as:

- The gradual subordination of the nation state—including the United States—and the increasing ascendance of a one-world polity, presided over by international organizations such as the United Nations and the World Trade Organization
- The enforcement of sanctions against nations and individuals that violate basic human rights, as defined by international declarations and approved by the *Times*
- The banning of nuclear testing and weapons
- The opening of trade and other connections with potentially hostile foreign powers, such as China

Such political observers as William Kristol, Robert Kagan, and Marvin Olasky have argued in the *Times* and *World* magazine that this approach to foreign policy, which has been pursued by the Clinton administration, is wrong headed. They preferred the tack taken by Teddy Roosevelt and later by Ronald Reagan, who stood for the proposition that America should enter the international arena from a position of great military strength. At the same time, they criticized the global style pushed by Woodrow Wilson and Jimmy Carter, who placed more of an emphasis on international agreements and cooperation than on American arms (10/25/99, p. A27; *World*, 6/26/99, p. 46).

Some recent editorial positions taken by the *Times* highlight specific ingredients of the paper's concept of globalism:

Ingredient #1: The Promotion of Human Rights. In a rather superficial historical overview entitled "THE POWERFUL IDEA OF HUMAN RIGHTS," the *Times* affirmed the growing international condemnation of genocide, slavery, torture, and arbitrary arrest and extolled the movement to provide everyone on earth with rights to freedom of speech and assembly. One of the main contemporary vehicles for these developments, the paper said, was the Universal Declaration of Human Rights approved by the United Nations in 1948 (12/8/99, p. A30).

As we've seen in other contexts, the *Times* also supports the broadening of international protections for journalists, women, and minority groups. In addition, the paper has voiced intermittent protests against religious persecution abroad, including occasional mild disapproval of the persecution of Christians. (Since the firing of columnist A. M. Rosenthal in 1999, however, the *Times*' opposition to Christian persecution has been even more muted.)

Ingredient #2: Attacks on Isolationism. Isolationism—the idea that it's best for the United States to minimize involvement in foreign affairs—is the antithesis of the *Times*' globalist philosophy. In an October 31, 1999, editorial attacking the return of isolationist advocacy, the paper called instead for "an expansive worldview that defines broader diplomatic engagement and leadership by the United States as necessary components of national security and global stability" (p. 14).

One practical way that the *Times* has parted company with those who advocate some form of American disengagement from the world scene is its support of United States participation in international peacekeeping forces to prevent mass murder or other violations of human rights.

For example, in a September 8, 1999, editorial headlined "EAST TIMOR UNDER SIEGE," the paper called for the United Nations Security Council to form a "quick-reaction international peacekeeping force" and use it to compel Indonesia to end the violence in its land (p. A28).

An Editorial Observer column signed by Tina Rosenberg and published as part of the regular editorial page went even further in stating the globalist position on outside intervention: ". . . the war in Kosovo punctured the sanctity of state sovereignty—the idea that a nation's actions within its borders are its own business" (8/2/99, p. A18).

In other words, the *Times* looks forward to a day when "state sovereignty is no more."

Ingredient #3: A Ban on Nuclear Tests. The *Times* has fought consistently to ban nuclear testing and eliminate the proliferation of nuclear weapons abroad.

For example, the paper favored the 1996 Comprehensive Test Ban Treaty, which must be signed by all nuclear powers to become binding. A strong editorial severely criticized Senate Republicans as well as presidential contender George W. Bush for opposing the treaty (9/5/99, p. 10). The paper also attacked the Republicans and Bush for supporting a stronger missile defense system (11/20/99, p. A26).

With this stand, the *Times* again placed heavy reliance on global agreements and international cooperation and deemphasized the role of American military might as the most effective means to ensure peace in the future.

Ingredient #4: Favoritism toward China. In general, the *Times* has favored opening American markets to potentially hostile nations like China and welcoming the Chinese into the World Trade Organization and other international bodies.

Furthermore, the paper has been rather selective in insisting that the Chinese observe principles of human rights within China. In particular, the *Times* has shown a willingness to embrace China without first requiring the country to institute strong sanctions against such rights abuses as freedom from religious persecution.

The reasoning, which has emerged in such editorials as "OPENING CHINA'S MARKETS," is that opening trade and other contacts immediately would be a step toward "committing [China] to obey rules that apply to all other major trading partners." Such contacts would also "strengthen the hand of domestic forces fighting for the rule of law for the rest of Chinese society" (11/16/99, p. A30).

Reduced American Power

Overall, these and similar positions taken by the *Times* add up to a form of globalism that is moving steadily toward the weakening and eventual removal of national boundaries. This approach would, in effect, establish the United States as a kind of "first among equals" in the international community—but the U.S. would be relegated to the role of a firmly leashed tiger.

In other words, under the *Times'* version of world cooperation, we would often be thrust into a position of leadership. But our ability to act independently in international affairs could apparently be restricted by the whim and vote of partner countries.

Exactly how far would the *Times* go with this type of globalism?

The jury is still out. But strong signals coming from the paper's editorial, op-ed, and news sections suggest that the world of the future, according to the *New York Times*, would be a world of reduced American power, governed by detailed international agreements that control all matters of trade, human rights, and military deployments. In any event, it's likely that the United Nations or a more powerful successor to that organization would oversee the entire show.

The Fate of Conservative Christianity

How would conservative religious groups, such as evangelical Christians and traditional Catholics, fare in this new global village?

The answer to this question comes back to the *Times'* definition of "human rights" for the world, which would undoubtedly have to include all the rights now pushed by the *Times* in the United States. These include an unlimited right to freedom of the press, the right of women to unlimited abortions, and the right of homosexual couples to the same benefits and recognition as heterosexual married couples.

But religious freedom and protection from persecution are not a priority now—and they certainly wouldn't be if the *Times* succeeded in projecting its utopian vision on the entire earth. In short, if the rights of conservative Christian groups were protected at all under the *Times'* brave new globalism, these rights would almost certainly be subordinated to other concerns, such as international trade.

The Great Global Army

Finally, these international agreements would have to be enforced by an international "peacekeeping" force under the jurisdiction of an officer corps drawn from many different countries. Theoretically, this force would have the power to enter any nation in the world, even the United States, to correct perceived violations of human rights.

In other words, it's conceivable that at some point in the not-too-distant future, a Chinese Communist general might be poised to lead a force into the American South or Midwest. His mission? To keep the peace after violent riots have broken out over some rights issue.

In short, it seems only logical to ask, "If international peacekeepers could enter East Timor or Kosovo today, why not Kansas or Texas tomorrow?"

When could these events occur? Certainly not tomorrow. Currently, the average American wouldn't stand for such intervention.

But like the proverbial frog in the gradually heating pot, we are becoming slowly accustomed to changes in our basic values through the process of Culture Creep. Before you realize what's happening, it might seem quite normal, or even right, to have that Chinese general operating on your own soil.

THE SPIRIT OF MULTICULTURALISM

An issue closely related to globalism is the "spirit" of *multiculturalism*. The difference is that while both emphasize a comprehensive international viewpoint, globalism tends to focus on events that occur abroad. Multiculturalism, by contrast, centers mainly on the domestic scene.

The term "multiculturalism" has become the popular catchword to refer to the racial, ethnic, and religious diversity in a given social or political system. Diverse groups and individuals remain an integral part of that social system, yet at the same time they retain and celebrate their own peculiar differences.

As time goes on, more people and groups tend to be accepted as a legitimate part of the multicultural mix and are endowed with special legal privileges and statuses. In the United States, for instance, some advocates of multiculturalism would now include those of various sexual orientations, economic levels, and physical handicaps in their diversity "tent."

An important feature of the multicultural ideal is *tolerance* for all groups and individuals in the culture as a whole. (For a detailed description of the *Times'* approach to tolerance, especially with regard to conservative Christian groups, see the discussion in chapter 5.)

In the conventional understanding of the term, tolerance means that members of any historically recognized group—such as an ethnic or religious minority—should be accepted under the law as equal to anyone else. So in a society that values multiculturalism, women and African-Americans should have civil rights equal to those of white males. Also, the government should not favor or "establish" one religion over another.

Few would quarrel with these issues of multiculturalism. But when it comes to the multicultural issue of immigration, there is some disagreement.

A Special Place in the Times' Heart for Immigrants

Typically, multiculturalists of all stripes—and that would include the large majority of all Americans—believe that immigrants should be given a reasonable package of rights when they enter the United States. Furthermore, they should have equal standing with everyone else when they become full citizens. This support for a policy that welcomes immigrants is a natural outgrowth of the basic American identity as a "nation of immigrants." After all, at some point in the relatively recent past, most of us came from somewhere else.

The *Times* has consistently been at the cutting edge of supporting a broad stream of immigrants into New York City, and through New York, to the rest of the country. A headline in the December 15, 1996, issue of the paper summed up this attitude quite well: "CITY OF IMMIGRANTS, PAUSING, OFFERS A BELATED WELCOME" (p. 39).

The story, which described how the *Times*' Neediest Cases Fund has served immigrants since its inception in the early twentieth century, emphasized the paper's depth of commitment to immigrants:

> "Adolph S. Ochs, publisher of the *Times*, began the fund after encountering a pauper, an immigrant, on Christmas night in 1911. Mr. Ochs believed that if readers of his newspaper knew how some of their neighbors lived, they would want to help" (p. 39).

Whenever possible, the paper highlights the diverse, multicultural nature of New York and the nation as a whole, and more often than not, the headlines carry a strong editorial message. After the New York Yankees won the World Series in 1999, for instance, the *Times* chose to couch the main story on the team parade as a celebration of the immigration theme.

The headline across the top of the Sports Section, "CELEBRATION IN A MELTING POT," echoed a powerful description in the body of the article on the nature of New York City's relatively advanced multiculturalism:

> ". . . to understand the Yankees one must look at the diversity of the crowd that showed up at City Hall and along the parade route to celebrate the Yankees. The fans were young, they were old, they were men and women, they were all variations of white. They were also all shades of black and brown. What has been striking during the Yankees' championship runs in the last four years has been the number of Hispanics, African-Americans and West Indians who described themselves as die-hard, long-time Yankee fans" (10/30/99, p. B17).

A similar pro-immigration message—but this time with a religious twist—appeared in the September 23, 1999, paper under the headline, "ACROSS AMERICA, IMMIGRATION IS CHANGING THE FACE OF RELIGION" (p. A16).

The article focused on recent Mexican immigrants who had established a thriving, distinctively ethnic Roman Catholic parish in Iowa. The reporter concluded in an editorialized flourish: "The life of organized religion in the United States has been growing more diverse than it was two or three decades ago" (p. A16).

Multicultural Limits?

Despite the nation's long history of welcoming immigrants, not all Americans support a policy that is as favorable to arriving foreigners as that of the *Times*.

For example, conservatives concerned with national safety have warned that security at our national borders must be tightened to thwart potential terrorists. Also, some states have worried that the increased payments they have to make for social services to illegal aliens are placing undue burdens on governmental budgets. Even liberal groups, such as the Sierra Club, have cautioned that an influx of too many immigrants may put too much pressure on the American environment.

Another problem with extreme multiculturalism is more subtle and philosophical. All variations of multiculturalism are rooted in an assumption that everyone and every group, including illegal immigrants, should be treated equally under the law and social customs. But the most radical multiculturalists may push equality to the edge of common sense by arguing for the removal of most, if not all, of our immigration or border security standards.

The problem with such an extreme leveling philosophy is that it runs counter to practical experience and the needs of a nation-state. The great French observer of American life in the 1830s, Alexis de Tocqueville, foresaw both the advantages and the dangers of the deep American commitment to equality—and by implication, the possible threat of socialism. As he put it in his *Democracy in America*:

"Equality urges them on, but at the same time, it holds them back; it spurs them, but fastens them to earth; it kindles their desires, but limits their powers" (Toqueville, 2:277).

Among other things, Tocqueville warned that when equality becomes too powerful in a society, a "tyranny of the majority" may result, with individual achievement and merit depreciated or reduced to the lowest common denominator (p. 307).

In a similar vein, extreme multiculturalism may lead to the political and economic leveling that is usually associated with old-fashioned, doctrinaire socialism. The *Times* may not want to take us quite to this extreme, but the paper's worldview certainly encompasses strong elements of the welfare state, as we'll see in chapter 15.

In the social sphere, a belief in virtually absolute equality can also pose problems for multiculturalism. Although a significant part of our multicultural society consists of different religious groups, the *Times* has shown an interest in wanting to promote the idea that practically any type of belief or moral behavior—such as a religious faith or choice of sexual activity—is as good as any other.

So an extreme multiculturalist, following the lead of the *Times*, might contend that Christianity is necessarily equal in truth and the potential for salvation to Buddhism. As a result, according to this argument, cultural institutions or laws should be molded to reflect this "equal" status—perhaps by prohibiting one religious group from trying to proselytize members of another group. Or rules might be passed to keep all references to religion out of public forums.

Similarly, multiculturalism rooted in extreme ideas of equality might lead to laws holding that unmarried heterosexual cohabitation (or homosexual cohabitation) is as valid as traditional marriage. This might result in a number of revolutionary social changes, such as the mandating of government benefits for "partners" in non-traditional sexual liaisons.

✥

To sum up, then, there are many degrees and variations of multi-culturalism. In fact, most fair-minded Americans would probably find, on close inspection, that they are multiculturalists by some definition.

But as we have seen in our previous discussions of religion, sexual orientation, and the like, the *Times* operates at the far left end of the spectrum on multiculturalism and globalism. Most Americans would not buy into multiculturalism or globalism to this degree.

But who can predict how the effects of Culture Creep will shape our views of ourselves and our world in the future? For that matter, who could have predicted how American views on sexuality would change in the final decades of the twentieth century?

CHAPTER 14

THE SPIRIT OF TOTAL SEXUAL FREEDOM

Since the 1960s, a true sexual and gender revolution has occurred in the United States—and in recent years the *Times* has led the way in fighting for these changes. The features of the revolution include:

- Growing power and independence of women
- Greater and more open acceptance of sexual freedom outside marriage
- Increased willingness to have children out of wedlock
- Higher public profile of gay advocacy and intensification of the movement to legitimize and normalize homosexual behavior
- Increased openness to highly unusual sexual practices and behavior, such as transsexuality and transvestitism

DETAILING THE SEXUAL REVOLUTION

Let's add some statistical flesh to the above facts. Perhaps the most striking change has been the rise of the American woman, especially in economic and occupational power and independence.

By 1995, for example, 48 percent of all employed married women provided half or more of their family's income. Also, almost one quarter of working married women said they expected their jobs to provide more long-term financial security for their families than the jobs held by their husbands, a figure that was up from only 9 percent in 1981 (*WSJ*, 5/11/95, p. B1).

On the sexual front, a study by the University of Chicago's National Health and Social Life Survey revealed that one quarter of married men in the United States and one-sixth of married women reported having had at least one extramarital affair (7/4/98, p. A13).

Some experts have suggested that these figures may be low because many people interviewed might not have wanted to admit they had been unfaithful. Adding some credence to this interpretation is the fact that 90 percent of men and 94 percent of women believe that extramarital sex is "always wrong" or "almost always wrong" (7/4/98, p. A13). In other words, many people may be messing around outside marriage, but they apparently don't feel quite right about it or are ashamed of their infidelity.

In addition to the issue of adultery, there has been a dramatic increase in sexual activity among unmarried teenagers and adults—to the point that unmarried women now account for about one-third of all births. In contrast, only about 20 percent of all babies were born to an unmarried mom in 1980 (National Center for Health Statistics, Miami *Herald*, 6/7/95, p. 1A).

Other studies suggest that what once qualified as "promiscuous" or "loose" or "sluttish" behavior—where a person engaged in sex with several partners outside marriage—is now ancient history. In fact, if current practices are any indication, those words have completely lost their meaning, according to a 1992 study by the University of Chicago's 1992 National Opinion Research Center.

In that investigation, 21 percent of American men and 32 percent of women said they had had two to four sex partners since age 18; and another 23 percent of men and 20 percent of women had five to ten partners since age 18 (10/9/94, p. 3).

Furthermore, according to this study, 16 percent of men had engaged in sex with 11–20 partners, and 17 percent had more than 21 partners! Only 23 percent of men and 35 percent of women reported having only one partner or no partners since they were 18.

Homosexuality is another sexual issue that has acquired an extremely high profile since the late 1960s, as gay rights advocates, with the help of such mainstream publications as the *Times*, have become more vocal. During the same time frame, the number of homosexuals has apparently remained the same. But public acceptance is on the rise. As indicated in chapter 3, only 34 percent of Americans considered homosexuality an "acceptable lifestyle" in 1982, but the figure rose to 50 percent in 1999 (Gallup poll, *www.gallup.com*).

The above University of Chicago study confirmed earlier studies to the effect that about 2.8 percent of American men and 1.4 percent of American women identified themselves as homosexual or bisexual (10/9/94, p. 3).

On the other hand, the homosexual population tended to be concentrated in large cities. Specifically, 9 percent of the men and 3 percent of the women in the nation's twelve largest cities said they were homosexual or bisexual. As the *Times* noted in this article, this tendency for gays to congregate in large cities helps explain why New York City and San Francisco have such active gay populations.

THE TIMES' LEADING ROLE IN THE SEXUAL REVOLUTION

Many factors have undoubtedly contributed to the changes in American sexual mores that have occurred during the past few decades. But the *New York Times*—especially since the early 1980s—has become the primary public relations organ for the sexual revolution. To illustrate, consider how active the paper has been in trying to push back the frontiers of sexual and gender freedom.

The Frontier of Women's Rights

The celebratory nature of the *Times'* coverage of feminism and women's rights was reflected in one of the "millennium series" that the Sunday Magazine ran in 1999. The issue was devoted exclusively to the progress and increasing power of women in our society. Articles ranged from the historic milestones that have marked the forward march of feminism and women's rights to modern-day sexuality (5/16/99).

One of the contributors was Naomi Wolf, the controversial writer and $15,000-per-month feminist adviser to Vice President Al Gore for his presidential candidacy. She gained a moment of fame in the fall of 1999 when she advised Gore to transform himself into an "alpha male."

Besides providing a liberal Democratic connection, Wolf's presence as a contributor provided other complexities for the *Times.* She was the wife of David K. Shipley, a former speechwriter for President Clinton, who was also an editor for the *Times* Sunday Magazine (11/1/99, p. A15).

Furthermore, when Wolf was criticized for her role in the Gore campaign, the *Times* immediately ran stories defending her. One of these, which was introduced by a six-column banner headline that ran across the entire top of a page, gave her side of the story in a nutshell:

> "NAOMI WOLF, FEMINIST CONSULTANT TO GORE, CLARIFIES HER CAMPAIGN ROLE — A WRITER DENIES SHE HAS BEEN COACHING GORE ON HOW TO BE DOMINANT" (11/5/99, p. A20).

The *Times* devoted prominent space for her defense to feminist advocates such as Patricia Ireland of the National Organization for Women, who has become a darling of *Times* editorial writers.

This Wolf incident is important mainly as a symbol of the pervasive radical feminist substructure that pervades the Times' organization and news coverage. In a very short space and time period, we see a gathering of several "strange bedfellows"—or at least they seem strange for any publication that aspires to objectivity and fairness in reporting. The cast of characters in this scenario might appear to be far too convoluted and implausible in any other context, even a political potboiler:

> A liberal Democratic vice president and presidential
> candidate . . .
> Is advised by a feminist political consultant and writer, author
> of books with such titillating titles as *Promiscuities* . . .
> Who in turn contributes an article to the most powerful
> Sunday newspaper magazine on earth . . .
> In a milestone issue on the status and power of women at the
> end of the millennium . . .
> The feminist political consultant, by the way, is married to a
> former Democratic presidential speechwriter . . .
> Who just happens now to be an editor on the self-same powerful Sunday newspaper magazine on earth for which his
> feminist political consultant wife has written . . .
> All the while, the feminist political consultant wife continues
> to advise the Democratic presidential candidate, who is
> seeking advice on how to be a real man . . .
> Until she is "outed" for her high-priced and provocative consulting role . . .
> And must be defended in the news pages of the aforementioned greatest newspaper on earth . . .
> Which relies for authority on a cadre of radical feminist advocates to make the feminist political consultant's case.

But again, this is only one example of a pervasive, strongly feminist pattern in the paper. On a regular basis, the *Times* keeps issues involving women's rights at the forefront of its news coverage. And in fact, it's important to recognize that many of those issues *should* be highlighted because they involve fundamental rights, such as equal pay for equal work and protection from sexual harassment.

A series of typical headlines tells the story:

- "As Asian Economies Shrink, Women are Squeezed Out" (front page, 6/11/98).

- "HARASSMENT? THE NEW SEX MONITORS ARE PATROLLING THE HALLS" (cover story on sexual harassment in public schools, Sunday Magazine, 6/13/99).
- "NO SEX, PLEASE. THIS IS A WORKPLACE" (cover story on harassment, Sunday Magazine, 5/3/98).
- "THE FALLOUT AS WOMEN'S SPORTS GAIN: SEXUAL HARASSMENT" (front page story, full page headline for jump page, 3/7/99, p. 1, 16).
- "HUNK, HE-MAN, MENSCH, MILQUETOAST: THE MASKS OF MASCULINITY" (feature on a tenet of feminist theory that gender is not inborn, and so there are no real, natural-born he-men, 2/13/99, p. A19).
- "FREE MARKETS LEAVE WOMEN WORSE OFF, UNICEF SAYS" (economic plight of women abroad, 9/23/99, p. A5).

Although this list provides just a sampling of the variety of gender-related issues, the *Times* advocacy for sexual liberation is far broader—and sometimes of more questionable validity. One of the more problematic frontiers, where the paper has been taking strong, controversial stands in recent years involves articles that advocate or in some way condone the legitimacy of sex outside marriage.

Extramarital Sex in Uniform

The *Times* doesn't attach much importance to the act of adultery—at least that's the strong implication that has come across in a number of articles and editorials in the paper, including a series of stories on adultery in the military. In the *Times'* view, the armed services should not only treat men and women who violate marriage vows the same way under the law, but should also downgrade the adultery to a meaningless peccadillo. Little or no consideration was given to the fact that extramarital sex in the services might undermine morale and discipline.

In a July 21, 1998, editorial headlined, "ADULTERY IN THE MILITARY" (p. A18), the *Times* supported a measure by President Clinton's Defense Secretary, William Cohen, for "reducing the crime," by making it more difficult to prosecute adultery and by easing penalties for the offense.

The editorial moguls concluded that it was important to "reduce fears of unreasonable prosecutions based on private matters that have nothing to do with military discipline."

The *Times'* relative lack of interest in the morality of adultery also is reflected in the number of stories it devotes to the topic. Over the two-and-a-half year period from 1998 to mid-2000, the paper ran 398 articles on "adultery" and a mere 33 on "extramarital sex"—and this time span covered the Clinton-Lewinsky extramarital sex scandal! By contrast, during the same period the *Times* ran 3,759 articles on "gay" relations; 1,439 articles on "homosexuality," and 943 articles on "lesbian" relations. Clearly, the paper is much less interested in adultery than in all varieties of same-sex relationships. Why? Perhaps the *Times* assumes the battle for heterosexual license has already been won, whereas much more needs to be accomplished in the cultural conflict over homosexuality.

If You've Got It, Flaunt It!

In general, the *Times* celebrates provocative sexuality in its pages—a practice that seems a clear approval of extremely lenient standards of sexual conduct.

Consider, for example, a feature headlined "THE ARTIST IS A GLAMOUR PUSS—YOUNG WOMEN IN FINE ART PRESENT THEMSELVES AS STYLISH AND SEXY, REFLECTING THEIR WORK." In the story, young female artists, pictured in revealing attire, were quite open in promoting their sexually free philosophies of life (4/19/99, p. B7).

One artist, displaying dramatic décolletage, said, "If I was in denial about my sexuality, I'd be in denial about aspects of my work, which deals with personal revelations."

Another, who was a sculptor, "wore leg warmers with garters and a see-through plastic miniskirt to an interview at Yale."

The pages dealing with society doings also frequently feature sexually titillating material, which would be the envy of any men's magazine. On February 8, 1999, for instance, one page (p. B8) was decorated with color shots of mature teenage girls dancing and prancing in miniskirts, some in same-sex embraces.

The article, which made the most of the sexual overtones of the event, began this way: "All the boys were talking about her hip-revealing Gucci skirt, as she swirled around the dance floor to the pounding beat of a Pull Daddy CD with her best girlfriend from school. . . .

"The guys gaped at . . . a tall size '0' blonde, whose waist and shoulders also played peekaboo in a black tube top. . . .

"When the music ended, she signaled to her friend . . . who was dressed every bit as stylishly—and as skimpily—and both teenage girls grabbed unsuspecting boys from the crowd to kiss them. Three minutes later, they ended the make-out sessions and pushed the boys away, then returned to dancing with each other" (p. B8).

To introduce a section dealing with the trend toward uncontrolled teenage partying, including the free use of alcohol, one fourteen-year-old boy was quoted as saying: "The rule in the whole entire thing is that the adults totally don't care, and they can't stop anything that's happening."

Later, in its usual practice of relying on "experts" who can give such events at least a veneer of respectability, the *Times* quoted an Upper East Side child psychiatrist. She contributed this bit of pseudo-historical psychobabble: "The time in boys' or girls' lives in which they become capable of reproduction is a time that has been celebrated since primitive days."

The message that came across was that flaunting one's sexuality and active sexual expression among teenagers should not only be encouraged, but is actually "in" or stylish. All the cool kids do it, so why are you middle-American kids who believe in abstinence or traditional values holding back?

Furthermore, if the child psychiatrist is to be believed, it's perfectly all right for our contemporary moral and sexual standards to be guided by ancient pagan rituals and primal urges.

There was no suggestion in the article that perhaps, in light of the epidemic of AIDS and sexually transmitted diseases, mature adults should intervene and encourage these children to put the brakes on their sexuality. Instead, the *Times* just quoted observers of the scene as offering the excuse, without making any moral judgments, that "what precocious teen-age girls are imitating are the lives of young celebrities."

One predictable result of such media-condoned behavior is our epidemic of sexually transmitted disease (STD). Another is the increasing public acceptance of abortions and illegitimate births.

Furthermore, the push for legal sanctions to protect those who engage in unrestricted sex outside marriage may be gaining momentum. A *Times* report on August 6, 1998, was entitled rather tellingly, "LAWSUIT ON SEX BIAS BY 2 MOTHERS, 17—PREGNANCY KEPT THEM FROM HONOR SOCIETY, THE GIRLS CONTEND." The story recounted a number of efforts across the country by pregnant, unmarried young women who wanted the courts to require schools not to penalize them for their behavior (p. A12).

The Gay Frontier

Much has already been said in the previous pages about the *Times*' unequivocal support for strengthening the rights of homosexuals above and beyond the rights enjoyed by the average citizen. So there is little need to retrace that ground here.

But what is worth noting is the wide variety of pro-gay advocacy pieces that the *Times* publishes in every section of the paper. On the op-ed page, for instance, columnist Frank Rich has led the attack, often dueling with his critics in other publications who take him to task for his vitriolic tone.

For example, on the opinion page of the *Wall Street Journal*, Amherst College jurisprudence professor Hadley Arkes criticized partisans of gay rights for showing no courtesy to those who have moral reservations about homosexuality. Instead, Arkes wrote, "Frank Rich and other columnists have spun out columns vibrant with a hatred of the Family Research Council and evangelical Christians who have run ads on television pointing up gays who have 'converted.' But those ads were put forth in a spirit of civil appeal; they cast no reproach, and sought to inspire no contempt" (*WSJ*, 11/20/98, p. W17).

Rich responded directly in a December 5, 1998, column:

". . . the same groups that worked overtime to stigmatize gay people have mounted a furious propaganda defense to assert that their words and ads demeaning gay people have nothing to do with any anti-gay crimes. . . . So they . . . attack those who call them on their game, hoping we might be intimidated and shut up. As one of their apologists, Hadley Arkes, wrote in a *Wall Street Journal* opinion piece, my columns on this subject are 'vibrant with a hatred of the Family Research Council and evangelical Christians.' It's a nice try at changing the subject" (p. A25).

The battle is also waged regularly in the paper's editorials, such as a June 29, 1999, opinion piece entitled "STONEWALL, THEN AND NOW." This statement by management affirmed the *Times*' long-standing support for the gay rights movement, which gay rights observers claim began at the Stonewall Inn in New York City's Greenwich Village in June of 1969.

The editorialists declared that the name "Stonewall" had "become synonymous with the struggle for gay civil rights and full protections under the law."

In the Sunday Magazine, the promotion of gay rights and the normalization of homosexual behavior in every part of American society have become a standard litany. A cover story on June 28, 1998—with a dramatic picture of a U.S. Marine saluting in his dress blues—was entitled "THE SHADOW LIFE OF A GAY MARINE— FOR THIS OFFICER, AS FOR COUNTLESS OTHER HOMOSEXUALS IN THE MILITARY, 'DON'T ASK, DON'T TELL' IS HELL."

It would be hard for anyone to argue that this picture, plus the slanted headline and other copy, is objective journalism. Clearly, the editors want to send a message that the military is full of homosexuals, their rights are being violated—and governmental policy should be changed to allow gays to operate more openly in the services.

The magazine also frequently runs short articles attempting to show that gay couples are just like regular married couples. A typical article was entitled "ELEGY: UPON MOURNING—WEEKS AFTER THE DEATH OF HIS PARTNER OF 32 YEARS, [A] DIARIST AND COMPOSER REFLECTS ON GRIEF, LOSS AND 'ECSTATIC MASOCHISM.'"

Whenever possible, the *Times* gives prominent play to stories involving gay clergy or the sanctioning of gay marriages by renegade churches and pastors. An article in point, which appeared on March 29, 1999 (p. A15), involved a Methodist pastor from Chicago who was suspended for officiating at a "wedding" of two gay men.

The headline left no doubt about the *Times'* positive stance toward the pastor and the concept of same-sex marriage: "SUSPENDED PASTOR'S FLOCK VOICES ITS SUPPORT—PRAYERS AND ANGER AFTER A SUSPENSION FOR A GAY UNION."

The kicker, or final two paragraphs, provided the reader with a highly positive sendoff, designed to evoke a sense of sympathy and warmth toward gay activists in the denomination:

> "It took until my 20's before a minister could look me in the eye without saying, 'You're evil and you're going to hell,'" [a gay] parishioner . . . said.
>
> "He smiled at [the pastor]. 'Because of you,' he said, 'there are Methodist kids all over the country—kids who thought they were the only ones—who now know that they're O.K. and that God loves them'" (p. A15).

In other words, the *Times* is not only aggressive in promoting gay rights but also doesn't hesitate to try to intervene in Christian religious customs and decision-making.

But after all, the paper accepts the mantle of cultural "cathedral" with aplomb, and its chief executive officer has referred to the *Times* as his religion. Furthermore, the beliefs espoused by the paper, including gay rights, are presented as absolutes. So it apparently seems quite natural for the staff to meddle in the affairs of real religious bodies and try to alter the standards of their faith.

The *Times* also uses the Sunday Book Review, as well as the arts sections to try to normalize homosexual behavior (see Book Review, 3/7/99, p. 10; Living Arts, 7/27, 99, p. B1).

One prominent story featured actor Jack Larson, who played Jimmy Olsen on the old "Adventures of Superman" television series (5/15/98, pp. B1, B26). Although the main thrust of the article was that Larson had become a playwright and librettist, the writer used the story to spread the word that he was also a homosexual.

According to the story, Larson was involved with actor Montgomery Clift and another actor and screenwriter with whom he had a "35-year-domestic partnership, much admired in Hollywood circles where relationships can be so fleeting" (p. B26).

In the lifestyle sections, many articles are devoted to the minutia of gay life, such as how gay men can get dates. One prominent feature in this category was headlined, "FOR GAY MEN, MATCHMAKING AS AN EXTREME SPORT" (12/7/98, p. B8). The gist of the article was that "high-tech mixers" are springing up to help homosexuals find companions who are compatible according to looks, interests, and HIV status.

Even the sports pages can't escape the pro-gay editorializing. A huge article by former pro football player David Kopay, a self-professed homosexual, launched an attack on Christian player Reggie White, who had taken a stand against homosexual behavior.

The headline was particularly biting and personal: "DEAR REGGIE WHITE: YOU JUST DON'T GET IT—HOMOSEXUALITY IS NOT THE ENEMY, AND VILIFYING IT IS HURTFUL AND DESTRUCTIVE."

All readers should be aware that guest columnists like Kopay don't write these headlines. The editorial staff, with the implicit approval of top management, handles that job. So when you read a headline like this, you should know you're getting a direct message from the *Times* staff, which is suggesting the paper's official position and convictions on a given topic.

Other headlines reveal the *Times'* pro-gay bias—and condescending attitude toward any person or group that would dare disagree—in almost every conceivable context and forum:

- "WHY SAME-SEX MARRIAGE IS THE CRUCIAL ISSUE" (Week in Review, Editorial Observer, 9/5/99, p. 10)
- "HAS JERRY FALWELL SEEN THE LIGHT?" (Frank Rich column on Rev. Falwell's decision to meet with homosexuals, 11/6/99, p. A27)
- "MR. FALWELL'S PROGRESS" (patronizing editorial on the same topic, 11/26/99, p. A30)

Note: articles and editorials on this and related topics represent a clear effort by the *Times* to nudge evangelical Christians away from their convictions about the biblical view of homosexuality and toward acceptance of the paper's doctrine of homosexual activity as normal.

- "BIGOTRY IN THE MILITARY" (editorial supporting greater openness of homosexuality in the services, 8/30/99, p. A22)
- "REFLECTIONS ON A SECRET LIFE IN SPORTS" (celebratory retrospective by sports columnist Robert Lipsyte on gays and lesbians in professional sports, 9/12/99, p. 42)
- "FEARING ISOLATION IN OLD AGE, GAY GENERATION SEEKS HAVEN" (front-page story on retirement arrangements for aging homosexuals, 10/ 21/99, p. 1)
- "NEW YORK STUDY FINDS GAY MEN USING SAFER SEX" (front page story on status of HIV and AIDS in New York City, 6/28/99, p. A1, A17)

Note: The issue of AIDS and the homosexual community has been one of the paper's prime interests for more than a decade. Quite commendably, the *Times* has focused on pushing for more effective treatment and sounding the alarm as the AIDS epidemic has intensified abroad. Also, as possible treatment breakthroughs have occurred, the *Times* has alerted readers and helped those suffering from the disease understand better the various options available to them.

From the *Times'* perspective the basic principles of gay rights now seem to have been firmly fixed. All that remains is for the paper to push, attack, argue, and publicize those principles over and over until the rest of the country accepts the *Times'* position.

But those who preside over the journalistic cathedral on Times Square are by no means ready to suspend their experimentation with the outer limits of sexuality and gender. Other frontiers remain to be conquered.

The Outermost Sexual Frontiers—Or Boldly Going Where Few Newspapers Have Gone Before

What is the nature of the sexual territory that the *Times* will try to explore in the future? Two major features in June of 1998 suggest the paper's direction.

One story focused on female surrogates who were giving birth to children of gay men. Although the number of such women is miniscule, and the *Times*, by its own admission, didn't know how many there were, the article still pictured the phenomenon as a building movement that would change the face of American family in the future.

The headline summarized the movement the *Times* was trying to create: "A SMALL-BUT-GROWING SORORITY IS GIVING BIRTH TO CHILDREN FOR GAY MEN—SURROGATES ARE CHALLENGING TRADITIONAL MODELS OF FAMILY LIFE" (6/25/98, p. A12). The body of the article was peppered with biased references to non-existent trends, which were identified by unnamed "experts."

Here is a sampling of the editorializing:

"The exact number [of surrogates] is unknown, but a few experts on surrogate parents said at least scores of women had acted, or agreed to act, as surrogates for gay men. . . . Other signs also indicated that surrogacy for gay men—arranged in rare cases for at least a decade—is taking firmer root . . . [One surrogate] believes that society should be more accepting of gay men and lesbians" (p. A12).

Another full-page feature highlighted the outlook for gay children of gay parents. It was entitled, "THE SECOND GENERATION—THE CHILDREN ARE GAY. SO ARE THEIR PARENTS. WHAT DO THEY FACE?" (6/8/98, p. B7).

The objective of this article was apparently to try to establish that homosexuality was predetermined genetically and couldn't be altered by therapy or religious influence. Furthermore, the pervasive underlying message was that it is perfectly normal to have a home with various homosexual variations among parents and children.

The kicker in this feature consisted of a rather surreal anecdote describing how a mother discovered that she was a lesbian, divorced so that she could live with her lover, and then reestablished a meaningful relationship with her son, who had, in the meantime, determined that he was gay. The illustration ended with the mother's lesbian lover also affirming her maternal love for the gay son.

The Transsexual Connection

If the above account was confusing, there is more to come. The *Times* has also become enamoured with normalizing other unusual sexual predilections, such as transsexuality.

Two major features in June 1999 make the point. One article was headlined, "A TRANSSEXUAL ECONOMIST'S SECOND TRANSITION—SHE SAYS GENDER DETERMINES ONE'S APPROACH TO HER FIELD." The story described the saga of a prominent economist—a former Harvard football player—who underwent a sex change operation. Now, the "new woman" is working on a feminist approach to economic theory (6/19/99, p. A19).

The other feature, "SPOTLIGHTING ISSUES OF GENDER, FROM PRONOUNS TO MURDER," highlighted another "male-to-female transsexual" who had become a "transgender rights advocate" (6/11/99, p. A27). The paper described the modus operandi of this particular activist, who specialized in hate crimes, this way:

"Every time a transsexual or cross-dresser or someone otherwise 'gender-different' is reported murdered in the United States, her group posts the news at its Web site" (p. A27).

The kicker, or final paragraph, of this particular story appears to sum up the *Times'* feelings about the brave new sexual scene being promoted by the paper:

"One of [the transsexual's] fondest dreams," she said, "is that a straight married man can decide to wear a dress into work and the worst thing anyone will say is: 'Nice outfit. Is that report done?'" (p. A27).

Even from this short overview of the *Times'* viewpoint on sexual and gender issues, it should be abundantly clear that the paper has been working diligently to establish moral and behavioral standards far different from what practically any American could imagine three or four decades ago. For that matter, many Americans today would be uncomfortable affirming the paper's current positions.

But much has changed in just a few decades. What may have seemed radical a few years ago—like the idea of multiple sex partners for both men and women before marriage—is now standard practice.

Traditional religious and spiritual values have fallen, and the gospel of the *Times* is fast filling the vacuum as the civil religion of choice. Unless some authentic force of morality can assert itself, what seems strange or bizarre in the sexual arena today is almost certain to become a normal way of life in the near future.

CHAPTER 15

THE SPIRITS OF ENVIRONMENTALISM AND ENTITLEMENT

The *New York Times*, like any other organization or individual with a strong neo-socialist bent, is favorably disposed toward government control and intervention in those matter that the paper feels may pose a threat to individual or group welfare.

Two of the most important of these danger areas are: the environment; and entitlements or special protective measures by the government for those perceived to constitute the poor or oppressed.

THE SPIRIT OF ENVIRONMENTALISM

The *Times* has provided a consistent, if low-key, voice in support of environmental concerns during the past few years. An editorial published on December 19, 1999—one of a series of

"Reflections on the Millennium"—summed up the broad outlines of the paper's policy.

First, the paper predicted that the past century would be remembered "as a moment when mankind, realizing the earth's resources were not finite and perhaps seeking expiation for years of predatory behavior, struck a truce with nature" (Week in Review, 12/19/99, p. 12).

The article then went on to say that for "the first time since the dawn of the industrial age there was, at least in the West and certainly in America, a rough armistice between the forces of economic growth and the forces of preservation."

In other words, the paper pictured a quasi-cosmic battle between capitalism and environmentalism and concluded that environmentalism was finally beginning to win the fight.

America, according to the editorial moguls, had fallen into the fallacy early in the century of regarding "nature . . . as an unruly force needing discipline. . . ." But now, the paper said, the outlook was brighter after "a citizens' revolt against environmental degradation," which produced "the first Earth Day in 1970, and . . . the creation of an astonishing body of environmental laws."

Finally, they said, this revolt had given the nation "the tools with which to heal itself [and] . . . conferred upon ordinary citizens the indispensable right to take even the government to court if it failed to carry out these laws."

At various times, the *Times* has entered the public fray to fight for an acceptance of the theory of global warming, saving the Florida Everglades, preserving endangered species (including rare crocodiles in Florida canals), eliminating garden-variety pollution, saving the whales, and a variety of other environmental causes (see articles, 1/24/99, p. 13; 1/24/99, p. 12; 10/24/98, p. A12; 10/24/98, pp. A1, A13; 12/15/96, pp. A1, A24; 6/30/99, p. A23; 6/29/99, p. A1; 6/29/99, p. D1; Week in Review, 12/19/99, p. 12; 6/25/99, p. A26).

Overall, the paper's position on environmentalism may be described as strongly pro-environment and strongly in favor of government intervention to protect the natural world—either through direct agency or executive action, or through lawsuits to enforce laws on the books.

THE SPIRIT OF ENTITLEMENT

In the spirit of American fair-mindedness and egalitarianism, the *Times* has taken a firm stand on the side of the poor, downtrodden, and disenfranchised.

Such a stance, which must be applauded, is certainly consistent with the principles established by John Locke, Thomas Jefferson, and others who gave us our system of individual and human rights. In fact, by promoting the equality of racial minorities and women in recent years, the *Times* has joined those intent on correcting early flaws in our system of government, such as the failure to give African-Americans, other racial minorities, and women the right to full equality.

The failure of Jefferson and many political leaders who followed him to include all citizens under the rights umbrella led to a catastrophic Civil War and extreme social disruptions at various times in our history, including the civil rights battles of the 1960s. At times during these crises, we have actually been in danger of losing entirely and permanently the consensus—or implied social agreement—about human rights and equality that has made our nation so strong and stable.

But the efforts of the *Times* to protect the downtrodden and disenfranchised have also raised a few questions. For one thing, as we have already seen, the paper, in discarding the divine and biblical controls that guided John Locke and others, has fallen into the subjective trap of extending rights in inconsistent, helter-skelter fashion to any group that is a darling of current mass media hype.

Consequently, according to the *Times*, convicted murderers get an unqualified right to life, while innocent unborn children die. Furthermore, those espousing unusual sexual proclivities or orientations get the right to operate and express themselves freely, but those who affirm traditional Christian morality and beliefs don't.

Also, the *Times* is anything but libertarian or small-government in its approach to protecting and enforcing either the well-established array of historic rights or the new "rights" that the paper is ardently trying to establish.

Specifically, the *Times* has made it clear that its first line of response to maintain and protect all rights, old or new, is a form of Democratic socialism. In other words, the tools of choice in the paper's program of social engineering are regular government intervention and strong federal programs, including affirmative action.

Here are a few of the most important groups that should be entitled to special treatment and extensive government help, according to the *Times*.

The Poor and Homeless

In a 1993 editorial entitled "DON'T DUCK WELFARE REFORM," the *Times* endorsed Bill Clinton's campaign promise for welfare reform—including programs to provide education and training for the poor, to extend childcare, and to encourage the able-bodied needy to find work (1/25/93, p. A16).

The editorial said, "The proposal embodied the notion that government has obligations to the needy, but the needy also have obligations to society. . . . Americans have a right to hold [President Clinton] to his lofty promises. The welfare system isn't working very well. Many poor have become long-term welfare recipients—doing them and their children little good."

Then the editorial gurus switched to New York self-interest. They called for Donna Shalala, Secretary of Health and Human Services , to lighten the welfare burden on city and state governments.

"The poor and homeless who roam the streets of New York are not New York's poor," the paper said. "They are America's poor.

Presidents Reagan and Bush ignored them for the last 12 years. Mr. Clinton promised to do better" (p. A16).

The *Times* appears to have settled on a welfare ethic that mixes Horatio Alger with a Great Society safety net. The paper regularly monitors the disparity in incomes between the rich and the poor in its newspapers (9/5/99, p. 16). At the same time, the editors have kept close track of how many welfare recipients were going to work under the overhaul of the welfare system engineered by Congress and endorsed by President Clinton in the mid-1990s (6/9/98, p. A21). Overall, the verdict seems to be that the new system is working rather well, and many former welfare recipients are indeed getting and holding down jobs.

But the *Times* still resists any measures that might further cut social programs. For example, a signed "Editorial Observer" editorial by Steven R. Weisman argued against a tax cut pushed by Republicans in 1999 (Week in Review, 8/22/99, p. 12). The rationale was that the rich would benefit too much from such a cut, and cutting taxes might jeopardize government programs such as Social Security, Medicare, education funding, environmental measures, and "other government services" (p. 12).

The Sick and Infirm

The paper's convictions about government entitlements for those in need of medical care came across clearly in a July 16, 1999, editorial headlined, "PATIENT RIGHTS AND WRONGS."

"Health care—like civil rights and environmental protection—is one of those areas where Americans want broad, consistent national policy," the *Times* declared (p. A20).

This particular editorial pushed for measures to protect the rights of patients in managed-care health programs, including broad rights to redress grievances in court for denial of care and to secure greater access to medical specialists. The *Times* accused Republicans who opposed the legislation of kowtowing to big-money health care conglomerates.

In another editorial, published on June 24, 1998 (p. A26), the organization came out swinging for stronger Medicare protections, including the needs of "38 million elderly and disabled beneficiaries, as more of them move into the managed-care system." The paper also called for an extension of health care protections and benefits "to all consumers, including those trapped in low-quality plans."

Overall, then, the paper regularly pushes for greater entitlements and more comprehensive health programs to provide a medical safety net for wider and wider segments of the general public.

Children and the Elderly

The *Times* has also conducted an ongoing campaign to protect and extend the rights of children. A sign of the paper's concern emerged in a one-year search of articles on "children" published by the editorial desk—including editorials, letters to the editor, and op-ed columns. The search, which covered the period from December 20, 1998 through December 20, 1999, turned up 1,011 articles. Another, more restrictive search over the same period focused on editorial desk articles about "children" and "rights." This effort resulted in 94 articles.

Typical articles focused on taking governmental steps to protect children's mental and physical health, to protect them from abuse, to enhance their education, to finance child care, and to provide them with health insurance.

An editorial published slightly earlier than the time period for these searches and entitled, "PROTECTING NEW YORK'S CHILDREN," called children in the city's welfare system a "vulnerable population." And the editorialists urged greater attention on the part of New York to protect them (7/11/98, p. A18).

A similar, if somewhat less intense editorial crusade has been conducted to help the plight of the elderly who are poor or infirm. A search for articles on the elderly produced by the editorial desk for the one-year period ending December 20, 1999, produced 137 "hits." The main topics included saving and shoring up Social Security, taking steps to make more nursing homes and facilities available, and improving the financial foundations of Medicare.

The paper also makes a concerted effort to alert the public to particular problems facing older people, such as special challenges to their health. A front-page story on September 5, 1999, for instance, was headlined, "GAPS SEEN IN THE TREATMENT OF DEPRESSION IN THE ELDERLY." Relying on solid studies and statistics, the editors highlighted the financial side of the issue in a provocative subheading: "ARE MENTAL HEALTH RESOURCES CAPABLE OF DEALING WITH AN AGING POPULATION?"

The *Times* also champions the extension of rights and entitlements to many other groups and subgroups, such as prison convicts and ethnic minorities, which could benefit from special remedial education programs (12/21/99, p. A30).

To be sure, many of these entitlement issues supported by the paper are worthy of special consideration or support by compassionate, fair-minded people. Even the *Times* has taken significant steps in the arena of volunteerism to help the poor by promoting programs like its own Neediest Cases Fund (see page 129).

But at the same time, the paper's preference for government-based solutions may be unattractive to many people. In this era of downsizing government and emphasizing greater self-reliance, any suggestion that throwing government money at social problems—no matter how dire the need—can be expected to meet with significant opposition.

Instead, the current trend seems to be to encourage more private than government aid and to provide training and job opportunities to enable the downtrodden to pull themselves up by their own bootstraps. If they are unable to do it themselves, according to this self-help philosophy, then the job should usually be left up to charitable or religious associations—not to the government.

The *Times'* obsession with spreading rights to new groups and with bolstering, enhancing, and financing rights that already exist, is apparently too deeply ingrained to accommodate a meaningful change in direction. So we can expect the paper to try not only to support future government incursion into the affairs of private citizens, but also to widen individual and human rights to encompass new and untested groups and issues.

A Bizarre New World for Rights and Entitlements?

In what new direction may the paper want to push for government support and entitlements?

As categories of rights relating to humans become exhausted—after old and young, gay and straight, male and female, and every racial and ethnic group has received its own special package of rights—some evidence suggests that the next frontier for the *Times* may be special rights for animals. This may even mean raising their legal status closer to the position enjoyed by human beings.

The *Times* paved the way for a remarkably serious debate on this issue—which the majority of Americans would probably regard as quite bonkers—in August 1999.

On August 18, William Glaberson wrote an article entitled, "LEGAL PIONEERS SEEK TO RAISE LOWLY STATUS OF ANIMALS." Among other things, he reported that "two of the country's most prestigious law schools, Harvard and Georgetown, announced that they would offer courses in animal law for the first time" (*partners.nytimes.com/yr/news/national/animal-law.htm*o p. 1).

One of the experts who was quoted, Professor Gary L. Francione, an animal law teacher at Rutgers, recommended that lawsuits should be filed on behalf of gorillas, arguing that "they should be declared to be 'persons' under the Constitution."

This seems to be a rather curious suggestion, especially in light of the fact that unborn babies do not enjoy the legal status of "persons."

A contrary view appeared in a guest op-ed column on August 20 under the headline, "WE THE PEOPLE (AND OTHER ANIMALS) . . ." (8/20/99, p. A23). The author, Frans B. M. De Wall, a primate scientist at Emory University, contended that "tender loving care" would be more appropriate for animals than some version of human rights.

Glaberson came back with another article in the Sunday Week in Review section on August 22, 1999, under the heading, "MONKEY TRIAL: REDEFINING A JURY OF THEIR PEERS." Again, he argued, though with more humor this time, that the animal rights movement was serious business, not just monkey business.

One suggestion he proposed for those representing the animals was to use slavery-era statutes, which enabled slaves to bring lawsuits. He also stated—and it was hard to believe the author was entirely serious here—that the best parties to the lawsuits might be primates that could engage in rudimentary speech.

The final kicker to the article went like this:

> "Last month an orangutan who had been taught to use a voice synthesizer in Atlanta said this: 'Please buy me a hamburger.'
>
> "Given the chance, a great ape might not make an eloquent plea for freedom. But its lawyers would hope that any words uttered from an animal to a judge would be powerful simply because they were uttered" (p. 14).

This movement toward widening the concept of rights to include animals hasn't yet received the imprimatur of the editorial page. But it may be getting close. Just two days after Glaberson's August 22 article, the *Times* did run a lead editorial calling for laws that would provide better treatment for bison—even though they had not yet been listed as an endangered species (8/25/99, p. A26).

Specifically, the paper's management affirmed their support for thirteen million dollars from federal funds to give the bison a place to graze. They also suggested that another one billion dollars that had been cut from President Clinton's environmental budget should be reinstated for similar programs.

So perhaps it's not so far fetched to suggest that if the *Times* had its way, rights and entitlements would proliferate as fast as the bison that roam the plains. Never mind that John Locke never had such strange notions in mind when he philosophized back in the late seventeenth century, or that Thomas Jefferson would have been thoroughly baffled by such absurd extensions of his work.

But the movers and shakers at the *New York Times* have moved well beyond the theories and convictions that drove Locke and Jefferson. They are beckoning us to enter a brave new world of burgeoning, virtually unrestricted entitlements, where any increasingly bizarre concept of rights can take on a life of its own.

Yet if we enter this strange new realm, the inevitable and voracious demand for government money may very well turn the tables on the *Times'* good intentions—and push us further and further back toward the big-government mentality of ages past.

CHAPTER 16

THE SPIRITS OF SCIENTISM AND HUMANISM

Two dominant "spirits" provide much of the impetus that shapes and underlies the entire *Times'* worldview—namely, the spirits of scientism and humanism.

THE SCIENTISM OF THE TIMES

The most common and basic definition of scientism is that it's a belief that the assumptions and methodology of the natural sciences, such as physics and biology, should be used to interpret all other aspects of existence—including religion, philosophy, and the humanities.

The Great Battle: Scientism Versus Revelation

The roots of scientism can be traced back at least to the Enlightenment of the seventeenth and eighteenth centuries, which was characterized by an increasing reliance on reason, rather than on faith and religion. Scientism, which involves looking only to science as the ultimate source of truth, was a philosophy that fit naturally into the Enlightenment emphasis on human effort as the best way to make sense of the world.

Ernst Cassirer, the influential German philosopher and educator (1874–1945), concluded that "the formative power" of the eighteenth century was reason, which "becomes the unifying and central point of this century, expressing all that it longs and strives for, and all that it achieves" (Koelln and Pettegrove, p. 5).

This preoccupation with reason led thinkers of the period to narrow their search for truth to nature and the natural sciences: "In one and the same intellectual process of emancipation the philosophy of the Enlightenment attempts to show the self-sufficiency of both nature and the intellect" (p. 45).

To put this Enlightenment form of scientism in its most extreme form: "For man is the work of nature, and he has no existence except in nature" (p. 65).

This reductionistic view of the world clearly runs counter to any belief system that would allow for the existence of a truth that might transcend the natural world. For example, Christian thinkers, with their affirmation of the validity of revelation by God from a realm beyond this existence, have typically found themselves in serious conflict *not* with mainstream scientific thinking and investigation, but with the atheistic philosophy of scientism that some antireligious scientists espouse.

In the words of one contemporary Catholic thinker, Brother Francis of the Saint Benedict Center, scientism is not synonymous with science, but rather, is "an abuse of the scientific method and of scientific authority" *(www.catholicism.org/pages/scient.htm)*.

In other words, instead of looking to theology or religious doctrine to explain how the universe began, adherents of scientism might seek an explanation in non-theistic astrophysical theories, or resort to the notion that the universe appeared as a result of some cosmic accident.

Similarly, a believer in scientism would most likely attribute the appearance of humans on earth to the operation of a theory of evolution that denies any divine intervention or guidance. Prevailing evolutionary theory, of course, is itself a prime illustration of contemporary scientism.

How the Times Promotes Scientism

A major forum where the *Times* pushes the power and authority of science is the Science Times section, which is published every Tuesday. This part of the paper contains much useful information about new scientific investigations and breakthroughs, as well as a Health & Fitness addendum with practical health guidance from columnist Jane Brody and others.

But one of the strongest threads that runs through the Science Times section and frequently spills over into other parts of the paper is the conviction that the natural world is a closed system with no room for intervention or influence from any divine source.

Symbolic of this bias are features such as an adulatory profile headlined: "A CONVERSATION WITH STEPHEN JAY GOULD: PRIMORDIAL BEASTS, CREATIONISTS AND THE MIGHTY YANKEES."

This interview with Professor Stephen Jay Gould, the paleontologist and evolution apologist from Harvard and New York University, appeared in the December 21, 1999, issue (p. D3). The *Times* has been quite taken with Gould, as with its other specially anointed Ivy League gurus. In fact, the paper featured the professor in twenty-five articles during the one-year period ending on December 22, 1999.

Sometimes Gould was mentioned in the context of other articles, where he was cited as a special authority. At other times he would author a column, such as the op-ed piece on July 2, 1999, "THE HUMAN DIFFERENCE," in which he suggested that there was no "difference in quality" between humans and chimpanzees. Predictably, his foray into radical scientism and evolutionary speculation triggered a rash of letters to the editor, several of which mocked his conclusions (see letters on 7/7/99).

But such controversy hasn't deterred the *Times* from fawning over the professor and promoting his career. In the above-mentioned "Conversation"—featured across the top of one Science Times page with a large, full-color picture of Gould—the reporter tossed out a series of softball questions, including several on his battles with creationists (12/21/99, p. D3). One of these questions sought to elicit Gould's response to a decision by the Kansas School Board of Education to make the teaching of evolution optional in public schools.

The introduction to the interview article noted that Gould had come under fire from some of his pro-evolution colleagues because they thought he had helped the creationist cause by letting it slip that a great deal of chance might be involved in the evolutionary process.

Gould has also indicated in other contexts that major evolutionary transition forms are rare in the fossil record—again, an observation that creationists have used against him.

A case in point is the book *Refuting Evolution*, by Jonathan Sarfati, an Australian chemist who is on the staff of Answers in Genesis, a creationist advocacy group. Employing a well-established debating strategy, Sarfati adeptly used Gould's own writings against him.

On one occasion, for instance, Sarfati said that Gould admitted that the ". . . absence of fossil evidence for intermediary stages between major transitions in organic design . . . has been a persistent and nagging problem for gradualistic accounts of evolution" (Sarfati, p. 48, quoting Gould's *Evolution Now: A Century After Darwin*, p. 140).

At another point, Sarfati pulled a Gould remark from a *Natural History* magazine article, where the paleontologist said: "I regard the failure to find a clear 'vector of progress' in life's history as the most puzzling fact of the fossil record" (Safarti, p. 48–49, taken from the issue of Feb. 1984, [93:14–23]).

According to Sarfati, Gould had become upset because creationists were using his own writings to trip him up. So it would be understandable for the professor to take advantage of any opportunity to launch a counterattack against his annoying pro-Creator adversaries.

In any event, in his *Times'* interview Gould left no doubt in anyone's mind that he was solidly on the anti-creationist side of the fence. For example, he labeled as "stupidity" and "absurd" the Kansas decision that favored the creationist cause. Then he bemoaned how embarrassing it was for him that "European intellectuals" don't understand "how you can possibly have an anti-evolutionary movement in a modern scientific country."

Note: Gould's point here about the attitudes of "European intellectuals" is a favorite ploy among those who follow his and the *Times'* liberal line.

The same argument was used by many Clinton supporters who said they were embarrassed by the disdainful reaction of "sophisticated" Europeans to the "puritanical" attitudes of those Americans who were offended by the president's dalliances with Monica Lewinsky in the Oval Office.

The point is that members of the European elite supposedly have an advanced moral and spiritual sense, which less sophisticated middle-Americans would do well to emulate. (Never mind that a member of the nineteenth-century French intellectual class, Alexis de Tocqueville, was considerably more impressed with American standards and values than with those of his own aristocracy.)

In a similar vein, another featured "Conversation" interview in the Science Times section with Sir Martin Rees, the "Astronomer Royal of England," served as a front for another attack on those who believe God had a part in the creation process (4/28/98, p. B15).

Rees made his belief in the non-theistic origins of humankind quite clear:

"What we don't know is whether given the right conditions, the emergence of life is automatic or a rare accident. Still less do we know whether simple life automatically evolves toward something we recognize as intelligent. So we don't know whether life is unique to the earth" (p. B15).

So there is a great deal that Rees doesn't know. But what he *does* know is this: "Neither creationism nor astrology are serious issues" (p. B15).

As might be expected, the *Times'* editorial management regularly provides strong backing for such anti-creation sentiment. Listen to the paper's response in an editorial to the Kansas Board of Education decision to make the teaching of evolution optional:

> ". . . evolution has become one of the best established of all scientific theories. The central concept of biological evolution—that all organisms have evolved from common ancestors through a process of "natural selection" in which those best able to reproduce themselves survived—is even more firmly supported today than in the time of Charles Darwin. . . .
>
> "The Kansas action is a victory for creationists. . . . They will be repelled only when the advocates of sound science mount an equally vigorous campaign to keep evolution in the curriculum" (8/13/99, p. A18).

WHATEVER HAPPENED TO GOD?

Over and above such blatant pro-evolution and anti-creation rhetoric, the *Times* consistently runs news stories that assume the truth of an evolutionary process without God.

One such article was a massive, front-page feature in the Science Times section entitled, "REARRANGING THE BRANCHES ON A NEW TREE OF LIFE" (8/31/99, p. D1, D7). A subhead highlighted a major point in the article—that DNA research has come to the remarkable, counter-intuitive conclusion that "GENETIC COMPARISONS PLACE FUNGI CLOSER TO MAN THAT TO PLANTS."

The lead, a masterful summary of one form of contemporary scientism, provided a classic statement of evolutionary theory, which left God completely out of the process of the development of life:

"A diner sits down to a salad containing mushrooms and lettuce. In the universal genealogy of life, the mushrooms are more closely related to the lettuce than to the diner, right?

"Wrong. As part of an outpouring of research that is revolutionizing notions about the genetic, biochemical, structural and evolutionary relationships among living things, fungi like mushrooms have now been revealed as being closer to animals like humans than to plants like lettuce" (p. D1).

The paper frequently employs front-page stories to push the pro-evolution, anti-creation argument forward. In a clear bit of editorializing, one of these front-page headlines read, "SCIENTISTS SAY CHINA FOSSILS PROVE DINOSAUR-TO-BIRD LINK" (6/24/98, p. A1, A14). The jump-page headline used exactly the same headline, again, apparently to be certain that the message would come across.

The operative word in the above headline was *prove* because it carried with it the implication that the debate had been settled: that there could be no argument against the position that birds evolved directly from dinosaurs. Yet the word "prove" was never used by a quoted expert in the story and wasn't even supported solidly in the text.

Furthermore, the second paragraph contained this qualifying sentence: "But a few skeptical adversaries are not ready to capitulate."

In other words, they were not prepared to agree that the fossils in question were evidence of a bird-dinosaur link.

But the *Times* is apparently not interested in opening its pages to a serious debate on the theory of evolution. The main objective seems to be to marshal headlines, interviews, and editorials to argue that evolution of almost any stripe is preferable to any version of a God-created universe.

Sometimes, the paper is not above issuing an implied threat when advocates of divine creation become too vocal or aggressive. In a lead story in the Week in Review—"TRUE BELIEVERS: SCIENCE AND RELIGION CROSS THEIR LINE IN THE SAND," the paper provided a quick overview of the tensions that have existed between scientists and theologians.

But in the midst of the generally light, entertaining prose, this rather ominous warning popped out on the jump page:

> "Any religion that outrightly rejects science's most powerful theories—like evolution and the big bang—will find itself relegated to society's fringes. . . . Religion needs to secure a niche for itself in an increasingly scientific world" (p. 18).

No authority was cited for this remark. It was simply the reporter's clearly editorialized statement of opinion tucked firmly in what was supposed to pass as an "objective" news story.

With such overheated rhetoric both in its "news" stories and editorials, the *Times* delivers an unmistakable, thinly veiled threat, which might be summed up in this way:

> You religious people who believe in creation had better be careful—or we'll take steps to ensure you become social outcasts.

But despite such sword rattling, the *Times* editors and managers aren't stupid. They understand that even though they have strong allies among Ivy League faculties and the scientific establishment, they are in a minority on this issue.

A June 25, 1999, poll conducted by CNN/USA Today/Gallup Poll revealed these facts about the general public's views of evolution and creation:

- An overwhelming 68 percent favored teaching creationism *along with* evolution in public schools. Only 29 percent were opposed, and 4 percent had no opinion.
- A startling 40 percent actually favored teaching creation *instead of* evolution in public schools! Another 55 percent were opposed to this idea, and 5 percent expressed no opinion (8/15/99, pp. 4–1, 4–4).

With such strong public affirmation of the creationist position, the *Times* apparently realizes that it must move slowly and stealthily if it hopes to mobilize support for evolution. There are several tactics that the paper has employed to reach this objective.

The Times' Anti-Creation Strategy

First, the *Times* occasionally features evolution proponents with some connection to traditional religion, evidently in an effort to round up those with a religious faith who would be happy to reconcile their belief in God with the typical evolutionist disbelief.

A striking instance of this approach was another "Conversation" interview in the Science Times section, this time with Professor Francisco J. Ayala, an evolutionary biologist at the University of California at Irvine (4/27/99, p. D5).

The article on Ayala was headlined in such a way as to signal that the text would definitely provide a satisfactory answer to reconcile evolution and traditional religion: "EX-PRIEST TAKES THE BLASPHEMY OUT OF EVOLUTION."

Note the declarative nature of the statement in the headline. The editors wanted to leave no doubt that Ayala—a former Dominican priest whom the interviewer praised as "the Renaissance man of evolutionary biology"—had indeed "taken the blasphemy" out of evolution.

In the body of the article, the interviewer plied Ayala with easy questions, which enabled him to expound extensively and freely upon why he felt religious believers should accept his evolutionary views. His main argument, however, was that the believers were wrong and should change their views. There was no hint that perhaps evolutionists should make some accommodations on their part.

With Catholics, for instance, he said he emphasizes that the pope endorsed evolutionary teachings in an address in October 1996. What he didn't say was that the pope would still place God behind all creation, unlike the non-theists who follow classic evolutionary theory.

With "Christian fundamentalists," he stressed that "many Protestant theologians . . . agree with evolution." Furthermore, he said, the Christians' affirmation of "special design" in creation is, in fact, "blasphemous," because the "Special-Design-God is a God who messes up."

To support his novel thesis, he pointed to the aches, pains, infections, and other health problems that have plagued human beings throughout history.

It's remarkable that the *Times* would allow such naive and weak arguments for evolution into its pages. Anyone with a modicum of biblical knowledge could immediately think of a variety of responses to punch holes in Ayala's logic—such as the classic view that health problems are a result of original sin and the Fall, not of God's creation.

A Sense of Desperation?

But the situation facing the *Times* and other proponents of evolution seems to be triggering a degree of desperation, which has prompted an avalanche of articles supporting evolutionists' attacks on creationism and creationists.

A one-year search of the paper's archives, ending on July 9, 1999, showed that the *Times* had run 764 articles on evolution during the previous year, or an average of two per day. In that same time frame, 14 articles dealt specifically with "creationism," 16 focused on "evolutionary biology," and 36 highlighted "Charles Darwin."

Typical of the articles that the paper publishes on this subject was one entitled, "EVOLUTIONARY BIOLOGY BEGINS TACKLING PUBLIC DOUBTS—THE WHOLE CREATION-EVOLUTION ISSUE REARS ITS HEAD EVERY TIME YOU TEACH" (7/8/98, p. C20).

The headline provides an interesting illustration of artful editorializing. When they read the phrase "rears its head," most people would probably automatically insert the word "ugly" before "head" to complete the common cliché. So the negative connotation is fixed in the reader's mind, even though the "ugly" word wasn't used.

In this piece, the reporter cataloged how evolutionary biologists were going to seminars and taking other steps to get their peculiar version of scientism out to the public.

Among other things, according to the report, they were encountering resistance from both high-school students and college students. In one survey mentioned in the article, 20 percent of graduate students in science education, who would eventually go on to a teaching career, said they didn't accept evolution—though they did say they would teach the subject.

After learning of such studies, the biologists apparently panicked and resolved to conduct what amounted to an old-fashioned evangelistic campaign to spread their gospel of scientism. Or, as the writer put it, "the evolutionary biologists came away from the conference committed to more outreach and perhaps even politics" (p. C20).

Another article published about a year later centered on the "enemy" that evolutionists were targeting, "IN SCHOOLS ACROSS THE LAND, A GROUP MOUNTS COUNTERATTACKS ON 'CREATION SCIENCE'" (8/29/99, p. 12).

In this case, the *Times* used several old but still effective journalistic editorializing techniques to give this article a positive slant toward evolution and a negative tone for the idea of creation.

First, note the use of quotation marks around "creation science" in the headline. The same punctuation is used when the term is used in the first sentence.

Quotation marks can have many purposes, of course. But in this case, they were employed to signal to the reader that "creation science" is a bogus concept, which no intelligent person should take seriously.

In effect, the implied message in the quotes might be restated this way:

> We are going to publish this report. But we want to make it clear that we at the *Times* are too smart to accept any of the claims of this so-called "creation science" nonsense, and we

are quite sure, dear reader, that you also are smart enough to follow our lead.

The article, which touted an anti-creation advocacy organization called the National Center for Science Education, also used another well-worn editorializing technique—featuring images and literary allusions that put evolutionists in a good light and creationists in a bad light.

For example, the writer described the efforts of the National Center as a "David and Goliath struggle," with creationists, of course, being the bad-guy, Goliath.

The story also described anti-creation tactics that might be followed by evolutionists who read the account. One of these, which was used by the National Center, involved packing public hearings with members of the clergy who believe in evolution—and also with pro-evolution scientists who believe in God.

The reporter noted that a *Scientific American* survey showed that "about 40 percent of scientists believe in God," and the National Center sought them out to testify before local school boards. At the public hearings, the testimony of people who believed in both God and evolution caused listeners to be "mightily impressed," the paper said (p. 12).

Note: Such tactics may indeed help the evolutionists' battle against creationism—if the advocates can scramble around and find some credible scientists in the God-believing 40 percent who can also testify convincingly for the evolutionary viewpoint.

But it may be that one reason the creationists have had more success promoting their views is that they are advocating a majority position to a broadly sympathetic public. Remember: surveys by Gallup and other organizations have consistently shown that, in contrast to the scientists' unbelief, about 94–95 percent of the general public believe in God.

The National Center "nettles advocates of creationism," the *Times* observed, apparently with some satisfaction. To support this conclusion, the paper quoted a strong opponent of evolution,

Duane Gish of the Institute for Creation Research, one of the two largest pro-creation organizations in the United States.

He was quoted as saying, "They're effective."

But he also charged that the evolutionists who work hard to keep creation literature out of the schools "are censors and book burners. . . . They were organized for the sole purpose of fighting creationists and to keep any evidence for creation science out of public schools" (p. 12).

Although Gish's statements were quite telling, the *Times*, as is its custom when dealing with those on its enemies list, avoided other facts or quotations that would give the creationist side of the story.

A Sop to Quell the Creationist Surge?

Very infrequently, perhaps with the idea of providing some semblance of journalistic objectivity, the *Times* does run reasonably straightforward articles on the creationist position. One of these was a feature on one of the leaders of creation advocacy, the Australian Christian apologist Ken Ham, who founded the pro-creationist group, Answers in Genesis (12/1/99, p. A15).

In remarkably evenhanded fashion, the editors introduced the article with a fairly straight headline, "CREATIONIST CAPTAIN SEES BATTLE 'HOTTING UP.'" Also, many of Ham's views, such as his interpretation of the word "day" in Genesis as a twenty-four-hour period, were presented without negative comment or implication.

On the other hand, a number of anti-creationist, editorialized phrases and comments were sprinkled about in the story, such as the description of Ham's full-sized dinosaur models as "an oddly dissenting chorus." (Apparently the writer meant the dinosaurs were dissenting to Ham's creationist position.)

Overall, the treatment Ken Ham received in this article was as balanced and favorable as any outspoken creation advocate can reasonably expect in a pro-evolution paper like the *Times*. Unfortunately, such articles are extremely rare, and as mentioned above, are probably printed so that if challenged, the paper can point to them and say, "Look here, we have given these creationists some decent coverage!"

Another area the *Times* cannot afford to overlook in this evolution debate is the research being done on the cellular and molecular level. Some embarrassing reports (for evolutionists and the *Times*) are emerging from the scientific establishment, which suggest strongly that intelligent design is a more reasonable explanation for life than the haphazard evolutionary process of natural selection.

One of these scientists is Michael J. Behe, a biochemist and professor of biological sciences at Lehigh University and author of the disturbing (to evolutionists) *Darwin's Black Box: the Biochemical Challenge to Evolution* (New York: The Free Press—Simon & Schuster Inc., 1996).

The gist of Behe's argument is that traditional evolutionists, such as Harvard's Stephen Jay Gould, have become so fixated on changes in organs and body parts that they have completely ignored biochemical issues. Yet these biochemical issues cannot be explained adequately by the usual evolutionary conjectures.

At one point in his book, Behe thoroughly roughed up Gould. First, he argued in a rather low-key academic tone that contrary to Gould's attempted evolutionary explanation, the panda's "thumb," a bony projection from the animal's wrist, can be explained best by an "intelligent-design theory." These are fighting words for an evolutionist because "intelligent design" is a code word implying the operation of a Super Intelligence—that is, God.

Then Behe really took off the gloves:

"Gould has never done the science to support his idea: he has not shown or calculated what the minimum extension of the wristbone would have to be to help the panda; he has not justified the behavioral changes that would be necessary to take advantage of the change in bone structure; and he has not mentioned how pandas ate before acquiring the thumb. He has not done anything except to spin a tale" (pp. 228–29).

The *Times'* editors simply can't ignore an intellectual heavy-weight like Behe, even when he rhetorically decks one of the paper's favorite science authorities. They even ran a positive review on Behe's book in the Sunday Book Review (8/4/96, p. 8).

Furthermore, the editors actually gave him a guest column in the much-coveted space on the op-ed page, which they headlined, "TEACH EVOLUTION—AND ASK HARD QUESTIONS" (8/13/99, p. A19).

Behe's column was probably acceptable to the paper not only because of his obvious credentials, but also because he adroitly backed into his skepticism about traditional evolutionary theory. First, he knocked possible opponents off balance by conceding that he felt the Kansas School Board decision, which made the teaching of evolution optional, was wrong. But the reason for his disapproval, he said, was not that he believed in evolution. Rather he believed children deserve to know all sides of this issue.

He then went on to assert that the theory of evolution is full of holes, and if the subject is to be taught, the flaws should be taught as well. His artful conclusion went like this:

"Teach Darwin's elegant theory. But also discuss where it has real problems accounting for the data, where data are severely limited, where scientists might be engaged in wishful thinking and where alternative—even 'heretical' explanations are possible" (p. A19).

The Origin of Life and the Universe—According to the Times

The evolution-creation controversy is only one illustration of how the scientism of the *Times* is at work in our culture. An even more basic scientific quest, which is covered regularly by the paper, is the search for the origin of life and of the universe itself.

A dramatically illustrated Science Times feature published on February 2, 1999, was headlined "IN SEARCH OF STAR DUST AND CLUES TO LIFE" (p. D1, D2). The theme, as the heading implied, was the status of investigations by astrophysicists on how comets might have transported to earth "interstellar dust," which laid the groundwork for the spontaneous rise of life.

The writer explained the concept in these terms:

"A rain of cosmic and cometary material is widely thought to have brought early Earth not only water but the carbon-rich molecules necessary for life.

"Indeed, some scientists believe the speeding mountains of dirty ice known as comets may themselves support primitive life" (p. D1).

A clearly implied message here, as well as in many other *Times'* stories, was that the origin of life was purely a physical phenomenon. The assumption was that all of reality, including the origin of life, could be understood as having occurred within a closed, naturalistic system. God had nothing to do with the process—at least not in the context of the paper's radical, non-theistic scientism.

It's also interesting that the scientific authorities referred to in this article—researchers who were supposed to have affirmed a naturalistic view of the world that was "widely thought" to be true—were not identified. To be sure, a few scientists were quoted later in the article. But the article offered no support for this broad reference to a large body of anonymous experts.

Finally, this feature—like practically every other *Times* article on the origin of life and the universe—contained no hint that perhaps divine intervention was involved as a First Cause. At first blush, it may seem naive to question the omission of any mention of a supernatural or extra-dimensional option as a source for the beginning of the cosmos.

But why should we necessarily assume that mentioning a divine option is inappropriate?

The only reason would seem to be the anti-supernatural assumption about reality that the *Times* has foisted on the public—again, through the process of Culture Creep. Here's another way to think about this issue:

Suppose you are the owner of a magazine or newspaper, and you really do believe that God had a hand in creating human beings or the universe. If you make this supernatural assumption, wouldn't you be likely to demand that your editors and reporters take this option into account in their articles?

Of course you would, and that's exactly what's happened with magazines like *World* and *Christianity Today*, which take the supernatural option seriously.

But the *New York Times*, like most other secular publications and television and radio outlets that it influences, makes the opposite assumption. The supernatural realm doesn't exist, or if it does, it has no relevance to daily life. The only thing that's really real is the here and now—the three-dimensional universe plus time, or the reality that we can perceive with the five senses.

So the principles of scientism—and not those that may exist in some dimension beyond our limited world—must control any interpretation we give to explain reality. To be true to these anti-supernatural assumptions, standard secular news coverage cannot possibly suggest that God might be capable of breaking through into the cosmos or the events of human history.

THE SPIRIT OF HUMANISM

The fundamental philosophy that constitutes the bedrock of the *Times'* worldview—a philosophy that is even more basic and comprehensive than the scientism that drives the paper's views on evolution and the origins of the universe—might best be described as humanism.

Specifically, the *Times* affirms a brand of this philosophy that might best be labeled "modern" or "secular" humanism. Although some types of contemporary humanism incorporate religious concepts, these two are notable for their extreme focus on human abilities and reason and their denial of God and the supernatural. (For a detailed summary of different types of humanism, see Frederick Edwords, "What Is Humanism?" American Humanism Association, *www.jcn.com/humanism.html*.)

But in practically any of its forms, today's versions of humanism differ markedly from what humanism was like when it first appeared in the West. In fact, the humanism of the Renaissance often provided Christian believers with a new means of expressing their faith. Specifically, the Christians of the Renaissance used language and allusions from ancient Greek and Roman cultures to express their own human experiences and their personal understanding of the world around them.

A case in point was the philosopher Petrarch (Francesco Petrarca), known as the "father of Humanism," who lived during the Italian Renaissance of the fourteenth century (Cassirer, Kristeller, and Randall, p. 3).

Petrarch, in interpreting his real-life experiences in the context of his Christian beliefs, wrote such classic essays as "The Ascent of Mont Ventoux." Reflecting in 1336 on his daring climb up this mountain, he compared his experience with the struggles and risks inherent in living the serious Christian life (pp. 36–46).

But over the years, the Christian underpinnings to humanism were lost, much as John Locke's reliance on biblical authority in explaining his concept of human rights was lost. By the end of the twentieth century, human reason, instead of being seen as one of several means to find truth, had become the only means.

These ideas were summed up in *Humanist Manifesto I*, published in 1933 and signed by such intellectuals as John Dewey, Charles Francis Potter, and Edwin H. Wilson. The Manifesto led off with these two affirmations:

"First: Religious humanists regard the universe as self-existing and not created.

"Second: Humanism believes that man is a part of nature and that he has emerged as a result of a continuous process" (*www.humanism.net/documents/manifesto1.html*).

A later version, *Humanist Manifesto II*, which was published in 1973, declared in part: "We believe . . . that traditional dogmatic or authoritarian religions that place revelation, God, ritual, or creed above human needs and experience do a disservice to the human species. . . . As nontheists, we begin with humans not God, nature not deity" (*www.humanism.net/documents/ manifesto2.html*).

To be sure, there are "Christian humanists" and even "theistic religious humanists" today. But in popular thought, the humanist movement is usually assumed to be antisupernatural, antireligious, and set in opposition to traditional religious belief.

What does this modern humanism have to do with the *New York Times*?

As you think about many of the topics discussed in this book, you'll see that the *Times'* belief system fits neatly into an antireligious, antisupernatural humanist mold.

Remember, for instance, how the paper has waged an ongoing campaign against evangelical Christianity and traditional Roman Catholicism. One important flash point in this controversy is the issue of supernaturalism—with the *Times* not only implicitly rejecting the presence of God in human affairs, but actually working actively against those who believe in his intervention.

Recall also how the concept of "rights" promoted by the newspaper and its followers has lost any significant connection with the original biblical roots, which were relied on by John Locke and even Thomas Jefferson.

Reflect on how a human-centered scientific worldview in various news articles and most columns in the paper has replaced any spiritual interpretation of the origin of man and the universe.

Consider how personal moral standards have either disappeared from the pages of the *Times*, or have become so flaccid and distorted that they have largely lost their power to provide meaningful guidance for individual conduct.

Think about the paper's assumption that humankind has the potential for perfection—if only humans will exercise their human reason wisely. The *New York Times* never seriously suggests that perhaps a fundamental spiritual piece is missing deep inside us—a piece that can only be replaced by establishing a connection with a divine reality that transcends human reason.

Again, a reader may object that a daily secular newspaper has no responsibility or business meddling with such spiritual issues.

That kind of speculation is best left to the preachers and theologians, this argument goes.

Yet suppose there is some possibility that the spiritual realm is real and that there actually may be other dimensions of reality out there—where God, angels, demons, and the like interact with one another and even intervene in human affairs. In such a case, shouldn't any news organization that claims to be fair and balanced (if not objective) in its reporting make some effort to explore spiritual claims seriously—and not just relegate them to an obscure "Beliefs" column or an infrequent op-ed piece?

When outlandish fringe groups, which feature bizarre patterns of personal behavior or display all the earmarks of cults or the occult, send out a press release, the *Times* is quick to respond. We've seen many examples of this in the preceding pages.

Also, no matter how cynical or anti-religious the Manhattan news mammoth may seem at times—or how hardheaded or skeptical its reporters and editors may appear—they have ears that "itch" for strange doctrines. Furthermore, they are driven by restless minds and hearts toward any "new thing," to use the words of one spiritual sage. In the end, the staff stands ready to promote to the hilt the most novel beliefs or outrageous lifestyles—especially those that are inconsistent with traditional Christianity.

Yet when a controversial issue supported by traditional Christians comes to the fore, hostility usually surfaces from beneath the paper's seemingly cool, calm, pluralistic exterior. Any pretense to open-mindedness disappears because traditional faith is the enemy of contemporary scientism and humanism. And the *New York Times* is the primary public relations outlet and standard bearer for these antitheistic worldviews.

So these are the broad outlines of this new fundamentalism, the "gospel according to the *New York Times*." As part of the discussion, you have been introduced not only to the tenets of the faith, but also to the dangers that the paper's use of Culture Creep may present to the general public—and to you personally.

What can be done to counter the incredible power of the paper to influence the American mind?

If you find that you agree with most or all of the *Times'* beliefs that have been described in these first three parts of the book, then the answer is simple: Do nothing.

Just allow the *Times* and the mass media organizations that follow it in lockstep to move you inexorably in the currently prevailing humanistic cultural direction. Permit them to influence and shape your mind in their own image, and soon you'll be able to regurgitate the paper's sacred word on every major social, moral, and political issue as easily and glibly as any *Times'* editorial writer.

But if you have serious problems with one or more of the cultural changes that the *Times* is promoting, then you need to consider some countermeasures. You need to take serious steps to develop your own personal program to counter the influence of the paper's insidious Culture Creep in your mind and in the minds of your family and loved ones.

To this end, I've summarized in the following chapter some suggestions for creating a protective program, which I trust will help you combat the moral corrosion of Culture Creep.

PART IV

RESPONDING TO THE NEW FUNDAMENTALISM

CHAPTER 17

A STRATEGY TO COMBAT CULTURE CREEP

S uppose that you have decided that you don't want to succumb to the *Times'* conversion tactics—and that you want to select your own belief system and not be influenced, consciously or subconsciously, to affirm the values of the newspaper.

What can you do to protect yourself?

Secondarily, what can you do to help your family and friends establish their own self-defense mechanisms?

Here are eight suggested defenses, any of which might make a dent in the *Times'* influence. The first six, which are most appropriate for use by individuals, should provide you and your family with the personal protection you need.

The final two would require major financing, along with huge levels of individual and corporate effort and commitment. But if either of these last two strategies should succeed, the power of the *Times* could be reduced on a much larger scale.

DEFENSE #1: LEARN TO READ AND LISTEN TO THE NEWS CRITICALLY AND ANALYTICALLY.

That's what this book has been all about, but here are some of the highlights once more.

The first thing to remember is that if you just accept what you read or hear uncritically, you'll almost certainly be influenced over time to accept the messages that come into your mind. As a result, your mind and belief system will inevitably change through the process of Culture Creep.

So as you read the *Times,* or as you read your daily paper or listen to news on the radio or TV—all of which have been influenced to some degree by the *Times*—stay alert and mentally active.

Note the fact selection, and remember that every paper or newscast always leaves out plenty of facts. The biases of the writers, reporters, and editors—not to mention the publisher—come into play in the choice of facts for publication. In particular, the organization will pile up facts that support its worldview and omit facts that don't. Also, the facts that supposedly present the "other side of the story" will frequently be "straw men," or weak arguments or points that the paper's primary quoted authorities can easily shoot down.

Also, watch how the *Times* and related media organizations orchestrate news reports, editorials, op-ed pieces, and other articles to emphasize a favored point or belief over and over, from many different angles. If you can see what the organization is doing, you'll be much less likely to lose control over how your attitudes are shaped.

In news stories, look for slanted headlines, photos with a message, and editorialized statements that convey an opinion rather than unadorned fact. Also, pay attention to the "lead" (first few sentences or first paragraph or two) and the "kicker" (final quotation, facts, or thoughts in the last paragraph or two). The lead will put your thinking on the track desired by the paper, while the kicker will fix in your mind the primary message you're supposed to take away from the article. Both can enhance the process of Culture Creep.

So always read or listen with these and other active techniques described in previous chapters. Also, teach your children and friends how to employ them. If you do, you'll be taking advantage of the most potent personal defense available to fend off the subtle influences of the *Times*.

DEFENSE #2: EXPOSE CONFLICTS OF INTEREST INVOLVING THE TIMES.

This defense tactic is harder to employ than the first because conflicts are often buried in obscure references. If you're not alert, conflicts can slip right past you. But if you keep your eyes open, interesting tidbits will emerge.

Consider, for instance, our discussion about the close ties that the *Times* has to the Pulitzer Prize organization. This group has awarded the paper more Pulitzers than any other news organization—a record that greatly bolsters the *Times*' reputation as the greatest newspaper.

Or reflect on our discussion about one of Vice President Al Gore's most important female advisers in his presidential bid for the 2000 nomination—a woman who also had written for the *Times* Sunday magazine. Furthermore, she was married to a top *Times*' magazine editor. And that editor, in turn, had been a speechwriter for President Bill Clinton. The *Times*, of course, has consistently and overwhelmingly endorsed Democratic political candidates, including Bill Clinton.

But even if you miss these potential conflicts, which are often buried in unobtrusive references, the paper's competitors, such as the *Wall Street Journal*, are always on the lookout for embarrassing connections. Exposing potential conflicts and inconsistencies always provides a good opportunity to tweak the "newspaper of record."

You'll recall, for instance, that the *Journal* ran a story showing that the *Times* was a big contributor to a Manhattan theater organization. The *Times* in turn ran editorials and articles designed to influence the theater to reinstate a pro-gay play, which the theater had originally dropped. (The theater eventually caved in and conformed to the *Times'* position by reinstating the play.)

The more conflicts you can find, the more information you'll have to identify the moral and political directions in which the news organization is trying to push you.

DEFENSE #3: LIMIT YOUR EXPOSURE TO THE TIMES.

The point here is not to stop reading the newspaper or listening to newscasts—though some who have become frustrated with biased national news coverage have chosen this route and seem quite happy with their decision.

Also, I personally wouldn't recommend that anyone rely only on publications, commentators, or newscasts that merely reinforce one's own opinions.

Instead, if you hope to shore up your beliefs and defenses as solidly as possible, it's important to know your opponents thoroughly. This way, you can identify subtle attempts to inject a message for humanism here, or a point for scientism there. You'll become more alert to the multitude of ways that the media can promote an unacceptable shift in your view on some basic moral issues, such as abortion, adultery, or divorce.

If you know what the *Times* and its cohorts are doing—and how they are doing it—you will be much better prepared to defend yourself than if you're ignorant.

On the other hand, I believe it's also important to balance your reading of the *Times* or similar secular news media with publications from strong news organizations that operate from entirely different perspectives. My personal program, in addition to the *Times*, includes reading the *Wall Street Journal* every day; consulting *Christianity Today*, *World*, and the *Weekly Standard* magazines regularly; and, listening whenever possible to the news from a Christian perspective on CBN or TBN. By relying on this variety of national outlets, I find I have access to intelligent, well-researched viewpoints that are quite different from those of the *Times*.

In other words, withdrawing from all exposure to the world's views can be counterproductive—and may even be unbiblical for a Christian. Or as Oswald Chambers, relying on New Testament authority, has written: "We are to be *in* the world but not *of* it; to be disconnected fundamentally, not externally" (Chambers, p. 332 [Nov. 27]; see also Matthew 5:14; 1 Corinthians 5:9–13; John 17:15–16).

DEFENSE #4: DEVISE AN EFFECTIVE SYSTEM OF APOLOGETICS THAT WILL ENABLE YOUR BELIEF SYSTEM TO PREVAIL IN DISPUTES WITH THOSE WHO FOLLOW THE TIMES' GOSPEL.

Many books are available on apologetics, or the art of defending the Christian faith or other belief systems. So I won't attempt to replicate or compete with them in this short subsection.

But here are a few general guidelines to keep in mind as you devise your own system of apologetics—guidelines that may help you ward off undue influences from the mass media in general and the *New York Times* in particular.

First of all, it's important to *have your own comprehensive worldview*, which you can use to test every point in the *Times'* worldview. This means you should know exactly how you feel about such issues as abortion, creation, capital punishment, and the like. Even more important, you must settle your views on God, Jesus Christ, and the means of salvation.

Second, in evaluating the beliefs of the *Times* or other publications or individuals who differ with your convictions, the best strategy is first to *identify the basic worldview or spiritual assumptions*.

For example, if you're exploring the issue of creation, it's important to know if your adversary is assuming that there is no God who intervenes in the universe or in human affairs. If you recognize an atheistic, agnostic, or deistic assumption, it would probably be pointless to argue beliefs or conclusions about creation that arise from that assumption. Rather, it will most likely be best to pinpoint and discuss the basic assumption first.

Suppose you're talking about creation with an atheist (one of the tiny percentage of Americans, about 1–3 percent, who believe there is no God). In this case, arguing about whether the world was created in six twenty-four-hour days or in millions of years would be pointless, because the atheist won't even accept your basic assumption that God exists.

Similarly, any biblical interpretation of creation will be irrelevant or unintelligible to the modern-day deist, who believes that a God created the universe but hasn't intervened since the first moment of creation.

To be sure, some atheists or deists may respond to a well-formulated argument for intelligent design over evolutionary natural selection (see the reference to the biochemist Michael Behe in chapter 16).

But unless you are an expert on this subject and also an exceptionally adept apologist, it will probably be best to deal first with your friend's basic assumptions about God, or his personal view of Jesus Christ. Then, if he or she ever decides to embrace your assumptions about God, you'll be in a stronger position to discuss creation, abortion, or some other related topic.

DEFENSE #5: LEARN TO IDENTIFY AND COMBAT CULTURE CREEP IN ENTERTAINMENT AND OTHER MEDIA.

The *Times* has a vast influence not only over other news organizations, but also over the public acceptance of entertainment vehicles, such as films, plays, and artistic exhibits. A favorable review in the *Times* will often assure a reasonably successful run in the theater or museum.

But the influence of mass entertainment offerings reaches far beyond the *Times* and can have a serious impact on personal beliefs, especially those of young people. So it's important to know what messages are being conveyed in movies and on television and to alert your family members—especially your children—to the ways they may be influenced by mass entertainment.

Two examples from contemporary popular culture that come to mind involve movies that received reviews that ranged from generally good to absolute raves: *Shakespeare in Love* and *Pleasantville*.

In the first, *Shakespeare in Love*, fine acting, a compelling plot, and an extremely well-written screenplay garnered some of the best reviews of 1999. But a closer evaluation of the film revealed two underlying assumptions: first, adultery may have some mild consequences but is basically acceptable and romantic; second, in many contexts, extramarital sex is mainly funny and a pleasurable diversion, not morally reprehensible.

Pleasantville, which moved along at a good clip, with an engaging plot and unusual special effects and cinematography, projected the basic message that free premarital and extramarital sex was far superior to traditional sexual morality. Not only that, free sex could enhance one's personal creativity.

The film also gave a clear message that the "old" or "traditional" moral standards of the mid-twentieth century were repressive and encouraged narrow thinking, right-wing violence, anti-intellectualism and book burning. The film stressed this point by picturing those who affirmed the "old" morality and culture in black and white. In contrast, the "new" and "enlightened" morality prevailing at the end of the twentieth century came across as exciting and stimulating, and the hope for the future. Those who finally caught on to this message started showing up on the screen in color.

The insidious nature of such movies is that they appear in extremely artful packages but convey immoral values. In fact, their messages conflict with traditional morality from a number of religious traditions, including evangelical Protestantism, Roman Catholicism, and Orthodox Judaism.

Furthermore, it's not really adequate to say R-rated movies are prohibited, but PG-13 or PG movies are all right. In fact, many PG-13 and even PG movies are built on premises that run directly counter to the moral messages that many families, churches, and synagogues are trying to teach.

Remember: most movie and TV ratings are devised by secular organizations—including the Motion Picture Association of America (MPAA) and the TV Parental Guidelines Oversight Monitoring Board. These groups have no particular connection to or interest in biblical or traditional morality. Their main objective seems to be to assuage public concern about violence and sex in the media so as to keep money flowing into the entertainment industry. They have shown little interest in reversing the moral decline of American culture.

DEFENSE #6: UNDERSTAND THE TIMES' CORPORATE CULTURE.

It's important to remember that the worldview propagated by the *Times* is not simply the result of some conscious conspiracy being fomented inside a dark room on Manhattan's 43rd Street.

To be sure, some of the beliefs that the paper is spreading are formulated and disseminated in a completely conscious manner. The editorial board, for instance, has regular meetings to determine the paper's positions on the various issues discussed in this book, and their conclusions appear as editorials.

But perhaps even more significant than these explicit decisions, the *Times* has developed a powerful corporate culture that causes those who are part of it—the editors, reporters, and columnists—to regurgitate the party line on a regular basis. There are a few dissenting voices, such as A. M. Rosenthal, who was finally fired. (*Overseas Press Club Bulletin*, Dec. 1999, p. 7). But the overwhelming majority—those who write the headlines, run the photos, draft the leads and kickers, and select the facts—operate in a way that is quite consistent with the corporate culture. This conformity may be subconscious, but the result is the same as any conscious decision.

So it's best not to accuse the *Times* or any other media organization of engaging in a conscious conspiracy to subvert American morality. Such an accusation smacks of the tactics of wacky conspiracy theory advocates who are easy to dismiss.

Instead, it's best to say that some of the *Times'* proselytism for its worldview, such as the editorial page, is most certainly conscious. Also, some is undoubtedly subconscious, or a consequence of the influence of the paper's corporate culture on the management and staff. In the end, however, the result is the same. The organization as a whole moves inexorably forward, influencing and changing public opinion and beliefs.

❖

These six "defenses" are most useful for those who hope to counter the influence exerted by the *Times* on themselves, their families, and their friends. But there are also some broader possibilities that reach well beyond such individual efforts.

DEFENSE #7: TAKE OVER THE TIMES.

One radical possibility that has been suggested for eliminating the *Times'* influence is to engineer a corporate takeover of the paper. But from all indications, that would be an extremely difficult if not impossible task.

The main problem is that even though the organization is publicly owned and listed on the New York Stock Exchange, the Ochs-Sulzberger family members and connections own the large majority of the voting stock. The public mainly has access to non-voting shares.

To effect a hostile takeover, a significant number of owners of the voting stock would need to defect. How might this occur?

A remote possibility is that one or more minority holders of a significant block of voting shares might at some point in the future "see the light" and defect from the majority mind-set. Then they could initiate a takeover attempt from within the company.

Another possibility is that other minority shareholders might take advantage of the variety of laws that are currently on the books to harass and snipe away at the parent organization and its worldview through lawsuits. Such a tactic might at least distract the paper and slow its process of proselytizing. But any such corporate efforts would require a huge war chest and a significant number of experts with a long-term commitment to the cause.

DEFENSE #8: ESTABLISH AN OPPOSING NEWS ORGANIZATION.

This final possibility for countering or reducing the impact of the *Times*—establishing a "counter-paper"—is a strategy that has been attempted by other news organizations in other contexts. But the results have been mixed.

One of these ventures has been the *Washington Times*, which was founded in 1982 as an alternative conservative voice to the *Washington Post*. The paper is controlled through News World Communications, a corporation affiliated with Rev. Sun Myung Moon's Unification Church (Infoseek Company Profile: News World Communications, *www.infoseek.go.com*). The *Washington Times*, in turn, has founded *Insight* magazine, which was designed to compete with the weekly newsmagazines.

Moon—who has published his own scriptures and has suggested that he may be the messiah—and his church officials have denied that they exercise any editorial control over these publications. Many staff members have also denied these accusations, though a few have resigned after claiming that the Unification Church dictated editorial policy *(www.rickross.com)*.

In any event, the *Washington Times* has added a generally respected, conservative daily newspaper voice to counterbalance to some extent the liberal posturing of the *Washington Post*. Up to this point, however, the *Washington Times* has not succeeded in challenging the *Post* seriously, either in circulation or in influence, as the premier resident newspaper of Washington, D.C.

In the 1970s, evangelical Christians, through the old Logos publishing company, attempted to establish a national weekly newspaper called *The National Courier*. Top editors, reporters, and writers from major newspapers and other publications around the country contributed to the effort, and the news features caught the attention of national politicians and other leaders. The coverage of Jimmy Carter's run for the presidency in 1976 was particularly extensive. But Logos lacked the financing to keep the publication going, and the *Courier* closed down only a few years after its inception.

CBN founder Pat Robertson launched a promising effort to make a major impact in television with his Family Channel, but he sold out to Rupert Murdoch and Fox shortly after the concept began to experience financial success. Fox renamed the channel the Fox Family Channel.

To his credit, Robertson has continued his *700 Club*, which includes a one-hour news and interview program on both the Fox Family Channel and the Trinity Broadcasting Network (TBN). National politicians and other leaders frequently appear on the program, and the result provides at least the beginning of a much-needed counterbalance to the secular network shows. But a much more extensive effort would be required for CBN or TBN to begin to make significant inroads into the secular news market.

More recently, the Paxson Communications Corporation, owner of the PAX TV network, has begun, with some success, to schedule family programs that tend to uphold traditional family and moral values, including reruns of sitcoms and other features. Their Web site, *www.paxtv.com*, provides an overview of their offerings.

But news programs are virtually nonexistent on PAX. Until a greater effort is made to cover the news, the impact of PAX programming on network-fostered Culture Creep is likely to be negligible. Also, Paxson recently cut a deal with NBC, which involved the transfer to NBC of a significant block of Paxson stock. The outcome of this arrangement on the future of PAX TV and its independence remains uncertain.

If past experience is any indication, at least three major problems will loom as large obstacles to any attempt to set up a news organization to counterbalance the *New York Times*:

Problem #1: The *Times* sits at the top of the journalistic pin-
nacle and has spent a century shoring up its
position.

Such dominance cannot be overcome in a few months, or even
years. Anyone with the desire to challenge or surpass this paper
must be ready for a long, expensive, and bloody fight.

Problem #2: Any effective counterbalance to the *Times* will
probably have to be established in a *Times*-related
news medium—either print, or the Internet, or
more likely, both print and the Internet.

Relying on a television newscast as the primary weapon to defy
the *Times* is probably doomed to failure. A major reason is that in
the journalism business, pundits tend to compare like to like: print
to print, TV to TV, and so on.

Furthermore, there is an assumption—though many TV news
stars would never admit it—that good print reporting is superior
to good TV reporting. The reason is obvious: the print reporter
has more time and space to research and present his point than
the TV or radio newsperson.

Finally, as we have seen frequently in the preceding pages,
most journalists assume that the best print reporters are those
who work for the *Times*. Ergo, the *Times* stands at the top of the
journalistic heap, print or electronic—and any organization that
plans to mount an effective challenge must do so on the *Times*'
own turf.

Still, the *Times* is protecting its flanks by moving steadily into
Internet-related news coverage. In fact, the paper has predicted in
its own pages that twenty-four-hour news reporting via the
Internet is the wave of the future—and it plans to be in the forefront of the movement (12/27/99, p. C1, C8).

Specifically, Richard J. Meislin, editor in chief of the *Times*'
unit, Times Company Digital, declared:

"Our gut instinct is going to be that people come to the New
York Times for news that is the quality of the New York Times

newspaper and they would like to have that throughout the day" (p. C8).

Problem #3: Perhaps the greatest challenge for anyone with the skill and means to challenge the paper will be the temptation to sell out, just as success seems within reach.

Anyone who is smart and experienced enough to give the *Times* a run for its premier position will also be smart enough to recognize the possibility of a huge business windfall as success draws closer. As offers pour in, the prospect of recouping all losses and walking away with an unimaginable fortune could be overwhelming. Only the most committed entrepreneur with a vision for shaping the future of American culture will be able to withstand the pressure and the temptation.

CHAPTER 18

IS THERE AN AUTHENTIC VOICE OF THE PEOPLE?

As things now stand, the *New York Times* is making a strong bid to become the voice of the American people. But is that voice authentic?

To answer this question, reflect for a moment on the paper's various moral and political biases. Consider the *Times'* frequently demonstrated hostility to evangelical Christianity and traditional Roman Catholicism . . . condoning of blasphemy against revered religious beliefs and figures . . . support of unlimited abortion . . . benign views toward open-ended sexual activity and relationships . . . advocacy of the dilution of United States power abroad . . . and affinity for government-financed welfare programs.

Do these *Times'* beliefs really reflect what most citizens want? More importantly, do they reflect the principles *you* believe are true and right?

Clearly, the *Times'* worldview is different in many ways from the majority American point of view. It also represents beliefs that depart significantly from those of most traditional American religious faiths.

But with the *Times'* prodding, American views are changing and conforming increasingly to the paper's belief system, or its peculiar "gospel," if you will. In other words, the *Times* has moved into the spiritual vacuum created by the weak or nonexistent value systems that permeate much of our culture. By default, the paper is leaving its imprint on our basic concepts of right and wrong.

For growing numbers of people, the *Times*, not traditional religious faith, now defines that which is ultimately right and true, and that which is just and good. The *Times*, instead of the Bible, has become our cultural scripture.

Yet by any measure, it seems absurd to allow any news media organization to set our basic moral and cultural standards and agenda. No single mass communications business—not even so august an enterprise as the *New York Times*—should occupy such a dominant and potentially dangerous position.

In short, the *Times* is not the single legitimate authentic voice of the people now, and it never should be. Rather, in a truly pluralistic society, the *Times* should be only one strong voice among many.

But to ensure that result, the majority who affirm values and views that differ from those of the *Times* must stand up and be counted. They must begin to bolster their defenses against the process of Culture Creep, which the *Times* is employing to spread its gospel far and wide.

If increasing numbers of Americans will simply begin to read and listen with discernment—and be willing to express their opinions freely—no false gospel, regardless of how compelling and seductive, can overpower them. Those who know what they believe and are able to defend those beliefs skillfully will always project a strong and influential voice in a free society.

In the end, then, the authentic voice of the people should be heard clearly. But that voice doesn't have to be sounded only through publications or other mass media outlets that advocate views different from those of the *Times*. Rather, the authentic voice of the people should emerge through the many voices that well up from the hearts and souls of average citizens. Perhaps most important of all, that authentic voice should always resonate from somewhere deep inside the wellsprings of your own mind and spirit.

APPENDIX:
RESEARCH METHODOLOGY

In this exploration of the belief system of the *New York Times*, I have attempted to allow the paper, through its pages, to reveal the issues and beliefs that its own editors, management, and reporters regard as most important.

My purpose has not been to try to divine how the individual worldviews of top management—such as the publisher, Arthur Ochs Sulzberger Jr., or the executive editor, Joseph Lelyveld—may interact with each other or influence other high-ranking news officials. Nor have I focused on any personality dynamics that may cause views at the top to seep down and affect the hiring or assignment of reporters and writers. Such forces are undoubtedly at work. But in general, identifying and evaluating them has been beyond the scope of my inquiry.

Instead, I've concentrated on the peculiar corporate culture and belief system that permeate the *Times*, and that are reflected in the actual pages of the paper. These are the messages that are most likely to enter your mind, directly or indirectly, through the multiple means available to modern-day news media.

In general, my methodology has been implemented in several distinct stages. First, I began to study seriously the journalistic techniques and impact of the *Times* when I was competing against its reporters for several years as a New York *Daily News* reporter and writer in the early 1970s.

Second, I began to assemble a personal "morgue" of *Times* articles for facts and background information when I left the paper to concentrate on writing books in the mid–1970s, and then founded and edited a national church management newsletter through the early 1980s.

Third, I have consulted the *Times* frequently and have cited the paper as a factual authority in the approximately eighty books that I have now authored, coauthored or ghostwritten over the past thirty years. During this book-writing phase of my career, I continued to assemble an extensive morgue of *Times* clips and references.

Fourth, as I proceeded through this extensive reading, study, and use of the *Times* in my own work, I began to notice trends in the paper's coverage, along with the apparent promotion of various causes and points of view. An evident orchestration of editorials, op-ed pieces, news stories and photos to support certain key issues emerged time and time again.

Fifth, in the mid-1990s, I embarked on a more formal study of how the paper handled a wide variety of issues—such as evangelical Christianity, capital punishment, gun control, abortion, and globalism. Also, I tried to determine if there were any specific strategies and techniques that the paper was employing to promote its favorite values and viewpoints.

To achieve these objectives, from the summer of 1995 through the summer of 1999, I collected thousands of articles and entered many of them into more than two dozen spreadsheet categories. Then, relying on my decades as a journalist in various types of news media, I evaluated and analyzed them in an effort to understand more thoroughly distinctive trends and possible biases in the *Times* coverage. Also, to determine weighting and frequency of coverage of different issues, I made extensive use of the archives on the *Times* Web site.

The end result of this effort was the listing and discussion of the "sins" and "spirits" of the *Times* in the text, as well the exploration of other issues, such as the peculiar approaches of the paper to the concept of tolerance and human rights. Also, to put the *Times*' coverage into a broader context, I have referred frequently to coverage by other news sources, such as the *Wall Street Journal*, the *Palm Beach Post*, the Associated Press, college magazines, professional journals, and news coverage on television.

Obviously, time and space constraints have made it impossible to cover every issue mentioned in this book in equal depth. But I trust that that the "gospel according to the *Times*"—the comprehensive worldview that the paper clearly supports and promotes—has emerged with some clarity in these pages. And I also hope that some readers will be inspired to consider a little more carefully the information that enters their minds every day through their favorite news sources.

GLOSSARY

[Sources include the *New York Times* Web site; Melvin Mencher's *News Reporting and Writing*; William L. Rivers, *The Mass Media: Reporting—Writing—Editing*, pp. 311ff.; William Metz, *Newswriting from Lead to "30"*; and my personal experience in the news business.]

"A" head. A single-column headline, used at the top of the front page.

Angle. Special viewpoint, thrust, or theme of a story.

Attribution. Identification of the person who is quoted or is used as the authority or source in a story.

Balance. Characteristic of a competently reported and edited story, where both sides of an issue or dispute are given.

Banner headline. A big headline that runs across the top of a page (usually the front page). Also called a "streamer," "screamer," or "the big one."

Beat. A reporter's regularly assigned territory of news coverage, such as the "criminal courts beat," the "police beat," or the "city hall beat." Also, the term may refer to an exclusive story (a "scoop") that a reporter has acquired ahead of competitors.

Bias. A personal belief or worldview that interferes with completely balanced or objective news reporting. Every reporter, editor, and corporate culture has some bias.

Body type. The typeface (usually 8-point or 9-point) in which most news stories are printed. The *Times'* body type style is called "Imperial."

Box. Short news story, list, or other material that is enclosed and set off from the rest of the copy on the page by lines. These graphics give the appearance of a two-dimensional "box" on the page.

Byline. The name of the writer or reporter of the story, which is printed just under the headline at the top of the text. When there is more than one name on the byline, the first will often be that of the person who has "reported" the story or gathered the facts, and the second will be that of the writer, or the rewrite man or woman.

Caption. A short explanation or description that accompanies pictures in a newspaper. Also called a "cutline."

Column. An article in which the writer expresses his opinion. Often, news columns are printed on the "op-ed" page, or the page opposite the editorial page. Other columns may appear in the sports section or other parts of the paper. The term also refers to a single, vertical section of type on a news page.

Columnist. A regular column writer or opinion writer for a newspaper or news syndicate.

Copy. The initial version of the newspaper article that is written up by the reporter or writer in preparation for printing and publication.

Copyright. The exclusive legal ownership of a nonfiction or fiction literary work, music, or art. Only the copyright owner, such as a newspaper or author, has the right to duplicate, publish, or sell material that is copyrighted, though there are some exceptions to this rule. For example, limited sections of a copyrighted work can be used or quoted under a "fair use" doctrine, or under educational use exceptions that allow limited copying of materials for classroom purposes.

Correspondent. A reporter who submits news material from a distant location.

Credit line. The name of the photographer or news service that supplies photographs or other pictures.

Dateline. The words immediately preceding an article that provide the time and place of the reporting. If there is no dateline in the *New York Times*, that usually means the story originated in New York City.

Deadline. The final second for getting copy into production for the next edition of the paper. If a reporter misses the deadline, the story won't make it into the next edition.

Ear. A small box on either side of the newspaper's "nameplate," or title (e.g., "*The New York Times*"), on page 1. The *Times'* slogan, "All the News That's Fit to Print," which can be found on the left ear, first appeared on February 10, 1897.

Edition. A particular version of a newspaper printed on a given day. Several editions of the *Times* and many other newspapers are printed each day, with updates of old stories and insertion of new stories. (Compare with "issue," which refers to all editions on a given day.)

Editorial. An article giving the opinion of the news organization's top editors or management on a given topic. Usually published on a separate editorial page.

Editorialize. Inject the opinion of the writer, reporter, editor, or headline or caption writer into an article (usually a news article), headline, or picture caption.

Feature. An article focusing on an unusual, entertaining, or human interest topic, as distinguished from a straight "news story." When used as a verb, the word refers to the act of highlighting or giving special prominence to a story.

First Amendment. The First Amendment to the U.S. Constitution, which guarantees several freedoms, including freedom of religion, speech, assembly, and the press.

Flag. See "nameplate."

Fourth Estate. The press or news media in a free society. Also sometimes called the "fourth branch of government," a term popularized by Douglass Cater in his book by the same name (*The Fourth Branch of Government*, Houghton Mifflin, 1959).

Graf. Abbreviation for "paragraph," often used as shorthand by editors.

Headline. The title of an article, often called a "head," which is printed in large bold type and summarizes the story beneath it. A separate group of editors usually writes headlines, but on the *Times*, regular op-ed columnists have traditionally had the right to draft their own heads.

House story. A story that affects the management or business side of the paper and, as a result, is closely watched or controlled by the editors and management.

Investigative reporter. A journalist who is given the freedom to dig and research beyond daily news coverage in an attempt to find the deeper meaning of an ongoing story, or to expose crime or other malfeasance.

Issue. All editions of a newspaper or magazine published on a particular date.

Journalist. Anyone who researches or writes news reports on a regular basis and has that material published, broadcast, or otherwise disseminated to the public in some fashion.

Jump line. A written notice that a story continues (or "jumps") to another page.

Jump page. The page on which a story continues from an earlier page.

Kicker. At its Web site, the *Times* defines a "kicker" as a headline for a caption, which may refer the reader to an article inside the paper. A more common use of the term is to associate a kicker with the dramatic, punchy ending of a story; or, the term may refer to a short phrase printed above a headline.

Kill. To eliminate all or part of a story. The term "spike" is also used—from the precomputer practice of spearing excess copy on a literal metal spike on the editor or reporter's desk.

Lead. First sentence or paragraph in an article, which sets the tone for the entire piece. Sometimes a lead may run on for two or three paragraphs if the writer is employing a "feature treatment," such as a suspense lead.

Lead story. The main story in a particular newspaper issue or broadcast. In the *Times*, the lead story is always placed on the upper right part of the front page.

Masthead. A descriptive section, usually on the editorial page, that provides information about the paper or magazine's officers, place of publication, and related facts.

Morgue. Library for the news organization containing old clippings, pictures, and other background references to help reporters, editors, and writers prepare for an article.

Nameplate. The newspaper's specially designed title, positioned at the top of page 1. Also called the "logo," or the "flag."

New journalism. A form of journalism popularized in the 1960s by such writers as Tom Wolfe, Truman Capote, and Norman Mailer. The approach involves using slang, colloquialisms, and highly colorful descriptions to make the subject matter seem more realistic. There has also been a trend toward employing fiction devices or "novelizing" techniques to dramatize events, especially in features or book-length writing. Some using these techniques have been criticized or disciplined by their news organizations for making up quotations and characters in stories in their effort to write articles with the greatest impact.

News hole (or "newshole"). The space in a newspaper that is used for news stories and related photos. Advertising is not part of the news hole. The *Times* tends to have the largest news hole among major daily American newspapers.

News story. Also called a "news article" or "news piece," this refers to the printed result of writing and reporting "straight" news, as opposed to clear opinion articles, such as editorials and op-ed columns. Unfortunately, the *Times*, as well as many other newspapers, slips into editorializing from time to time, both in the text of news stories and in headlines that introduce them. (In its most recent advisories, by the way, the *Times* has cautioned that it prefers the word "article" rather than "story" because of the possible suggestion that what is contained in the article isn't factual!)

News analysis. An advanced phase of reporting, which requires the reporter to make sense out of the facts and in some cases interpret them. Though absolutely essential, especially for complex stories, this analysis phase can be abused by reporters and editors who want to impose their own beliefs or worldview on the facts that are being presented. Critical readers should regard the analysis or interpretation sections as major red flags that may signal the presence of fact-slanting and editorializing.

Not for attribution. A quotation or factual reference that is published without naming the source. On occasion, this practice is necessary, but it can also signal bad or dishonest journalism.

Sometimes, a not-for-attribution reference may be used at the insistence of an interviewee, who doesn't want to be identified for some reason, and the only way to get the information is to omit the person's name.

At other times a reporter may elect to omit a named source because one doesn't exist or because the reporter wants to cloak his or her own opinion under the guise of an anonymous "authority" or an unnamed group of authorities.

Objectivity. A state of being, aspired to by some naïve cub reporters or promoted by certain journalism pundits, that supposedly involves being completely fair and even-handed, free of personal prejudices and biases, and immune to the tendency or temptation to distort facts or inject personal interpretations or opinions into news stories. Ain't no such animal.

Off the record. According to the general meaning, information gathered from the subject who says it's "off the record" can't be used at all. But some reporters interpret this to mean it can be used as "background" (can be quoted, but not for attribution or not to be attached to an identifiable source), or "deep background" (can be used, but no direct quotations). Also, many reporters assume that if they get the information from a separate, independent source, it can be used so long as the original source is not identified. Most seasoned reporters will arrive at a definite mutual understanding of the meaning of these terms with their important sources before they print anything.

On background. The subject interviewed can be quoted but cannot be identified by name or characteristics.

Op-ed page. The page opposite the editorial page, which contains columns and other signed opinion articles.

Play. To give a particular emphasis or prominence to a story, such as by placing it on the front page or giving it a banner headline.

Puff piece. A highly positive, entirely non-objective story that promotes the main person, organization, or other subject.

Reefer. A sentence or two, usually on the front page or another early page, that sum up one or more articles inside the paper.

Rewrite. To combine accounts from several different reporters to produce one integrated presentation of a complex event or series of events. Also, to write a story a second or third time to provide extra polish and stylistic impact.

Rewriteman. A member of the paper's editorial staff who specializes in rewrites (see above). Also, "rewrite man" or "rewrite woman."

Sidebar. A relatively short article that explains or elaborates upon the main news story.

Slant. To editorialize, or inject one's opinion into a story that is supposed to be straight news.

Slug. A word or short phrase placed on every page of a story's copy to provide easy identification of the story; also used as a safeguard in case one page should be separated from the others.

Source. The individual, organization, or document that is the foundation of the particular information contained in the story.

Spike. Delete or eliminate, such as "spike" part or all of a particular story.

Stringer. Reporter or correspondent who is not a member of the organization's staff but is paid separately for each article assigned or used.

Subheading. A secondary headline; also called a "subhead."

Syndicate. A special news service that sells news reports and features to more than one news organization. Syndicates may market not only articles but also cartoons and other products. News services, in contrast, focus mainly on news reports.

Tabloid. In general, a newspaper that is printed on smaller sized paper, such as the New York *Daily News* or the *New York Post*. The term has also been used disparagingly to refer to smaller papers that specialize in personal attacks, false reports, or excessive sensationalism of the type that has characterized some of the so-called "supermarket tabloids."

Typeface. Size and type of font used in the publication.

Volume and issue numbers. In the *Times*, the Roman numerals in the upper left part of the front page indicate the volume number, which refers to the number of years the paper has been published. The Arabic numerals reflect the number of issues published by the paper since its founding. The *Times* published its first issue on September 18, 1851.

Weather ear. This entry in the upper right corner of the front page provides the reader's regional weather and the particular edition of the paper for that day.

Wires, wire services. These are news organizations, also known as "press associations," such as the Associated Press and Reuters, to which most major newspapers subscribe. They feed stories to their client papers throughout the day, and will tailor their reporting to fit the needs of clients with specific regional needs or special interests.

SELECTED REFERENCES

Note on citations: Throughout the text, references to printed articles in the *New York Times* national editions have been referred to by the slash method of dating, plus page numbers and section references where necessary. When the text makes it clear that the reference is to the *Times*, specific references to the paper have been omitted. When references could be confused, the initials *NYT* have been inserted to indicate the *Times*. Also, *WSJ* indicates a reference to the *Wall Street Journal*. In accordance with a common journalistic practice, the article "The" has not been capitalized or italicized for the *Times*, the *Journal*, or any other publication, despite the fact that the article may be part of the publication's official title. In the following list of Selected References, major Web sites have been included, but secondary sites have not. Internet addresses for these additional sites can be found at appropriate spots throughout the text. Also, as every Web-savvy reader knows, Web addresses tend to change with some frequency.

Associated Press, 1995–1999.

Audit Bureau of Circulations, May 1999.

Ballenger, Josephine. "Uncovering Abortion: Sisterhood is cautious." *Columbia Journalism Review*. March/April 1992. *www.cjr.org/year/92/2/abortion.asp.*

Behe, Michael J. *Darwin's Black Box: The Biochemical Challenge to Evolution*. New York: The Free Press, 1996.

Belz, Mindy. "Powerful pen." World on the Web. *www.world-mag.com/world/issue/0314-98/cover_1.asp*

Bennett, William J. *The Index of Leading Cultural Indicators*. New York: Touchstone/Simon & Schuster, l994.

Berger, Meyer. *The Story of the New York Times*, 1851–1951. New York: Simon and Schuster, 1951.

Booknotes – Cspan. *www.booknotes.org/transcripts/50148.htm*.

Carroll, Lewis. *Through the Looking-Glass and What Alice Found There*. Electronic Text Center, University of Virginia Library. http://etext.lib.virginia.edu. Chapter 6, p. 123.

Cassirer, Ernst, Paul O. Kristeller, John H. Randall, Jr. *The Renaissance Philosophy of Man*. Chicago: University of Chicago Press, 1948.

Cassirer, Ernst. *The Philosophy of the Enlightenment*, trans. by Fritz C. A. Koelln and James P. Pettegrove. Boston: Beacon Press, 1951, 1955, 1961.

Chambers, Oswald. *My Utmost for His Highest*. New York: Dodd, Mead & Company, 1935.

"Changing Definitions of News." Committee of Concerned Journalists Study. *www.journalism.org/lastudy.htm*.

Choices: Women Speak Out About Abortion. *www.feminist.com/choices.htm*.

Clinton Crisis and the Press: A New Standard of American Journalism? Committee of Concerned Journalists. *www.journalism.org/Clintonreport.htm*

Clinton Crisis and the Press: A Second Look. Committee of Concerned Journalists. *www.journalism.org/DCreport2g.htm*.

Columbia University News. *www.columbia.edu*.

"Commencement." *Mount Holyoke Alumnae Quarterly*. Summer 1999, pp. 15–16.

Commins, Saxe, and Robert N. Linscott. *Man & the State: The Political Philosophers*. New York: Washington Square Press, 1947, 1966.

Committee of Concerned Journalists Web site. *www.journalism.org*.

"Conscience Clauses—a growing threat to health care." ProChoice Resource Center. *www.prochoiceresource.org/html/news/issues_new.htm*

Corry, John. *My Times: Adventures in the News Trade.* New York: G. P. Putnam's Sons, 1993.

Cose, Ellis. *The Press.* New York: William Morrow, 1989.

"Covering the Epidemic: AIDS in the News Media, 1985–1996." *Columbia Journalism Review.* 11/21/97. *www.cjr.org/html/aids-introduction.*

Cox Newspapers Inc. *www.coxnews.com*

Croteau, David. "Examining the 'Liberal Media' Claim." A FAIR (Fairness & Accuracy in Reporting) Report. *www.fair.org/reports/journalist-survey.html.*

Dadlec, Dan. "How Bloomberg Pressures Editors." *Columbia Journalism Review.* September/October 1997. *www.cjr.org/html/97-09-10-bloomberg.html*

Davis, Elmer. *History of The New York Times, 1851–1921.* New York: New York Times, 1921.

Editor & Publisher Web site. *April 18, 1998, www.mediainfo.com*

Forse, Don T., Jr. "Media Bias? The Liberal Slant of Mass Media." American Family Association. *www.afatexas.org/document/news/other/mediabias.htm*

Freedom Forum. *www.fac.org*

Freedom Forum Media Studies Center. *www.mediastudies.org*

Gay Place News. GLAAD Press Release. *Gayplace.com/pages/news/press_releases/nc3276.html*

Ginsburg, Ruth Bader. "The Benjamin N. Cardozo Lecture." *The Record of the Association of the Bar of the City of New York.* May/June 1999, p. 275-309.

GLAADAlert. www.glaad.org/glaad/alert/971121/971121message03.html

Goulden, Joseph C. *Fit To Print: A. M. Rosenthal and His Times.* Secaucus, N.J.: Lyle Stuart Inc., 1988.

Hacker, Andrew. *Two Nations: Black and White, Separate, Hostile, Unequal.* New York: Ballantine, 1992.

Hartz, Louis. *Liberal Tradition in America.* New York: Harcourt, Brace and Company, 1955.

Harvard Magazine. July–August, 1999.

Harvard Magazine. March–April, 1999.

Heard, Alex. *Apocalypse Pretty Soon.* New York: W.W. Norton & Company, 1999.

Humanist Manifesto I. *www.humanism.net/documents/manifesto1.html*

Humanist Manifesto II. *www.humanism.net/documents/manifesto2.html*

Irvine, Reed, and Cliff Kincaid. "Feminazi at the *New York Times.*" June 8, 1998. *www.aim.org/mm/1998/07/08.htm*

Irvine, Reed, and Cliff Kincaid, "New York Times Discovers Christian Persecution." Accuracy in Media. *www.aim.org/mm/1998/12/02.htm*

Kennedy, Dan. "Left Out—Why conservatives are wrong about liberal media bias." *Salon*—PoliticallyBlackDotCom. *www.salonmagazine.com/media/media960729.html*

Lichter, S. Robert, Linda S. Lichter, and Daniel R. Amundson. *Media Coverage of Religion in America, 1969–1998.* Center for Media and Public Affairs. *www.cmpa.com/archive*

Local Laws of the City of New York for the Year 1998. *http:leahcouncil.nyc.ny.us/law98/int0303a.htm*

Mattingly, Terry. "Research compares today's religion journalists to writers of '80s." Scripps Howard News Service. 5/27/00.

Mencher, Melvin. *News Reporting and Writing*, 7th ed. Chicago: Brown & Benchmark Publishers, 1997.

Metz, William. *Newswriting From Lead to "30."* Englewood Cliffs, N.J.: Prentice-Hall, Inc., 1977.

National Gay and Lesbian Task Force Web site. *www.ngltf.org*

New York City Council Newswire. *www.council.nyc.ny.us/newswire*

New York Times on the Web. www.nytimes.com

New York Times, The, national edition. July 1995–August 1999.

"News junkies, News critics." *Newseum. www.newseum.org/survey/index.html.*

Newseum Web site. *www.newseum.org*

Operation Rescue Web site on "Corpus Christ" play. *www.orn.org/theStreets/corpusChristi.htm*

Palm Beach Post, The. 1996–1997.

Proctor, William. *The Resurrection Report: A Journalist Investigates the Most Debated Event in History.* Nashville: Broadman & Holman, 1998.

Proctor, William. *The Templeton Prize.* New York: Doubleday, 1983.

Pulitzer Prizes Web site. *www.pulitzer.org*

Quindlen, Anna. *Thinking Out Loud.* New York: Fawcett Columbine, 1993.

Quinn, Kathleen. "Defend the Moral High Ground." *www.motherjones.com/mother_jones/ND93/quinn.html*

Religious Tolerance. *www.ReligiousTolerance.org*

Rivers, William L. *The Mass Media: Reporting—Writing— Editing*. New York: Harper & Row, 1964, 1966.

Roper Center. "Are the Media Biased in Partisan and Ideological Terms?" *www.ropercenter.uconn.edu*

Roe v. Wade at 25. Stanford Law School. *www.law.stanford.edu/programs/Roe25.shtml*

Rosenthal, A. S. "Persecuting the Christians." *Explorations*. American Interfaith Institute/World Alliance of Interfaith Organizations. Vol. 11, No. 2, 1997, p. 1.

Saint Benedict Center. *www.catholicism.org/pages/scient.htm*

Sarfati, Johathan. *Refuting Evolution*. Green Forest, Ark.: Master Books, 1999.

Shea, Nina. *In the Lion's Den*. Nashville: Broadman & Holman, 1997.

Shepard, Alicia C. "The Media Get Religion." AJR NewsLink. *www.newslink.org/ajrshep2.html*

Study on Religion and the Media. Freedom Forum First Amendment Center, Vanderbilt University. *www.fac.org/publicat/gap*

Tifft, Susan E., and Alex Jones. *The Trust: The Private and Powerful Family Behind the New York Times*. Boston: Little Brown & Company, 1999.

Tocqueville, Alexis de. *Democracy in America, Vols 1 and 2*. New York: Vintage Books, 1945, 1961.

Turner, Richard. "The Gray Lady Applies Rouge and Lip Gloss." *Newsweek*, Sept. 15, 1997, p. 76.

United States Constitution.

Wall Street Journal, The. July 1995–August 1999.

Washington Times, various issues.

World Magazine. Various issues.

Zamorsky, Tania. "Media; Liable to Lose in Libel and Related Cases?" *Authors Guild Bulletin*. Fall 1997, p. 7.

Index

304